The Simple Genetic Algorithm

The Simple Genetic Algorithm
Foundations and Theory

Michael D. Vose

A Bradford Book
The MIT Press
Cambridge, Massachusetts
London, England

This book was set in Times Roman by Windfall Software and the author using ZzTEX and Postscript and was printed and bound in the United States of America.

Library of Congress Cataloging-in-Publication Data

Vose, Michael D.
  The simple genetic algorithm: foundations and theory / Michael D.
  Vose.
    p.   cm. — (Complex adaptive systems)
  "A Bradford book."
  Includes bibliographical references and index.
  ISBN 0-262-22058-X (hc: alk. paper)
  1. Genetic algorithms. I. Title. II. Series.
QA402.5.V68   1999
005.1—dc21   97-31932
                                                 CIP

To Ramon, whose regrets and dreams shaped my life

Contents

Preface

The scope of material considered is limited, for reasons of manageability, to a classical form of genetic search, referred to as the Simple Genetic Algorithm (SGA). Given it as object of interest, there are no alternative foundations; the formalization provided by this account quite literally *is* the SGA.

The viewpoint taken is that the Simple Genetic Algorithm is a mathematical object. Upon reflection, there is hardly an alternative. Mathematics is a precise language, and the subject and terms of discourse must somehow be described. Definition by way of carefully worded English prose or computer code would be, if unambiguous, mathematics in disguise.

The goals of this book extend beyond definition however, which is why mathematics is unveiled from the outset. My central purpose in writing this book is to provide an introduction to what is known about the theory of the Simple Genetic Algorithm. The rigor of mathematics is employed so as not to inadvertently repeat myths or recount folklore.

The decision to accept assertions only when proved is not without price. Few (certainly not I) have mastered enough mathematics to make its application trivial. Another cost is that one is forced to trade what is believed to be true for what can be verified. Consequently, this account is silent on many questions of interest for lack of proof.

With few exceptions (due to oversight, not willful neglect) the exclusion of certain elements of standard "GA theory" is due to: absence of well defined meaning, absence of nontrivial relevance, or absence of proof. Since I do not intend to throw stones, readers perusing the text for missing tenets must speculate as to which reason applies. I will say— since it is no longer controversial—that the "schema theorem" explains virtually nothing about SGA behavior. On the other hand, the subject of "schema utilities" is not considered for lack of proof.

This book lays out theoretical foundations upon which provable results about SGA behavior can be based. Several such applications are provided, but the subject is far from complete. Given the complexity of the Simple Genetic Algorithm, it is conceivable that simplifying assumptions may be the best route to further theoretical advances. Even so, assumptions made should be in terms of the formalization, relating to cases in which it may be reduced, in a provable way, to a more tractable form. Proceeding in this manner sharply delineates what is being studied, what simplifying assumptions represent, and to what extent conclusions are proved rather than merely conjectured.

My secondary purpose in writing this book is to make available algorithms for the computation of mathematical objects related to the Simple Genetic Algorithm. Relatively efficient methods (though still with exponential complexity) have been obtained which extend the range of simulations. I expect theory will ultimately profit from an interplay with computational experiments and empirical studies.

Acknowledgments

I owe a lot to friends, colleagues, and the National Science Foundation, for supporting this line of inquiry which so radically departs from the classical schemata-based "GA theory". Many have provided inspiration and companionship along the way, but Alden Wright and Gary Koehler deserve special mention. I should also thank the International Society for Genetic Algorithms whose sponsored conferences and workshops have provided a forum for this work for nearly a decade. Finally, I am indebted to Bart Naudts; without his help with fonts, I might never have completed the typesetting.

The Simple Genetic Algorithm

1 Introduction

Language describing the Simple Genetic Algorithm (SGA) in terms of heuristic search is used throughout this book. Recognizing that an implicit message conveyed by such language is that SGAs are search/optimization algorithms, the language is nevertheless too convenient to abandon. However, this book is not about search or optimization per se. The focus is on the simple genetic algorithm as an evolutionary system. Applications are not considered. Foundation, formalization, and emergent behavior are the subjects of concern.

The choice of topics is partly a matter of taste, and partly dictated by the current state of the art; what gets said is often what can be said. The range of material is also limited by the approach taken, which is depth-first, and by the level of difficulty, which is appropriate for senior level college or beginning graduate students.

A broad audience is anticipated. Although nontechnical readers might at first be deterred by the mathematical presentation, patience and willingness to learn will be rewarded. Nothing beyond the rudiments of algebra, calculus, probability, and topology is required. To make the material more widely accessible, selected mathematical background is summarized in the appendix. It is hoped that this book will be considered by the dauntless as an outline for exploring topics in mathematics and computer science in a goal oriented way.

The organization of material is linear. Skipping over sections is not recommended. Each section in some fashion depends on something which went before. Read in sequence, a clean, coherent picture of the simple genetic algorithm will emerge, developed from first principles.

The exercises are an integral part of the text. They are meant to develop, generalize, inform, aid, and challenge the reader. Some questions may suggest a visit to the library. The importance of the exercises cannot be overemphasized. The assumption that they would at least be read, if not worked through, underlies the design of the book. Part of learning is participation.

Exposition is deliberately terse. The precision and economy of mathematics is favored over prose. An attempt has been made to minimize everything which does not convey subject information. Extraneous material such as biological parallels, philosophical musings, or historical accounts is simply not included.

Proofs sketch the essential ideas behind theorems. A reader interested in the subject's broad outlines may skim over them at first reading. The level of detail given in the proofs is adequate for an expert. For an apprentice, the proofs will seem more like a workbook leading towards mastery; though at times challenging, filling in the details will be a rewarding exercise.

The student already acquainted with the simple genetic algorithm should find this account modern, refreshing, and even controversial. For the expert, the presentation (though elementary) should be a provocative reflection of the state of the art.

2 Notation

This section introduces some standard mathematical terms and notation used throughout the text, as well as some nonstandard but useful conventions. The reader is referred to the appendix for a review of selected topics from analysis, algebra, and probability.

The set of integers is $\mathbb{Z} = \{\ldots, -1, 0, 1, \ldots\}$, and the set of integers modulo c is $\mathbb{Z}_c = \{0, \ldots, c-1\}$. The symbol $\Re$ denotes the set of real numbers, and for any collection C of real numbers, vectors, or functions, the sub collection of positive members is denoted by C^+. The *positive orthant* is the set $\Re^{n+}$. The *nonnegative orthant* refers to the closure of the positive orthant. A collection C multiplied by a number α, as in αC, denotes the collection whose members are those of C multiplied by α.

Angle brackets $\langle \cdots \rangle$ denote a tuple that is regarded as a column vector. The vector of all 1s is denoted by $\mathbf{1}$, and the zero vector is denoted by 0. To make explicit the dependence of $\mathbf{1}$ on the dimension n, it may be written as $^n\mathbf{1}$. The identity matrix is I, and the jth column of the identity matrix is the vector e_j. Indexing of vectors and matrices begins with 0. For vector x, $\mathrm{diag}(x)$ denotes the square diagonal matrix with i, ith entry x_i.

Two vectors x and y are said to have similar direction, denoted $x \sim y$, if there exists a nonzero number α such that $x = \alpha y$. Transpose is indicated with superscript T, and inverse transpose with superscript $-T$. Two vectors x and y are *orthogonal* if $x^T y = x$. The set of vectors orthogonal to x is denoted by $x^\perp$. The symbol "·" is used as a place holder, except when occurring between column vectors as in $x \cdot y$ where it indicates $\mathrm{diag}(x)y$. Except where otherwise indicated, the standard vector norm is $\|x\| = \|x\|_2 = \sqrt{x^T x}$. The vector norm given by the sum of the modulus of components is $\|\cdot\|_1$, and the norm given by the maximum modulus over components is $\|\cdot\|_\infty$. The open ball of radius ε about the element or set x is denoted by $\mathcal{B}_\varepsilon(x)$, the closed ball by $\overline{\mathcal{B}}_\varepsilon(x)$.

The restriction of a function h to B is denoted by

$$h\Big|_B$$

Composition of functions h and g is defined by $h \circ g(x) = h(g(x))$. The ith iterate h^i of h is defined by

$$h^0(x) = x$$

$$h^{i+1}(x) = h \circ h^i(x)$$

Modulus (or absolute value) is denoted by $|\cdot|$, though other functions (depending on the chapter and context) use the same notation. The notation $O(h)$ denotes a function (with similar domain and codomain as h), call it g, such that pointwise $|g| \leq c|h|$ for some constant c. The notation $o(h)$ represents a function (with similar domain and codomain as h), call it g, such that pointwise $|g|/|h| \to 0$. In the case where h is a vector or matrix,

$|\cdot|$ is to be interpreted as a norm. The notations $O^+(h)$ and $o^+(h)$ carry the additional information that g is positive. The notation $(expr)^+$ denotes $\max\{0, expr\}$, and $(expr)^-$ denotes $-\min\{0, expr\}$ where $expr$ is a real valued expression.

Curly brackets $\{\cdots\}$ are used as grouping symbols and to specify both sets and multisets (a multiset is a set except that repetition of elements is allowed). The probability of the event *event* is denoted by

$$\Pr\{event\}$$

Square brackets $[\cdots]$ are, besides their standard use as specifying a closed interval of real numbers, used to denote an indicator function: if *expr* is an expression which may be true or false, then

$$[expr] = \begin{cases} 1 & \text{if } expr \text{ is true} \\ 0 & \text{otherwise} \end{cases}$$

The delta function is defined by $\delta_{i,j} = [i = j]$.

Standard logical symbols are used; $\wedge$ denotes conjunction, $\vee$ denotes disjunction, $\implies$ denotes implication, and $\iff$ denotes logical equivalence. For any objects x and y, the notation $x \equiv y$ indicates their equivalence, where context determines the meaning of equivalence.

The *supremum* of a set A is the least upper bound of its elements, and is denoted $\sup\{A\}$. The *infemum* of a set A is the greatest lower bound of its elements, and is denoted $\inf\{A\}$. The floor of x is

$$\lfloor x \rfloor = \sup\{z : z \in \mathcal{Z} \wedge z \le x\}$$

The ceiling of x is

$$\lceil x \rceil = \inf\{z : z \in \mathcal{Z} \wedge z \ge x\}$$

The *diameter* of a set $S \subset \mathfrak{R}^n$ is

$$\sup\{\|x - y\| : x, y \in S\}$$

If S is a finite set of vectors, then $\mathcal{L}S$ denotes their linear span,

$$\mathcal{L}\{s_0, \ldots, s_k\} = \{\alpha_0 s_0 + \cdots + \alpha_k s_k : \alpha_i \in \mathfrak{R}\}$$

and $\mathcal{H}S$ their convex hull,

$$\mathcal{H}\{s_0, \ldots, s_k\} = \{\alpha_0 s_0 + \cdots + \alpha_k s_k : \alpha_i \in \mathfrak{R} \wedge \alpha_i \ge 0 \wedge \sum \alpha_i = 1\}$$

The *spectrum* of a matrix (linear operator) A is denoted by $\text{spec}(A)$.

3 Random Heuristic Search

This chapter is the foundation of the entire development. A broad class of algorithms, *Random Heuristic Search* (RHS), is defined and some of its most basic properties are touched upon. The Simple Genetic Algorithm will emerge from this general context (in the next chapter) as a special case.

Central to the definition of Random Heuristic Search is the concept of state and transition between states. Here basic machinery is constructed for representing state and defining transitions. Reasonable attention is given to generality even though, for the Simple Genetic Algorithm, the underlying space is binary (the general cardinality case is dealt with in the exercises).

The first section is devoted to erecting a representational framework and defining RHS in approximate terms. There, its fundamental structure in terms of state and transition is explained. The next section refines the concept, incorporating the stochastic components of RHS within the representational framework. Qualitative aspects of the stochastic behavior of RHS are touched upon. The final section summarizes RHS in abstract terms and classifies instances according to properties of their heuristic. Every instance of random heuristic search is seen to be a Markov chain.

3.1 Representation

Random heuristic search can be thought of as an initial collection of elements P_0 chosen from some search space Ω of cardinality n together with some *transition rule* τ which from P_i will produce another collection P_{i+1}. In general, τ will be iterated to produce a sequence of collections

$$P_0 \xrightarrow{\tau} P_1 \xrightarrow{\tau} P_2 \xrightarrow{\tau} \cdots$$

The beginning collection P_0 is referred to as the *initial population*, the first population (or *generation*) is P_1, the second population (or generation) is P_2, and so on. Populations are multisets.

Not all transition rules are allowed. Obtaining a good representation for populations is a first step towards characterizing admissible τ. Define the *simplex* to be the set

$$\Lambda = \{\langle x_0, \ldots, x_{n-1}\rangle : \mathbf{1}^T x = 1, x_j \geq 0\}$$

An element p of Λ corresponds to a population according to the following rule for defining its components

$p_j =$ the proportion in the population of the jth element of Ω

For example, if $\Omega = \{0, 1, 2, 3, 4, 5\}$ then $n = 6$. The population $\{1, 0, 3, 1, 1, 3, 2, 2, 4, 0\}$ is represented by the vector $p = \langle .2, .3, .2, .2, .1, .0 \rangle$, given that

Coordinate	Corresponding element of Ω	Percentage of P_0
p_0	0	2/10
p_1	1	3/10
p_2	2	2/10
p_3	3	2/10
p_4	4	1/10
p_5	5	0/10

The cardinality of each generation $P_0, P_1, \ldots$ is a parameter r called the *population size*. Hence the proportional representation given by p unambiguously determines a population once r is known. The vector p is referred to as a *population vector*. The distinction between population and population vector will often be blurred. In particular, τ may be thought of as mapping the current population vector to the next.

To get a feel for the geometry of the representation space, Λ is shown in the following sequence of diagrams for n equals 2, 3, and 4. The (bold) figures represent Λ (a line segment, triangle, and solid tetrahedron). The (thin) arrows show the coordinate axes of the ambient space (the projection of the coordinate axes are being viewed in the second figure, which is three dimensional, and in the last figure where the ambient space is four dimensional).

In general, Λ is a tetrahedron of dimension $n - 1$ contained in an ambient space of dimension n. Note that each vertex of Λ corresponds to a unit basis vector of the ambient space; Λ is their convex hull. For example, the vertices of the solid tetrahedron (right most figure) are at the basis vectors $\langle 1, 0, 0, 0 \rangle$, $\langle 0, 1, 0, 0 \rangle$, $\langle 0, 0, 1, 0 \rangle$, and $\langle 0, 0, 0, 1 \rangle$. Assuming that Ω is the ordered set $\{0, 1, 2, 3\}$, they correspond (respectively) to the following populations:

r copies of 0, r copies of 1, r copies of 2, and r copies of 3. The center diagram will later be used as a schematic for general Λ, representing it for arbitrary n.

It should be realized that not every point of Λ corresponds to a finite population. In fact, only those rational points with common denominator r correspond to populations of size r. They are

$$\frac{1}{r}X_n^r = \frac{1}{r}\{\langle x_0, \ldots, x_{n-1}\rangle : x_j \in \mathbb{Z}, x_j \geq 0, \mathbf{1}^T x = r\}$$

As $r \to \infty$, these rational points become dense in Λ. The next theorem makes this precise. Since, if r is not specified, a rational point may represent arbitrarily large populations, a point p of Λ carries little information concerning population size. A natural view is therefore that Λ corresponds to populations of indeterminate size. This is but one of several useful interpretations. Another is that Λ corresponds to sampling distributions over Ω: since the components of p are nonnegative and sum to 1, p may be viewed as indicating that i is sampled with probability p_i.

Theorem 3.1 Let $p, q \in \Lambda$ denote arbitrary population vectors for population size r, and let ξ denote an arbitrary element of Λ. Then

$$\inf_{p \neq q} \|p - q\| = \sqrt{2}/r$$

$$\sup_{\xi} \inf_{p} \|\xi - p\| = O(1/\sqrt{r})$$

where the constant (in the "big O") is independent of the dimension of Λ.

Proof The first equality is an exercise. Given $\xi \in \Lambda$ with irrational components, choose p according to

$$p_0 = \lfloor r\xi_0 \rfloor / r$$

$$p_{i+1} = \begin{cases} \lfloor r\xi_{i+1} \rfloor / r & \text{if } p_i \leq \xi_i \text{ and } \xi_{i+1} - \lfloor r\xi_{i+1} \rfloor / r + \sum_{j \leq i}(\xi_j - p_j) < 1/r \\ \lceil r\xi_{i+1} \rceil / r & \text{if } p_i \leq \xi_i \text{ and } \xi_{i+1} - \lfloor r\xi_{i+1} \rfloor / r + \sum_{j \leq i}(\xi_j - p_j) \geq 1/r \\ \lceil r\xi_{i+1} \rceil / r & \text{if } p_i > \xi_i \text{ and } \xi_{i+1} - \lceil r\xi_{i+1} \rceil / r + \sum_{j \leq i}(\xi_j - p_j) > -1/r \\ \lfloor r\xi_{i+1} \rfloor / r & \text{if } p_i > \xi_i \text{ and } \xi_{i+1} - \lceil r\xi_{i+1} \rceil / r + \sum_{j \leq i}(\xi_j - p_j) \leq -1/r \end{cases}$$

Note that $1/r > |\sum(\xi_j - p_j)| = |1 - \sum p_j|$. Since the p_j have common denominator r, it follows that $p \in \Lambda$. The components of p can be divided into the contiguous groups

$$p_{k_0}, \ldots, p_{k_1-1}; \ p_{k_1}, \ldots, p_{k_2-1}; \ \cdots; \ p_{k_{j-1}}, \ldots, p_{k_j-1}$$

such that the sign of $\xi_i - p_i$ changes between groups but does not oscillate within any group. It follows that there can be at most $O(r)$ groups since if the ith group has positive sign, then $\xi_{k_i} + \cdots + \xi_{k_{i+1}} \geq 1/r$. The observation that

$$\sum (\xi_i - p_i)^2$$

$$= \sum_i \sum_{j=k_i}^{k_{i+1}-1} (\xi_j - p_j)^2$$

$$\leq \sum_i \left(\sum_{j=k_i}^{k_{i+1}-1} (\xi_j - p_j) \right)^2$$

$$\leq \sum_i (2/r)^2$$

$$= O(1/r)$$

completes the proof.   ■

In summary, random heuristic search appears to be a *discrete dynamical system* on Λ through the identification of populations with population vectors. That is, there is some transition rule

$$\tau : \Lambda \longrightarrow \Lambda$$

and what is of interest is the sequence of iterates beginning from some initial population vector p

$$p, \tau(p), \tau^2(p), \ldots$$

This view is incomplete however, because the transitions are in general nondeterministic and not all transition rules are allowed. In the next section the stochastic nature of τ will be explained and admissible τ will be characterized.

Exercises

1. Construct a diagram of Λ for $n = 4$ and identify lattice points corresponding to the following populations $\{0, 1, 2, 3\}$, $\{0, 1, 0, 0, 1, 1, 0, 1\}$, $\{1, 2, 3, 2, 1, 3\}$, $\{0, 0, 0, 1, 3, 2, 2, 1\}$.

2. Prove that the number of possible populations is the binomial coefficient $\binom{n+r-1}{r}$.

3. Prove that Λ is *compact*. That is, it is closed and bounded.

4. How is it that a rational point in Λ may represent arbitrary large populations?

5. Prove the first part of theorem 3.1.

6. What advantage is there, in the proof of theorem 3.1, of dealing with irrational points of Λ? How does it suffice to consider them?

7. Show that $\frac{1}{r} X_n^r$ is a subset of the translate by e_0 of the lattice

$$\frac{1}{r} \{ \alpha_1 b_1 + \cdots + \alpha_{n-1} b_{n-1} : \alpha_i \in \mathbb{Z} \}$$

where $b_i = e_i - e_0$.

8. A *cell* of a lattice is a parallelepiped having lattice points as vertices. Does there necessarily exist some cell (of dimension $n-1$, the dimension of Λ) of the translated lattice (described in the previous problem) having vertices contained in $\frac{1}{r} X_n^r$?

3.2   Nondeterminism

Given the current population vector p, the next population vector $\tau(p)$ cannot be predicted with certainty because τ is stochastic. It is most conveniently thought of as resulting from r independent, identically distributed random choices. Let $\mathcal{G} : \Lambda \to \Lambda$ be a *heuristic function* (heuristic for short) which given the current population p produces a vector whose ith component is the probability that the ith element of Ω is chosen (with replacement). That is, $\mathcal{G}(p)$ is that probability vector which specifies the sampling distribution by which the aggregate of r choices forms the next generation. A transition rule τ is admissible if it corresponds to a heuristic function $\mathcal{G}$ in this way. The following diagram depicts the relationship between p, Λ, Ω, $\mathcal{G}$, and τ through a sequence of generations (the illustration does not correspond literally to any particular case, it depicts how transitions between generations take place in general):

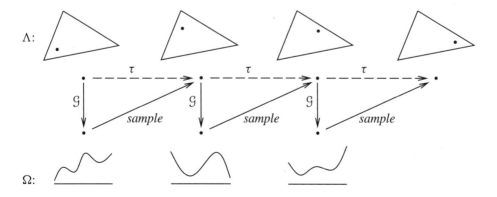

The triangles along the top row represent Λ, one for each of four generations. Each Λ contains a dot representing a population. These same populations are also represented in the second row with dots; τ maps from one to the next. The transition arrow for τ is dashed to indicate that it is an induced map, computed by following the solid arrows. The lower row of dots are images of populations under $\mathcal{G}$. Below each is a curve, suggesting the sampling distribution over Ω which it represents. The line segments in the bottom row represent Ω.

The transition from one generation (upper dot) to the next proceeds as follows. First $\mathcal{G}$ is applied to produce a vector (lower dot) which represents a sampling distribution (curve) over Ω (line segment). Next, r independent samples, with replacement, are made from Ω according to this distribution (represented in the diagram by *"sample"*) to produce the next generation.

For example, let Ω be the ordered set $\{0, 1, 2, 3\}$ and suppose the heuristic is

$$\mathcal{G}(p) = \langle 0, p_1, 2p_2, 3p_3 \rangle / \sum i p_i$$

Let the initial population be $p = \langle .25, .25, .25, .25 \rangle$. Since $\mathcal{G}(p) = \langle 0, 1/6, 1/3, 1/2 \rangle$, the probability of sampling 0 is 0, of sampling 1 is 1/6, of sampling 2 is 1/3, and of sampling 3 is 1/2. With population size $r = 100$, the transition rule corresponds to making 100 independent samples, with replacement, according to these probabilities.

A plausible next generation is therefore $\tau(p) = \langle 0, .17, .33, .50 \rangle$. Note that $\mathcal{G}(p)$, representing the sampling distribution used in forming the next generation $\tau(p)$, depends on the current population p. Going one generation further, the new current population is $\tau(p)$ and the sampling distribution for producing the next generation is represented by $\mathcal{G}(\tau(p)) \approx \langle 0, .07296, .28326, .64377 \rangle$. It is therefore plausible that the second generation is $\tau^2(p) = \langle 0, .07, .28, .65 \rangle$.

Note the conceptually dual interpretation of Λ. It serves as both the space of populations and as the space of probability distributions over Ω. The first natural question is: What is the expected next generation? The following lemma will be useful in answering this question.

Lemma 3.2 (Multinomial Theorem)   For $k, n \in \mathcal{Z}^+$,

$$(\mathbf{1}^T x)^k = k! \sum_{v \in X_n^k} \prod_{j < n} \frac{x_j^{v_j}}{v_j!}$$

Proof   Induct on n. The base case $n = 1$ is trivial. The inductive step is

$$k! \sum_{v \in X_{n+1}^k} \prod_{j \le n} \frac{x_j^{v_j}}{v_j!}$$

$$= k! \sum_{u=0}^{k} \sum_{v \in X_n^{k-u}} \frac{x_n^u}{u!} \prod_{j<n} \frac{x_j^{v_j}}{v_j!}$$

$$= \sum_{u=0}^{k} \binom{k}{u} x_n^u (k-u)! \sum_{v \in X_n^{k-u}} \prod_{j<n} \frac{x_j^{v_j}}{v_j!}$$

$$= \sum_{u=0}^{k} \binom{k}{u} x_n^u \left(\sum_{j<n} x_j \right)^{k-u}$$

Appealing to the binomial theorem completes the proof. ∎

Theorem 3.3 Let p be the current population vector. The expected next population vector is $\mathcal{G}(p)$.

Proof Without loss of generality, $\Omega = \{0, \ldots, n-1\}$. The first step is to determine for each possible population vector the probability that it represents the next generation. Feasible populations are $\frac{1}{r} X_n^r$. To obtain a general population vector $q = v/r$, it must happen that v_0 choices out of r are 0, which has probability

$$\binom{r}{v_0} (\mathcal{G}(p)_0)^{v_0}$$

and v_1 choices out of the remaining $r - v_0$ must be 1, which has probability

$$\binom{r - v_0}{v_1} (\mathcal{G}(p)_1)^{v_1}$$

and so on until finally v_{n-1} choices out of the remaining $r - v_0 - \cdots - v_{n-2}$ must be $n - 1$, which has probability

$$\binom{r - v_0 - \cdots - v_{n-2}}{v_{n-1}} (\mathcal{G}(p)_{n-1})^{v_{n-1}}$$

The product of these probabilities reduces (after expanding the binomial coefficients) to

$$r! \prod_{j<n} \frac{(\mathcal{G}(p)_j)^{v_j}}{v_j!}$$

It follows that the expectation is given by

$$r! \sum_{v \in X_n^r} \frac{v}{r} \prod_{j<n} \frac{(\mathcal{G}(p)_j)^{v_j}}{v_j!}$$

Applying the operator $\sum e_i x_i \frac{\partial}{\partial x_i}$ to both sides of the multinomial theorem (lemma 3.2) yields

$$kx(\mathbf{1}^T x)^{k-1}$$

$$= k! \sum_i e_i x_i \sum_{v \in X_n^k} \frac{v_i x_i^{v_i-1}}{v_i!} \prod_{j \neq i} \frac{x_j^{v_j}}{v_j!}$$

$$= k! \sum_{v \in X_n^k} v \prod_j \frac{x_j^{v_j}}{v_j!}$$

Using this formula to simplify the expectation completes the proof.   ∎

During the course of the preceding proof, an explicit formula was obtained for the probability that the next population is a particular element of $\frac{1}{r} X_n^r$ (the set of possible next populations) given that the current population is p. This is an important formula and it will be useful to have an approximation for it. Stirling's theorem says that given $x \in \mathcal{Z}^+$, there exists $0 < \theta < 1$ such that

$$x! = \left(\frac{x}{e}\right)^x \sqrt{2\pi x} \exp\left(\frac{1}{12x + \theta}\right)$$

Solving this equality for θ defines it as a function of x. The function θ appears in the next theorem.

Theorem 3.4   Let p be the current population vector. The probability that $q \in \frac{1}{r} X_n^r$ is the next population vector is

$$r! \prod \frac{(\mathcal{G}(p)_j)^{rq_j}}{(rq_j)!}$$

$$= \exp\left(-r \sum q_j \log \frac{q_j}{\mathcal{G}(p)_j} - \sum \left(\log \sqrt{2\pi r q_j} + \frac{1}{12r q_j + \theta(r q_j)}\right) + O(\log r)\right)$$

where summation is restricted to indices for which $q_j > 0$.

Proof   Using Stirling's theorem to eliminate factorials, the exponent of the right hand side of

$$r! \prod \frac{(\mathcal{G}(p)_j)^{rq_j}}{(rq_j)!} = \exp\left(\log r! + \sum (rq_j \log \mathcal{G}(p)_j - \log(rq_j)!)\right)$$

is

$$r \log r + \sum (rq_j \log \mathcal{G}(p)_j - rq_j \log rq_j) - \sum \left(\log \sqrt{2\pi rq_j} + \frac{1}{12rq_j + \theta(rq_j)}\right)$$

$$+ O(\log r)$$

The first two terms can be expressed as

$$-r \sum (q_j \log rq_j - q_j \log \mathcal{G}(p)_j - q_j \log r) \qquad \blacksquare$$

Theorem 3.4 provides qualitative information concerning probable next generations. The expression

$$\sum q_j \log \frac{q_j}{\mathcal{G}(p)_j}$$

is called the *discrepancy* of q with respect to $\mathcal{G}(p)$ and is a measure of how far q is from the expected next population $\mathcal{G}(p)$. Using the inequality $\log x \geq 1 - 1/x$ shows it to be at least

$$\sum q_j(1 - \frac{\mathcal{G}(p)_j}{q_j}) = \sum q_j - \mathcal{G}(p)_j = 0$$

Since the inequality is sharp at $q = \mathcal{G}(p)$, discrepancy is nonnegative and is zero only when q is the expected next population. Hence the factor

$$\exp\left(-r \sum q_j \log \frac{q_j}{\mathcal{G}(p)_j}\right)$$

occurring on the right hand side of theorem 3.4 indicates the probability that q is the next generation decays exponentially (with constant $-r$) as the discrepancy between q and the expected next population increases.

In the derivation of Theorem 3.4, keeping track of what goes into the sum

$$\sum \left(\log \sqrt{2\pi rq_j} + \frac{1}{12rq_j + \theta(rq_j)}\right)$$

(more precisely, replacing θ by its definition and simplifying) shows it to be

$$\sum \log(e^{x_j} x_j! / x_j^{x_j})$$

where $x_j = rq_j$. This expression measures the *dispersion* of the population vector q. The following observations can be made (their proof is an exercise). A minimally disperse population is homogeneous (r identical population members) and corresponds to $q = e_i$ for some i. The corresponding dispersion is $O^+(\log r)$. If $n \geq r$, a maximally disperse population has no duplication (q has r nonzero components which are all $1/r$) and dispersion r. The following diagram illustrates this for $\ell = 2$, $r = 4$. Populations are represented by dots, where smaller dots have lower dispersion and larger dots have higher dispersion.

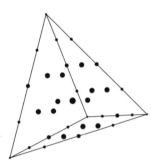

The factor

$$\exp\left(-\sum(\log\sqrt{2\pi rq_j} + \frac{1}{12rq_j + \theta(rq_j)})\right)$$

occurring on the right hand side of theorem 3.4 indicates the probability that q is the next generation decays exponentially with increasing dispersion. This is related to fluctuations in finite populations induced by sampling; finite populations have a natural tendency under sampling to converge.

The combined effect of the two influences of discrepancy and dispersion is that random heuristic search favors a less disperse population near the expected next generation. In particular, if the current population is near the expected next generation, then the first factor does not contribute a strong bias for change. When $\mathcal{G}(p)$ is nearly the initial population p, the influence of discrepancy favors p as the next generation since the alternatives, being lattice points, are constrained to be some distance away from the expected next generation. This phenomenon is expressed quantitatively by theorem 3.4. Moreover, the second factor may exert a stabilizing effect provided the current population has low dispersion compared to the alternatives.

According to theorem 3.3, the expected next generation from population p is known, but what about the variance? The next theorem shows it decreases like $1/r$ and depends upon the distance of $\mathcal{G}(p)$ from a vertex of Λ.

Theorem 3.5

$$\sum_{q \in \frac{1}{r} X_n^r} \|q - \mathcal{G}(p)\|^2 r! \prod_j \frac{(\mathcal{G}(p)_j)^{rq_j}}{(rq_j)!} = (1 - \mathcal{G}(p)^T \mathcal{G}(p))/r$$

Proof   Let $x = \mathcal{G}(p)$. Theorem 3.3 may be used to simplify the left hand side,

$$\sum_{q \in \frac{1}{r} X_n^r} (q^T q + x^T x - 2x^T q) r! \prod_j \frac{x_j^{rq_j}}{(rq_j)!} = -x^T x + r! \sum_{q \in \frac{1}{r} X_n^r} q^T q \prod_j \frac{x^{rq_j}}{(rq_j)!}$$

Since $\mathbf{1}^T x = 1$, applying the operator $\sum x_i (\frac{\partial}{\partial x_i} + x_i^2 \frac{\partial^2}{\partial x_i^2})$ to both sides of the multinomial theorem (lemma 3.2) leads to

$$k + k(k - 1)x^T x = k! \sum_{v \in X_n^k} v^T v \prod_j \frac{x_j^{v_j}}{v_j!}$$

Using this formula to simplify the preceding expression completes the proof.   ∎

Theorem 3.5 points to another influence in support of stasis when the current population is near the expected next generation and in an area of low dispersion. Since $\|\mathcal{G}(p)\|^2 \leq 1$ with equality precisely when $\mathcal{G}(p)$ is at a vertex of Λ, the variance is small in areas of low dispersion which favors populations near the expected next generation.

This section closes with terminology. Let $X(p)$ be a method (which may depend on $p \in \Lambda$) to sample an element from Ω, and suppose $\mathcal{G} : \Lambda \to \Lambda$. To say "the heuristic $\mathcal{G}$ corresponds to X" means

$$\mathcal{G}(p)_i = \Pr\{i \text{ is sampled from } \Omega \text{ according to } X(p)\}$$

Exercises

1. Show how RHS with arbitrary Ω is equivalent to the special case where Ω is given by $\{0, \dots, n - 1\}$.

2. In view of the previous exercise, write general purpose computer code implementing RHS as follows:

(a) Input an initial population vector x.

(b) Compute the distribution represented by $\mathcal{G}(x)$.

(c) Select $i \in \{0, \ldots, n-1\}$ for the next generation with probability $\mathcal{G}(x)_i$.

(d) Repeat the previous step until the next generation is complete.

(e) Replace x by the population vector describing the new generation just formed.

(f) Terminate or go to (b).

The heuristic $\mathcal{G}(x)$ should be an external function which can be linked in.

3. Is the heuristic of the example in this section continuously differentiable?

4. Write general purpose computer code to calculate discrepancy and dispersion.

5. Use the program of exercise 2 to empirically verify theorem 3.3.

6. Use the program of exercise 2 to compare the behavior of $\tau(p)$ with $\mathcal{G}(p)$ as $r \to \infty$.

7. Use the program of exercise 4 to empirically investigate which, discrepancy or dispersion, has the greater effect on the next generation.

8. Interpret dispersion geometrically in terms of the simplex and prove the remarks made concerning its extreme values. *Hint:* Use Lagrange multipliers to find the extreme points of $\sum \log(e^{x_j} x_j! / x_j^{x_j})$ over the domain $[0, r]^n$ subject to the constraint $\mathbf{1}^T x = r$ (replace the factorial with a gamma function).

9. Interpret RHS in terms of a "signal" (provided by the heuristic) and "noise" (provided by sampling according to theorem 3.4).

3.3   Markov Chain

The characterization of random heuristic search completed in the previous section was in terms of the sequence

$$p, \tau(p), \tau^2(p), \ldots$$

produced by sampling Ω. This can be thought of as a sequence of random vectors (p may be regarded as the random vector which with probability one assumes only the single value p). Moreover, each random vector in the sequence depends only on the value of the preceding one. This is a special situation; such a sequence is called a *Markov chain*. The matrix defined by

$$Q_{p,q} = r! \prod \frac{(\mathcal{G}(p)_j)^{rq_j}}{(rq_j)!}$$

for $p, q \in \frac{1}{r} X_n^r$, is the *transition matrix* of the Markov chain. By theorem 3.4, $Q_{p,q}$ is the probability that $\tau(p) = q$. The definition of τ in the previous section rests ultimately on Ω, as τ is the induced map

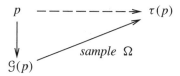

This conceptualization can now be replaced by an abstraction which makes no reference to Ω at all: from current population p, produce $q = \tau(p)$ with probability $Q_{p,q}$. This provides a fairly simple decomposition of τ into a deterministic *signal* component, given by $\mathcal{G}$, and a stochastic *noise* component, given by sampling the multinomial distribution. Theorem 3.4 shows, for any r, that $\tau(p)$ is given by a single sample from a multinomial distribution having mean $\mathcal{G}(p)$. By theorem 3.5, the noise in this sample (or variance from the mean) decreases as $1/r$. Note how, in this decomposition into signal and noise, the signal is *invariant* in the sense that it is *independent* of population size.

Associated with the stochastic progression of random heuristic search from one generation to the next is the deterministic dynamical system on Λ obtained by iterating $\mathcal{G}$ instead of τ. This is the underlying flow which provides the signal.[1] Locally (i.e., for a single transition) the expected result of $\tau(p)$ is $\mathcal{G}(p)$. But is $\mathcal{G}^2(p)$ the expected second generation? A counter example is provided by $n = 2, r = 1$, and suitable $\mathcal{G}$ satisfying

$$\mathcal{G}(\langle 1, 0 \rangle) = \mathcal{G}(\langle 0, 1 \rangle) = \langle 1/2, 1/2 \rangle$$

Here the possible populations are elements of $X_2^1 = \{\langle 1, 0 \rangle, \langle 0, 1 \rangle\}$. They can be thought of as "heads" and "tails". So far, this heuristic is a fair coin toss: 50% "heads", 50% "tails" from either initial condition of "heads" or "tails". Clearly, the expectation of the second toss is the same as that of the first, namely $\langle 0.5, 0.5 \rangle$. This need not coincide with $\mathcal{G}(\langle 0.5, 0.5 \rangle)$ however.

---

1. In dynamical systems theory (see E. Akin (1993), *The General Topology of Dynamical Systems*, American Mathematical Society), *flow* is a technical term which does not relate to iterating $\mathcal{G}$, but rather to an extension of that discrete time dynamical system to continuous time by interpolating between successive iterates. While a standard construction might be used to embed a discrete dynamical system in a flow, the domain of the extension differs, in general, from that of the original dynamical system. The use of the word "flow" in this book is metaphorical, intended to suggest that populations (in the infinite population case) are being swept along an evolutionary trajectory under the influence of an underlying current provided by $\mathcal{G}$.

Any question concerning $\tau(p)$ may be answered in terms of the transition matrix Q, since it defines the stochastic behavior of random heuristic search. To illustrate, the expected kth generation will be determined. Let v be a vector having sth component (s is a population) the probability that $p = s$ (thus v is indexed by populations). Note that the probability that $\tau(p) = q$ is

$$\sum_s \Pr\{p = s\} \Pr\{\tau(s) = q\}$$

which in matrix form is the qth component of $v^T Q$. This observation is essentially the inductive step in showing the probability that $\tau^k(p) = q$ is the qth component of $v^T Q^k$. Hence the expected kth generation is

$$\sum_q q v^T Q^k e_q$$

In light of this and the counter example above, why might the dynamical system with transition function $\mathcal{G}$ have any simple relation to the behavior of random heuristic search with stochastic transition τ? One answer lies in the previous characterization of RHS in terms of signal and noise; thus $\mathcal{G}$ provides the underlying flow which drives the stochastic system and also characterizes the noise. Another answer lies in the fact that the noise decreases as the population size r grows. The exploration of some consequences of these facts—among which are connections between iterates of $\mathcal{G}$ and iterates of τ—forms the latter part of this book.

Before considering the Simple Genetic Algorithm in the next chapter, RHS algorithms are first classified according to the behavior of $\mathcal{G}$. An instance of random heuristic search is *focused* if $\mathcal{G}$ is continuously differentiable and for every $p \in \Lambda$ the sequence

$$p, \mathcal{G}(p), \mathcal{G}^2(p), \ldots$$

converges. In this case $\mathcal{G}$ is also called focused. In terms of search, the latter condition means that the path determined by following at each generation what τ is expected to produce will lead to some state ω. By the continuity of $\mathcal{G}$,

$$\mathcal{G}(\omega) = \mathcal{G}(\lim_{l \to \infty} \mathcal{G}^l(p)) = \lim_{l \to \infty} \mathcal{G}^{l+1}(p) = \omega$$

Hence such points ω satisfy $\mathcal{G}(\omega) = \omega$ and are called *fixed points* of $\mathcal{G}$. The sequence (or set) $p, \mathcal{G}(p), \mathcal{G}^2(p), \ldots$ is called the *orbit* (or *trajectory*) of p under $\mathcal{G}$. It will turn out that fixed points are particularly relevant to both the *transient* (short term) and *asymptotic* (long term average) behavior of focused random heuristic search.

Exercises

1. Extend the counter example to "$\mathcal{G}^2(p)$ is the expected second generation" to a focused heuristic.

2. Adapt the program of exercise 2, section 3.2 to compare the orbit $p, \tau(p), \tau^2(p), \ldots$ with $p, \mathcal{G}(p), \mathcal{G}^2(p), \ldots$ and use it to investigate what happens as $r \to \infty$ for the heuristic of the previous exercise.

3. Adapt the program above (exercise 2) to investigate the relationship between the stochastic transition $p \longrightarrow \tau(p)$ and the vector field on $\frac{1}{r} X_n^r$ which at p has vector $\mathcal{G}(p) - p$.

4. Write general purpose computer code to compute the transition matrix Q.

5. Adapt the program above (exercise 4) to investigate the distribution of probability on $\frac{1}{r} X_n^r$ given current population p. Construct a tetrahedral diagram (like the one illustrating dispersion on page 13) where the size of a lattice point corresponds to its probability of being the next generation.

6. Let ν and Q be the initial population distribution and transition matrix (respectively) for RHS. Show the probability that $\tau^k(p) = q$ is the qth component of $\nu^T Q$.

7. Suppose the goal of RHS is to produce a population which contains some element w of Ω. Let ν and Q be the initial population distribution and transition matrix (respectively), except that all entries (rows and columns) corresponding to populations p satisfying $p_w > 0$ are omitted. Show the expected number of generations to encounter a population containing w is $\nu^T (I - Q)^{-1} \mathbf{1}$. *Hint:* Let S be the set of populations not containing w. Show the expected number of transitions beginning from $s \in S$ till reaching a population not in S is m_s where

$$m_s = 1 + \sum_{q \in S} Q_{s,q} m_q$$

8. Using the programs from previous exercises, empirically investigate the result of exercise 7.

9. Write computer code to compute fixed points of $\mathcal{G}$ by iteration (i.e., find the limit of $p, \mathcal{G}(p), \mathcal{G}^2(p), \ldots$).

10. Empirically investigate whether there seems to be a connection, given a focused heuristic $\mathcal{G}$, between the fixed points of $\mathcal{G}$ as determined by the code from the previous exercise and where in Λ the Markov chain is spending time.

4 The Simple Genetic Algorithm

This chapter develops what have traditionally been regarded as genetic algorithms. There have come to be endless variations on the basic theme which is explored here. No attempt is made to follow or even acknowledge alternate possibilities. Within the confines of the structure gained by limiting consideration to a simple genetic algorithm, the treatment is fairly general, at least with respect to the operators considered.

Naturally enough, the Simple Genetic Algorithm (SGA) is realized by specifying the search space Ω and identifying the heuristic function $\mathcal{G}$. Given the framework provided by the previous chapter, nothing else is required to define the SGA; it is merely a special case of random heuristic search.

The definition of $\mathcal{G}$ proceeds through steps analogous to a procedural prescription for τ (the treatment, however, is not procedural, it is functional). A section is devoted to each: *selection*, *mutation*, and *crossover*. The concluding section brings these elements together to define the simple genetic algorithm.

To the reader already familiar with genetic algorithms, it may not be apparent how some of the definitions presented in this chapter correspond to standard operators used in practice. The interpretation and computation of τ and $\mathcal{G}$ in procedural terms is postponed to a later chapter where it will be shown how the definitions given here may be recognized as describing familiar objects. The purpose of this chapter is to define the SGA as a mathematical object; whether the result is immediately intuitive is beside the point. Proceed, and faith will come.

4.1 Algebra

This first section establishes an algebraic framework which will be used extensively throughout the book.

For integer $\ell > 1$, the set of length ℓ binary strings is the Cartesian product

$$\Omega = \underbrace{\mathcal{Z}_2 \times \cdots \times \mathcal{Z}_2}_{\ell \text{ times}}$$

Since the ℓ-digit binary representations of integers in the interval $[0, 2^\ell)$ coincide with the elements of Ω, they are regarded as being the same. When elements of Ω are written as strings, the standard practice of putting least significant bit to the right is followed. For example, if $\ell = 3$ then $n = 2^\ell$ and

$$\Omega = \{000, 001, 010, 011, 100, 101, 110, 111\} \equiv \{0, 1, 2, 3, 4, 5, 6, 7\}$$

Elements of $\mathcal{Z}_2$ form a finite field under the operations of addition and multiplication modulo 2.

$\oplus$	0	1
0	0	1
1	1	0

$\otimes$	0	1
0	0	0
1	0	1

These operations are extended to Ω by applying them coordinate-wise. By convention, $\otimes$ takes precedence over $\oplus$, and both bind more tightly than operations which are not modulo 2. When representing elements of Ω as column vectors, the least significant bit is at the top. Continuing in the context of the example above (recall that $\langle \cdots \rangle$ denotes a column vector),

$$3 \oplus 5 \equiv 011 \oplus 101 \equiv \langle 1 \oplus 1, 1 \oplus 0, 0 \oplus 1 \rangle \equiv 110 \equiv 6$$

$$6 \otimes 2 \equiv 110 \otimes 010 \equiv \langle 0 \otimes 0, 1 \otimes 1, 1 \otimes 0 \rangle \equiv 010 \equiv 2$$

For $x \in \Omega$, let $\overline{x}$ abbreviate $\mathbf{1} \oplus x$. In standard computer science nomenclature, $\oplus$ is *exclusive-or* on integers, $\otimes$ is *and*, and $x \mapsto \overline{x}$ is *not*. Note that $\otimes$ distributes over $\oplus$. Because $\oplus$ differs from inclusive-or, De Morgan's laws do not hold with respect to $\{^-, \oplus, \otimes\}$.

For $k \in \Omega$, let those l for which $k \otimes 2^l > 0$ be $l_0 < l_1 < \cdots < l_{m-1}$ where $m = \mathbf{1}^T k$. The *injection corresponding to k* is the $\ell \times m$ matrix K defined by $K_{i,j} = [i = l_j]$.

To make explicit the dependence of Ω on the string length ℓ, it may be written as $^\ell\Omega$. The *embedding corresponding to k* is the image under K of $^m\Omega$ (elements of Ω are regarded as column vectors) and is denoted Ω_k. Integers in the interval $[0, 2^m)$ and elements of Ω_k can be (though seldomly) regarded as the same through the correspondence given by K. For example, $\ell = 6$ and $k = 26 \equiv 011010$ gives and $m = \mathbf{1}^T 26 = 3$, $l_0 = 1$, $l_1 = 3$, $l_2 = 4$, and

$$K = \begin{pmatrix} 0 & 0 & 0 \\ 1 & 0 & 0 \\ 0 & 0 & 0 \\ 0 & 1 & 0 \\ 0 & 0 & 1 \\ 0 & 0 & 0 \end{pmatrix}$$

integer	element of $^3\Omega$	corresponding element of Ω_{26}
0	000	000000
1	001	000010
2	010	001000
3	011	001010
4	100	010000
5	101	010010
6	110	011000
7	111	011010

Embedding an element of $^m\Omega$ intuitively corresponds to distributing its bits among the locations where k is nonzero. The utility of embeddings follows from the fact that each $i \in \Omega$ has a unique representation $i = u \oplus v$ where $u \in \Omega_k$ and $v \in \Omega_{\bar{k}}$. This follows from the identity

$$i = i \otimes k \oplus i \otimes \bar{k} = u \oplus v$$

From a more abstract perspective, this is essentially the observation that

$$(\mathbb{Z}_2)^\ell \equiv (\mathbb{Z}_2)^{\mathbf{1}^T k} \times (\mathbb{Z}_2)^{\mathbf{1}^T \bar{k}}$$

Let σ_k be the permutation matrix defined by

$$(\sigma_k)_{i,j} = [i \oplus j = k]$$

The permutation σ_k corresponds to applying the map $i \mapsto i \oplus k$ to subscripts. That is,

$$\sigma_k \langle x_0, \ldots, x_{n-1} \rangle = \langle x_{0 \oplus k}, \ldots, x_{(n-1) \oplus k} \rangle$$

It is easily verified that the σ_k are symmetric matrices and that $\sigma_i \sigma_j = \sigma_{i \oplus j}$. It follows that the σ_k commute and are self inverse.

Exercises

1. Prove the following

(a) if $i = u \oplus v$ where $u \in \Omega_k$ and $v \in \Omega_{\bar{k}}$, then u and v are unique.

(b) $i \otimes \bar{j} = 0 \Longleftrightarrow i \in \Omega_j \Longleftrightarrow \bar{j} \in \Omega_{\bar{i}} \Longleftrightarrow j \in i \oplus \Omega_{\bar{i}}$

(c) $i \otimes \bar{j} = 0 \Longrightarrow i \leq j$

(d) $\Omega_i \cap \Omega_j = \Omega_{i \otimes j}$

2. Prove the following

(a) $i^T j = \mathbf{1}^T i \otimes j$

(b) $KK^T x = k \otimes x$

(c) $K^T K = I_m$

(d) $K^T \mathbf{1} = {}^m \mathbf{1}$

3. For all expressions a, b, and c taking values in Ω, show that $[a = b]$ is equivalent to $[a \otimes c = b \otimes c][a \otimes \bar{c} = b \otimes \bar{c}]$.

4. Prove that Ω_k is an *Abelian group* under $\oplus$. That is, $\oplus : \Omega_k \times \Omega_k \to \Omega_k$ is commutative, associative, there is an identity element, and every $\omega \in \Omega_k$ has an inverse.

5. Is Ω_k an Abelian group under $\otimes$? A group whose operation is commutative is called Abelian. Does the collection $\{\sigma_k\}$ of permutations form a group?

6. Show, for $i, j \in \Omega$, that $\mathbf{1}^T i = \mathbf{1}^T j$ if and only if there exists a permutation matrix σ such that $\sigma i = j$ (a permutation matrix is the result of permuting rows or columns of I). Moreover, for general i, j and permutation matrix σ, show that

(a) $\sigma(i \oplus j) = \sigma i \oplus \sigma j$

(b) $\sigma(i \otimes j) = \sigma i \otimes \sigma j$

(c) $i^T j = (\sigma i)^T \sigma j$

(d) $\sigma(i \cdot j) = (\sigma i) \cdot \sigma j$

7. Although this text deals with the binary case (i.e., $\Omega = \mathcal{Z}_2^\ell$), the entire development can be extended to length ℓ strings over $\mathcal{Z}_c$ (i.e., the components of $x \in \Omega$ come from the integers modulo c). The extension to this more general case, begun by Gary Koehler and Siddhartha Bhattacharyya, will be outlined in the exercises and will be referred to as the *general cardinality case*. Show the following:

(a) The correspondence of $\mathcal{Z}_2^\ell$ with integers in the interval $[0, 2^\ell)$ can be extended to identify $\mathcal{Z}_c^\ell$ with integers in the interval $[0, c^\ell)$ by way of their base c representation.

(b) $\oplus$ can be extended to coordinate-wise addition modulo c.

(c) $\otimes$ can be extended to coordinate-wise multiplication modulo c.

(d) $\overline{j}$ can be extended to $\mathbf{1} \ominus j$, where $\ominus$ is coordinate-wise subtraction modulo c.

(e) $i \otimes j \oplus i \otimes \overline{j} = i$.

(f) $u \otimes k = i \otimes k \wedge v \otimes \overline{k} = i \otimes \overline{k} \Longleftrightarrow u \otimes k \oplus v \otimes \overline{k} = i$, provided $k \in \{0, 1\}^\ell$.

(g) The permutation matrices σ_k can be extended to $(\sigma_k)_{i,j} = [j \ominus i = k]$.

(h) The injection and embedding corresponding to k can be extended by replacing 2 with c and replacing m with the number of nonzero components of k.

4.2   Selection

The symbol s will be used for three equivalent (though different) things. This overloading of s does not take long to get used to because context makes meaning clear. The benefits are clean and elegant presentation and the ability to use a common symbol for ideas whose differences are often conveniently blurred.

First, $s \in \Lambda$ can be regarded as a *selection distribution* describing the probability s_i with which i is selected (with replacement) from the current population for participation in forming the next generation. A selected element is an intermediate step towards producing the next population, not typically a member of it. In total, $2r$ such selections are typically made, the aggregate of which is sometimes referred to as the *gene pool*.

Second, $s : \Lambda \to \Omega$ can be regarded as a *selection function* which is nondeterministic.

The result $s(p)$ of applying the selection function s to p is i with probability given by the ith component s_i of the selection distribution. Of course, for there to be a nontrivial dependence on p, the selection distribution must be some function $\mathcal{F}$ of p. The function $\mathcal{F}$ is referred to as the *selection scheme*.

Third, $s \in \Lambda$ can be regarded as a population vector (sometimes referred to as a *selection vector*).

An integral part of selection is an injective *fitness function* $f : \Omega \to \Re$ which is used (in a variety of ways) to determine a selection scheme.[1] The value $f(i)$ is called the *fitness* of i. Through the identification $f_i = f(i)$, the fitness function may be regarded as a vector.

Proportional selection refers to the selection function corresponding to the selection scheme

$$\mathcal{F}(x) = f \cdot x / f^T x$$

When proportional selection is being used, it is assumed that the fitness function is positive. Note that the proportional selection scheme is the identity function if $f \sim \mathbf{1}$ and is a linear transformation when magnitude is ignored (recall $f \cdot x$ denotes $\text{diag}(f)x$). Moreover, proportional selection does not depend on r. In fact, any focused heuristic $\mathcal{F}$ satisfying $p_i = 0 \implies \mathcal{F}(p)_i = 0$ can be used as a selection scheme. A heuristic $\mathcal{F}$ of this type used in this way (i.e. $s = \mathcal{F}(p)$) is referred to as *arbitrary selection*. An arbitrary selection scheme is called *positive* if $p_i > 0 \implies \mathcal{F}(p)_i > 0$.

Ranking selection refers to the selection function corresponding to the selection scheme

$$\mathcal{F}(x)_i = \int_{\sum [f_j < f_i] x_j}^{\sum [f_j \leq f_i] x_j} \varrho(y) \, dy$$

where ϱ is any continuous increasing probability density over $[0, 1]$.

For example, let $n = 4$, let $p = \langle .2, .3, .1, .4 \rangle$, and assume $f(x) = \log(1 + x)$ so that $f_0 < f_1 < f_2 < f_3$. The following table corresponds to $\varrho(y) = 2y$:

i	$\sum [f_j < f_i] x_j$	$\mathcal{F}(x)_i$	$s_i = \mathcal{F}(p)_i$
0	0	$\int_0^{x_0} \varrho(y) \, dy$	0.04
1	x_0	$\int_{x_0}^{x_0 + x_1} \varrho(y) \, dy$	0.21
2	$x_0 + x_1$	$\int_{x_0 + x_1}^{x_0 + x_1 + x_2} \varrho(y) \, dy$	0.11
3	$x_0 + x_1 + x_2$	$\int_{x_0 + x_1 + x_2}^{1} \varrho(y) \, dy$	0.64

1. In practice f is not necessarily injective, but an arbitrarily small perturbation would make it so. Because the assumption simplifies analysis, it is made throughout this book.

Therefore 0 is chosen for the gene pool with probability 0.04, while 2 is chosen with probability 0.11. This example illustrates that with ranking selection the selection distribution depends on how the elements of Ω are ranked by f; any increasing fitness function ($i < j \implies f(i) < f(j)$) would yield these same results. Also note that no reference to population size was made (there is no dependence on r).

Tournament selection refers to the selection function corresponding to the selection scheme

$$\mathcal{F}(x)_i = k! \sum_{v \in X_n^k} \mathcal{F}'(v/k)_i \prod_{j<n} \frac{x_j^{v_j}}{v_j!}$$

where $k > 1$ is an integer parameter and $\mathcal{F}'$ is any ranking selection scheme. Again, there is no dependence on population size.

By letting the heuristic $\mathcal{G}$ be the selection scheme, results from the previous chapter apply to selection. With population size $2r$, $\tau(p)$ becomes the gene pool. Invoking theorem 3.3, the expected gene pool is described by the population vector $s = \mathcal{F}(p)$. Theorem 3.4 gives the probability with which any $q \in \Lambda$ is the gene pool, and theorem 3.5 gives the variance.

For example, if $f = \mathbf{1}$ and the selection scheme is proportional, then $\mathcal{F}$ is the identity function on Λ, and (as the chapter on implementation will show) selection corresponds to choosing (with replacement) among equally likely population members. Therefore applying theorem 3.4 with population vector x and population size k yields

$$k! \prod_{j} \frac{x_j^{kq_j}}{(kq_j)!} = \Pr\{q \text{ results from uniformly choosing } k \text{ members of } x\}$$

Applying ranking selection to the result q, the probability of both producing q and selecting i is

$$k! \mathcal{F}'(q)_i \prod_{j} \frac{x_j^{kq_j}}{(kq_j)!}$$

Summing over all possible $q = v/k$ yields

$$k! \sum_{v \in X_n^k} \mathcal{F}'(v/k)_i \prod_{j<n} \frac{x_j^{v_j}}{v_j!}$$

It follows that tournament selection is ranking selection applied to the population vector q resulting from k uniform choices (with replacement) from the population x.

It will be shown in a later chapter that each of the selection schemes is continuously differentiable; they are in fact focused heuristics. Unless otherwise specified, reference to a selection scheme $\mathcal{F}$ indicates one of the three introduced in this section (proportional, ranking, or tournament).

Exercises

1. Show that $\mathcal{F} : \Lambda \to \Lambda$ for each of the selection schemes introduced in this section. In particular, prove

$$\mathbf{1}^T \mathcal{F}(x) = \int_0^{\mathbf{1}^T x} \varrho(y)\, dy$$

for ranking selection, and

$$\mathbf{1}^T \mathcal{F}(x) = (\mathbf{1}^T x)^k$$

for tournament selection.

2. Show each of the selection schemes introduced in this section is positive.

3. Interpret proportional selection in terms of choosing (with replacement) *population members* rather than selecting population member *types* from Ω.

4. Interpret ranking selection in terms of sorting (ranking) the population followed by choosing members according to a distribution based on rank.

5. Assuming that $\mathcal{G}$ is chosen to be $\mathcal{F}$, show $\tau(p) \subset p$ (recall that p and $\tau(p)$ may be regarded as populations). Hence selection does not explore beyond the confines of the population.

6. Assuming that $\mathcal{G}$ is $\mathcal{F}$, show that iterates of τ will, with probability one, converge.

7. What are the fixed points of $\mathcal{F}$?

8. Write a computer program to compute $\mathcal{F}$ for proportional, ranking, and tournament selection.

9. Adapt the program of the previous exercise to allow for arbitrary selection.

10. Why is there no reason to modify selection for the general cardinality case?

4.3   Mutation

As seen in the previous section (exercise 5) selection is not an explorative heuristic. Mutation is one mechanism for injecting new strings into the next generation, giving RHS the ability to search beyond the confines of the initial population.

The symbol μ will also be used for three different (though related) things. First, $\mu \in \Lambda$ can be regarded as a distribution describing the probability μ_i with which $i \in \Omega$ is selected to be a mutation mask (additional details follow).

Second, $\mu : \Omega \rightarrow \Omega$ can be regarded as a *mutation function* which is nondeterministic. The result $\mu(x)$ of applying the mutation function μ to x is $x \oplus i$ with probability given by the ith component μ_i of the distribution μ. The i occurring in $x \oplus i$ is referred to as a *mutation mask*. The application of μ to x is referred to as *mutating* x.

Third, $\mu \in [0, 0.5)$ can be regarded as a *mutation rate* which implicitly specifies the distribution μ according to the rule

$$\mu_i = (\mu)^{\mathbf{1}^T i}(1 - \mu)^{\ell - \mathbf{1}^T i}$$

The distribution μ need not correspond to any mutation rate, although that is certainly the classical situation. Any element $\mu \in \Lambda$ whatsoever is allowed.

The effect of mutating x using mutation mask i is to alter the bits of x in those positions where the mutation mask i is 1. When mutation is affected by a rate, the probability of selecting mask i depends only on the number of 1s that i contains.

If the mutation rate is nonzero (the typical case) then every element of Ω has a positive probability of being the result of $\mu(x)$ for any x. Mutation is said to be *zero* if $\mu = e_0$. For arbitrary $\mu \in \Lambda$, mutation is called *positive* if $\mu_i > 0$ for all i.

The heuristic $\mathcal{F}_\mu$ corresponding to mutating the result of selection is defined by

$$\mathcal{F}_\mu(p)_i = \Pr\{i \text{ results} \mid \text{population } p\}$$

$$= \sum \Pr\{j \text{ selected} \mid \text{population } p\} \; \Pr\{j \text{ mutates to } i\}$$

$$= \sum \mathcal{F}(p)_j \mu_{j \oplus i}$$

In the positive mutation case, this heuristic results in an ergodic Markov chain. In particular, the sequence

$$p, \tau(p), \tau(\tau(p)), \dots$$

visits every population infinitely often. This is essentially the observation that positive mutation will produce any element of Ω with nonzero probability.

Mutation is called *independent* if for all j and k

$$\mu_j = \sum_{k \otimes i = 0} \mu_{i \oplus j} \sum_{\bar{k} \otimes i = 0} \mu_{i \oplus j}$$

Independent mutation is of interest because of its relationship to the crossover operator considered in the next section.

Theorem 4.1   If μ corresponds to a mutation rate, then μ is independent.

Proof   The rightmost factor in the definition of independence is

$$\sum_{\bar{k}\otimes(i\oplus j)=0} \mu_i = (1-\mu)^\ell \sum_{\bar{k}\otimes i=\bar{k}\otimes j} \left(\frac{\mu}{1-\mu}\right)^{\mathbf{1}^T i}$$

Note that if $i = \bar{k} \otimes j \oplus k \otimes u$ then $\bar{k} \otimes i = \bar{k} \otimes j$. Hence summation over the range of i appropriate to the right hand side above corresponds to summation over $u \in \Omega_k$. Letting $m = \mathbf{1}^T k$, the summation in the right hand side is

$$\sum_{u\in\Omega_k} \left(\frac{\mu}{1-\mu}\right)^{\mathbf{1}^T\bar{k}\otimes j+\mathbf{1}^T u} = (1-\mu)^{-m}\left(\frac{\mu}{1-\mu}\right)^{\mathbf{1}^T\bar{k}\otimes j} \sum_{u\in^m\Omega} \mu^{\mathbf{1}^T u}(1-\mu)^{m-\mathbf{1}^T u}$$

Since the rightmost sum above is 1, it follows that

$$\sum_{k\otimes i=0} \mu_{i\oplus j} \sum_{\bar{k}\otimes i=0} \mu_{i\oplus j}$$

$$= (1-\mu)^{\ell-\mathbf{1}^T k}\left(\frac{\mu}{1-\mu}\right)^{\mathbf{1}^T\bar{k}\otimes j}(1-\mu)^{\ell-\mathbf{1}^T\bar{k}}\left(\frac{\mu}{1-\mu}\right)^{\mathbf{1}^T k\otimes j}$$

$$= \mu_j \qquad\qquad\qquad\qquad\qquad\qquad\qquad\qquad\qquad\qquad\qquad\qquad \blacksquare$$

Exercises

1. Prove that $\mu(x) = x$ (and hence $\mathcal{F}_\mu = \mathcal{F}$) when mutation is zero.

2. Prove that $\mathcal{F}_\mu$ is projectively (i.e., ignoring magnitude) a linear transformation when the selection scheme is proportional, and that its fixed points correspond to eigenvectors.

3. Prove that $\mathcal{F}_\mu$ is focused when the selection scheme is proportional and mutation is positive. *Hint:* Use the fact that $\mathcal{F}_\mu$ is projectively linear (see the previous exercise). Since the corresponding matrix, call it A, is positive, there is a basis $b_0, \ldots, b_{n-1}$ and $\lambda > 0$ such that

$$A^k p = A^k \sum_{j=0}^{n-1} c_j b_j = \lambda^k \left(c_0 b_0 + o(1) \sum_{j=1}^{n-1} b_j\right)$$

and the coefficient c_0 in the representation of p is nonzero for any $p \in \Lambda$ (see appendix). Thus

$$\lim_{k\to\infty} \mathcal{F}_\mu^k(p) = \lim_{k\to\infty} \frac{A^k p}{\|A^k p\|_1}$$

4. Show by example that if mutation is not positive, then $\mathcal{F}_\mu$ need not be focused.

5. Can μ be independent without corresponding to a mutation rate?

6. Interpret mutation in the general cardinality case. That is, explain the three meanings of μ when Λ is the state space of RHS corresponding to $\Omega = \mathcal{Z}_c^\ell$. *Hint:* In the case of a rate, define the distribution according to

$$\mu_i = (\mu/(c-1))^{\#i}(1-\mu)^{\ell-\#i}$$

where $\#i$ denotes the number of nonzero components of i.

7. In the general cardinality case, independent mutation is defined with the restriction that k be binary (i.e., $k \in \{0, 1\}^\ell$). Show theorem 4.1 carries over to the general cardinality case.

4.4 Crossover

It is convenient to use the concept of *partial probability*. Let $\zeta : A \to B$ and suppose $\phi : A \to [0, 1]$. To say "ξ is $\zeta(a)$ with partial probability $\phi(a)$" means, for all b, that ξ takes the value b with probability $\sum[\zeta(a) = b]\phi(a)$.

The description of crossover parallels the description of mutation given in the previous section; the symbol χ will be used for three different (though related) things.

First, $\chi \in \Lambda$ can be regarded as a distribution describing the probability χ_i with which i is selected to be a crossover mask (additional details follow).

Second, $\chi : \Omega \times \Omega \to \Omega$ can be regarded as a *crossover function* which is nondeterministic. The result $\chi(x, y)$ is $x \otimes i \oplus \bar{i} \otimes y$ with partial probability $\chi_i/2$ and is $y \otimes i \oplus \bar{i} \otimes x$ with partial probability $\chi_i/2$. The i occurring in the definition of $\chi(x, y)$ is a *crossover mask*. The application of χ to x, y is referred to as *recombining* x and y.

Arguments x and y of the crossover function are called *parents*, the pair $x \otimes i \oplus \bar{i} \otimes y$ and $y \otimes i \oplus \bar{i} \otimes x$ are referred to as their *children*. Note that crossover produces children by exchanging the bits of parents in those positions where the crossover mask i is 1. The result $\chi(x, y)$ is called their *child*.

Third, $\chi \in [0, 1]$ can be regarded as a *crossover rate* which specifies the distribution χ according to the rule

$$\chi_i = \begin{cases} \chi c_i & \text{if } i > 0 \\ 1 - \chi + \chi c_0 & \text{if } i = 0 \end{cases}$$

where $c \in \Lambda$ is referred to as the *crossover type*. Classical crossover types include *1-point crossover*, for which

$$c_i = \begin{cases} 1/(\ell - 1) & \text{if } \exists k \in (0, \ell) . \, i = 2^k - 1 \\ 0 & \text{otherwise} \end{cases}$$

and *uniform crossover*, for which $c_i = 2^{-\ell}$. The situation where the crossover distribution is $\mathcal{X} = e_0$ (equivalent to a zero crossover rate), is referred to as *zero crossover*.

The following theorem says that when mutation is independent, it may be performed either before or after crossover; the effects are probabilistically the same.

Theorem 4.2 If μ is independent, then for arbitrary $\mathcal{X}$

$$\Pr\{\mathcal{X}(\mu(x), \mu(y)) = z\} = \Pr\{\mu(\mathcal{X}(x, y)) = z\}$$

Proof The left hand probability is

$$\sum_{i,j,k} \mu_i \mu_j \mathcal{X}_k \frac{1}{2} ([(x \oplus i) \otimes k \oplus \bar{k} \otimes (y \oplus j) = z] + [(x \oplus i) \otimes \bar{k} \oplus k \otimes (y \oplus j) = z])$$

Splitting the sum across the "+", performing the change of variable $k \mapsto \bar{k}$ and recombining yields

$$\sum_{i,j,k} \mu_i \mu_j \frac{\mathcal{X}_k + \mathcal{X}_{\bar{k}}}{2} [(x \oplus i) \otimes k \oplus \bar{k} \otimes (y \oplus j) = z]$$

$$= \sum_{k} \frac{\mathcal{X}_k + \mathcal{X}_{\bar{k}}}{2} \sum_{h} [x \otimes k \oplus \bar{k} \otimes y = z \oplus h] \sum_{i \otimes k \oplus j \otimes \bar{k} = h} \mu_i \mu_j$$

Note that $i \otimes k \oplus j \otimes \bar{k} = h$ is equivalent to the pair of relations $k \otimes i = k \otimes h$ and $\bar{k} \otimes j = \bar{k} \otimes h$. Thus the last sum above is

$$\sum_{k \otimes (i \oplus h) = 0} \mu_i \sum_{\bar{k} \otimes (j \oplus h) = 0} \mu_j$$

which, by the independence of μ, is μ_h. Substituting μ_h for this sum yields

$$\sum_{k} \frac{\mathcal{X}_k + \mathcal{X}_{\bar{k}}}{2} \sum_{h} [x \otimes k \oplus \bar{k} \otimes y = z \oplus h] \mu_h$$

Splitting the sum across the "+", changing variables, and recombining as before yields

$$\sum_{k,h} \mu_h \mathcal{X}_k \frac{1}{2} ([x \otimes k \oplus \bar{k} \otimes y = z \oplus h] + [x \otimes \bar{k} \oplus k \otimes y = z \oplus h])$$

which is equal to $\Pr\{\mu(X(x, y)) = z\}$.   ∎

Exercises

1. The *2n-point crossover* of parents x and y has the following procedural description. Let $0 \le b_1 < \cdots < b_{2n} < \ell$ be $2n$ distinct random choices. Interpreting subscripts of x and of y modulo ℓ, the two children are obtained from the strings

$$x_{b_1} \cdots x_{b_2-1} y_{b_2} \cdots y_{b_3-1} x_{b_3} \cdots x_{b_4-1} \cdots y_{b_{2n}} \cdots y_{\ell+b_1-1}$$

$$y_{b_1} \cdots y_{b_2-1} x_{b_2} \cdots x_{b_3-1} y_{b_3} \cdots y_{b_4-1} \cdots x_{b_{2n}} \cdots x_{\ell+b_1-1}$$

by cyclicly permuting their bits so that the resulting strings begin with x_0 and y_0 (respectively). What is the corresponding crossover type $c \in \Lambda$?

2. *n-point crossover* results from making n random choices $0 \le b_1 < \cdots < b_{2n} < \ell$ and interchanging, with probability X, bits $x_{b_k} \cdots x_{b_{k+1}-1}$ of parent x with bits $y_{b_k} \cdots y_{b_{k+1}-1}$ of parent y for $0 < k \le n$ (subscripts of x and of y are interpreted modulo ℓ). What is the corresponding crossover type $c \in \Lambda$?

3. Show by example that theorem 4.2 could fail if mutation were not independent.

4. Interpret crossover in the general cardinality case. *Hint:* Do not allow arbitrary $X \in \Lambda$, but restrict to binary masks (i.e., $i \notin \{0, 1\}^\ell \implies X_i = 0$).

5. Show theorem 4.2 carries over to the general cardinality case.

4.5   Mixing

Obtaining child z from parents x and y via the process of mutation and crossover is called *mixing* and has probability denoted by $m_{x,y}(z)$. Formulas for these probabilities (which are contained in the proof of theorem 4.2) are recorded in the following theorem.

Theorem 4.3   Whether or not μ is independent, if mutation is performed before crossover, then

$$m_{x,y}(z) = \sum_{i,j,k} \mu_i \mu_j \frac{X_k + X_{\overline{k}}}{2} [(x \oplus i) \otimes k \oplus \overline{k} \otimes (y \oplus j) = z]$$

and if mutation is performed after crossover, then

$$m_{x,y}(z) = \sum_{j,k} \mu_j \frac{X_k + X_{\overline{k}}}{2} [x \otimes k \oplus \overline{k} \otimes y \oplus j = z]$$

When mutation and crossover are both zero, mixing is referred to as *cloning*. Mixing has many symmetries. The most fundamental are given by the following theorem.

Theorem 4.4   Whether or not μ is independent, and whether or not mutation is performed before or after crossover,

$$m_{x,y}(z) = m_{y,x}(z) = m_{x\oplus z, y\oplus z}(0)$$

Proof   Theorem 4.3 is symmetric in x and y. The indicator function in theorem 4.3 corresponding to mutation before crossover is equivalent to

$$[((x \oplus z) \oplus i) \otimes k \oplus \overline{k} \otimes ((y \oplus z) \oplus j) = 0]$$

The case of mutation after crossover is analogous.   ∎

The matrix M with i, jth entry $m_{i,j}(0)$ is called the *mixing matrix*. It is symmetric by theorem 4.4. The *mixing scheme* $\mathcal{M} : \Lambda \to \Lambda$ is defined by the component equations

$$\mathcal{M}(x)_i = (\sigma_i x)^T M \sigma_i x$$

Theorem 4.5   The heuristic $\mathcal{M}$ corresponds to mixing the results of uniform choice (with replacement) from the population.

Proof   Let $\mathcal{F}$ be the proportional selection scheme corresponding to $f = \mathbf{1}$. By theorem 4.4 and the discussion in section 4.2,

$$\mathcal{M}(x)_i$$

$$= \sum_{u,v} x_u x_v M_{u\oplus i, v\oplus i}$$

$$= \sum_{u,v} \mathcal{F}(x)_u \mathcal{F}(x)_v m_{u,v}(i)$$

$$= \sum_{u,v} \Pr\{u \text{ selected} \mid x\} \Pr\{v \text{ selected} \mid x\} \Pr\{i \text{ is the child} \mid \text{parents } u, v\} \qquad ∎$$

The next theorem decomposes $\mathcal{M}$ into a composition of operators, one corresponding to mutation, and the other corresponding to crossover.

Theorem 4.6   If the selection scheme for the operator $\mathcal{F}_\mu$ is proportional, then

$$\mathcal{M} = \left(\mathcal{M}\Big|_{\mu=e_0}\right) \circ \left(\mathcal{F}_\mu\Big|_{f=\mathbf{1}}\right)$$

Proof   It is easily verified that

$$(\mathcal{F}_\mu\Big|_{f=1})(x)_i = \sum x_j \mu_{j\oplus i}$$

and

$$(\mathcal{M}\Big|_{\mu=e_0})(x)_i = \sum_{u,v} x_u x_v \sum_k \frac{\chi_k + \chi_{\bar{k}}}{2}[u \otimes k \oplus \bar{k} \otimes v = i]$$

Therefore,

$$(\mathcal{M}\Big|_{\mu=e_0}) \circ (\mathcal{F}_\mu\Big|_{f=1})(x)_h$$

$$= \sum_{u,v} \sum_i x_i \mu_{i \oplus u} \sum_j x_j \mu_{j \oplus v} \sum_k \frac{\chi_k + \chi_{\bar{k}}}{2}[u \otimes k \oplus \bar{k} \otimes v = h]$$

$$= \sum_{i,j} x_i x_j \sum_{u,v,k} \mu_{i \oplus u} \mu_{j \oplus v} \frac{\chi_k + \chi_{\bar{k}}}{2}[u \otimes k \oplus \bar{k} \otimes v = h]$$

$$= \sum_{i,j} x_i x_j \sum_{u,v,k} \mu_u \mu_v \frac{\chi_k + \chi_{\bar{k}}}{2}[(u \oplus i) \otimes k \oplus \bar{k} \otimes (v \oplus j) = h]$$

$$= \sum_{i,j} x_i x_j M_{i \oplus h, j \oplus h}$$

$$= \mathcal{M}(x)_h \qquad\qquad\qquad\qquad\qquad\qquad\qquad\qquad\qquad\qquad\blacksquare$$

The restriction of the operator $\mathcal{F}_\mu$ to $f = 1$, given that its selection scheme is proportional, is referred to as the *mutation scheme*, and the restriction of the operator $\mathcal{M}$ to $\mu = e_0$ is referred to as the *crossover scheme*.

In a later chapter, necessary and sufficient conditions for $\mathcal{M}$ to be focused will be determined. Although a sufficient condition is positive mutation, $\mathcal{M}$ is focused under far more general conditions.

Exercises

1. Theorem 4.5 implies $\mathcal{M} : \Lambda \to \Lambda$. Give alternate justification for the invariance of Λ under $\mathcal{M}$, using only the identity $1 = \sum_z M_{x \oplus z, y \oplus z}$ which follows from theorem 4.4.

2. Write computer code to compute the mixing matrix for 1-point, n-point, $2n$-point, and uniform crossover, given crossover rate χ and mutation rate μ.

3. Write a computer program to compute the mixing matrix for arbitrary distributions χ and μ.

4. Write a computer program to compute $\mathcal{M}$ for arbitrary mixing matrix M.

5. Prove that if mutation is independent then the mutation scheme and the crossover scheme commute, i.e.,

$$(\mathcal{M}\Big|_{\mu=e_0}) \circ (\mathcal{F}_\mu\Big|_{f=1}) = (\mathcal{F}_\mu\Big|_{f=1}) \circ (\mathcal{M}\Big|_{\mu=e_0})$$

6. Is the hypotheses of proportional selection necessary in theorem 4.6?

7. Show that if mutation is zero, then for every k,

$$\sum_{i \in \Omega_k} M_{i,i \oplus k} = 1$$

8. Show the following theorems carry over to the general cardinality case:

(a) Theorem 4.3. *Hint:* See exercise 4 of section 4.4.

(b) Theorem 4.4, provided $\oplus$ is replaced by $\ominus$.

(c) Theorems 4.5 and 4.6.

4.6 SGA's Heuristic

The heuristic $\mathcal{G}$ defining the simple genetic algorithm is the composition of mixing and selection

$$\mathcal{G} = \mathcal{M} \circ \mathcal{F}$$

As mentioned previously, the heuristic $\mathcal{F}$ is focused, and under quite general conditions so is $\mathcal{M}$. Formulas will be derived for their fixed points (when $\mathcal{M}$ is not focused, its iterates converge towards a periodic orbit which will be explicitly determined). The situation for $\mathcal{G}$ appears to be considerably more complex. Very little is known concerning when it is focused, although empirical evidence points towards that being the typical case when mutation is given by a rate $\mu < 0.5$.

Since the simple genetic algorithm's heuristic has been defined, the transition rule τ of random heuristic search can be implemented as outlined in exercise 2 of section 3.2 (the exercises have asked for the requisite computer code to be completed by this point). Such an implementation is most natural since it corresponds directly to the definition of RHS.

From a complexity standpoint, naive computation of $\mathcal{G}$ takes $O(8^\ell)$ time. Even though this can be improved to $O(3^\ell)$ (and, in the special case where mixing is via a mutation rate and one-point crossover, to $O(\ell 2^\ell)$), computation remains limited to somewhere around $\ell = 20$. The best implementations of τ are based on procedures which generate an element for the next generation with appropriate probability without calculating $\mathcal{G}$. That is, exponential complexity is avoided by sampling without computing the distribution which governs the sampling. The next chapter shows how this may be accomplished. A consequence is that, in practice, computation of τ takes time $O(\ell)$.

As described in the previous section, $\mathcal{M}$ may depend on the order of mutation and crossover. Since $\mathcal{G}$ based on mutation after crossover is analogous (and simpler), the remainder of this book will assume mutation occurs before crossover.

In the general case, a heuristic of random heuristic search is called *ergodic* if RHS using that heuristic is an ergodic Markov chain for all r (in that case RHS is also called ergodic). This section closes with a formal statement of the fact that, with positive mutation, the SGA's heuristic is ergodic.

Theorem 4.7   If μ is positive, then $\mathcal{G}(x)$ is positive for every $x \in \Lambda$. In particular, $\mathcal{G}(x)$ is ergodic.

Proof   Consider the mixing matrix

$$M_{x,y} = \sum_{i,j,k} \mu_i \mu_j \frac{\chi_k + \chi_{\overline{k}}}{2} [(x \oplus i) \otimes k \oplus \overline{k} \otimes (y \oplus j) = 0]$$

Let k be such that $\chi_k > 0$, and let $i = x \oplus \overline{k}$, $j = y \oplus k$. The sum above consists of nonnegative terms, and the term corresponding to i, j, k is

$$\mu_i \mu_j \frac{\chi_k + \chi_{\overline{k}}}{2} > 0$$

Thus M has positive entries. It follows that $\mathcal{G}(x)$ is positive. Hence (by theorem 3.4) every population has a nonzero probability of being the next generation.   ∎

Exercises

1. Write computer code implementing the SGA as outlined in exercise 2 of section 3.3. Include the following options:

- arbitrary fitness function f.

- proportional, ranking, tournament or arbitrary selection scheme.

- 1-point, n-point, $2n$-point, uniform, or arbitrary crossover distribution.

- arbitrary mutation distribution or mutation rate.
- arbitrary mixing matrix M.

This only requires integrating code from previous exercises.

2. Extend the computer code of the previous exercise to the general cardinality case.

3. Since the SGA is ergodic, it visits every population infinitely often. Use code from the previous exercise to investigate how long it takes to visit each population at least once.

4. Suppose the goal of RHS is to produce a population which contains some element w of Ω. A crude estimate of how long this might take is the time required to visit every population at least once. Another estimate is provided by the method of exercise 7 in section 3.3. Compare these two estimates empirically.

5. Consider the instance of the simple genetic algorithm determined by proportional selection and the parameters

$\ell = 2$

$r = 5$

$f = \langle 1.000, 0.001, 0.002, 0.003 \rangle$

$\chi = \langle 1.000, 0.000, 0.000, 0.000 \rangle$

$\mu = \langle 0.001, 0.001, 0.001, 0.997 \rangle$

What is the typical behavior of an orbit $p, \tau(p), \tau^2(p), \ldots$? Contrast that with the behavior of the orbit $p, \mathcal{G}(p), \mathcal{G}^2(p), \ldots$. *Hint:* Compute orbits under τ, but appeal to exercise 3 of section 4.3 to characterize orbits under $\mathcal{G}$.

6. Explain the results of the previous exercise in terms of the coarseness of the lattice available to populations for occupation. How do the results of the previous exercise change as r increases?

7. Show theorem 4.7 carries over to the general cardinality case.

8. The definition of the simple genetic algorithm involves $\mu \in \Lambda$ (mutation), $\chi \in \Lambda$ (crossover), and f (fitness). Show that without loss of generality $f \in \Lambda$. *Hint:* For proportional selection, f may be arbitrarily scaled. Tournament selection reduces to ranking selection which allows f to be translated as well as scaled.

5 Implementation

This chapter will show how to implement τ efficiently. The key is to appropriately sample Ω without computing $\mathcal{G}$. Some readers may be wondering whether the SGA as defined in previous chapters is the same simple genetic algorithm they are already familiar with. Among other things, this chapter shows that it is.

The first three sections are devoted to efficient procedural counterparts of selection, mutation, and crossover. The fourth section implements τ by assembling these elements, and the classical, procedurally defined genetic algorithm emerges. The final section is devoted to efficiently making random choices, a subject important to every implementation of the SGA.

5.1 Selection

Efficient implementation of an arbitrary selection scheme is in general not possible (though the methods of section 5.5 may be helpful to some extent). This section therefore considers proportional, ranking, and tournament selection.

Proportional selection is considered first. Let f be a positive fitness function and let $P = \{x_0, \ldots, x_{r-1}\}$ be the current population (a multiset). The corresponding population vector p is

$$p_i = \frac{1}{r} \sum_{j \in P} [i = j]$$

The selection distribution is $s = f \cdot p / f^T p$. Note that

$$e_i^T \operatorname{diag}(f) p = \frac{f(i)}{r} \sum_{j \in P} [i = j] = \frac{f(i)}{r} \sum_k [x_k = i]$$

Moreover, $f^T p$ is

$$\sum_i e_i^T \operatorname{diag}(f) p$$

$$= \sum_i \frac{f(i)}{r} \sum_k [x_k = i]$$

$$= \frac{1}{r} \sum_k \sum_i f(i) [x_k = i]$$

$$= \frac{1}{r} \sum_k f(x_k)$$

Therefore, the selection function chooses i with probability

$$s_i = \frac{f(i)}{\sum f(x_k)} \sum [x_k = i]$$

Now consider choosing x_j (with replacement) from P with probability

$$\frac{f(x_j)}{\sum f(x_k)}$$

The probability of choosing i is

$$\sum_j \frac{f(x_j)}{\sum f(x_k)}[x_j = i] = \frac{f(i)}{\sum f(x_k)} \sum_j [x_j = i]$$

which is identical to s_i. Therefore, *choosing population members in proportion to their fitness implements the proportional selection function.* Choosing k elements (with replacement) from a population P of size r with respect to an arbitrary probability distribution over P can be accomplished in $O(k + r)$ time.

Next consider ranking selection (f need not be positive). Let the elements of P be indexed so that $f(x_0) \leq \ldots \leq f(x_{r-1})$. The selection distribution is

$$s_i = \int_{\sum [f_j < f_i] p_j}^{\sum [f_j \leq f_i] p_j} \varrho(y) \, dy$$

If $i \notin P$ then $p_i = 0$, and in that case the upper and lower limits of the integral are

$$\sum_j [f_j \leq f_i] p_j = \sum_j [f_j < f_i] p_j$$

Hence $s_i = 0$ since the limits of the integral coincide. If $i \in P$, the lower limit is

$$\frac{1}{r} \sum_j [f_j < f_i] \sum_{k \in P} \delta_{j,k}$$

$$= \frac{1}{r} \sum_{k \in P} \sum_j [f_j < f_i] \delta_{j,k}$$

$$= \frac{1}{r} \sum_{k \in P} [f_k < f_i]$$

$$= \text{(the smallest } j \text{ such that } i = x_j)/r$$

Similarly, the upper limit is

(the largest j such that $i = x_{j-1}$)/r

It follows that

$$s_i = \sum [i = x_j] \int_{j/r}^{(j+1)/r} \varrho(y)\, dy$$

Now define

$$t_j = \int_{j/r}^{(j+1)/r} \varrho(y)\, dy$$

and consider choosing x_j from P with probability t_j. The probability of choosing i is

$$\sum [i = x_j] t_j$$

which is identical to s_i. Therefore, *sorting the population followed by choosing members (based on rank) according to the distribution t implements the ranking selection function.* Because of the required sort, choosing k elements (with replacement) takes $O(k + r \log r)$ time.

Tournament selection has already been interpreted in terms of ranking selection (section 4.2): *Applying the ranking selection function to the result of k uniform choices (with replacement) from the population implements the tournament selection function with parameter k.*

The situation where $f \sim \mathbf{1}$ and selection is proportional, or else $\varrho = 1$ and selection is either ranking or tournament, is referred to as *uniform selection* . In this case $\mathcal{F}(x) = x$ and the selection function corresponds to a uniform choice from the population.

Exercises

1. Verify the claims made for uniform selection.

2. Write an efficient computer implementation of the proportional, ranking, and tournament selection functions.

3. Show how the implementations discussed in this section imply that the standard basis vectors are fixed points of the proportional, ranking, and tournament selection schemes.

4. Are there any other fixed points of section besides those noted in the previous exercise?

5. Extend the computer code of exercise 2 to the general cardinality case.

5.2   Mutation

Mutation is allowed to be any distribution $\mu \in \Lambda$. An efficient implementation of the mutation function at that level of generality is not possible (though the methods of section 5.5 may be helpful to some extent). This section therefore considers mutation affected by a rate.

The result of mutating x is $x \oplus i$ with probability $(\mu)^{\mathbf{1}^T i}(1 - \mu)^{\ell - \mathbf{1}^T i}$. Suppose each bit of x is considered independently and is changed to its binary complement with probability μ. Then $x \oplus i$ results from this process provided that complementing bit x_j coincides with $i_j = 1$. This has probability

$$\prod \mu^{i_j}(1 - \mu)^{1 \oplus i_j} = \mu^{\mathbf{1}^T i}(1 - \mu)^{\ell - \mathbf{1}^T i}$$

Hence "bit flipping" with probability μ implements mutation without explicit computation of the mutation distribution. Since there may be many bits to consider, it is usually impractical to implement bit flipping in the obvious way. A reasonably fast implementation can be based on the following considerations.

In what follows, j, k, l, u are integer parameters. Regard the population as one long string of bits (concatenate its members), and consider the probability that the first bit to be flipped is the $j + 1$st. This event has probability $\mu(1 - \mu)^j$.

Let l be positive, choose $u \geq 0$ with probability $(1 - \mu)^{lu}(1 - (1 - \mu)^l)$, and choose $0 \leq k < l$ with probability $\mu(1 - \mu)^k / (1 - (1 - \mu)^l)$. The event $lu + k = j$ where $j \geq 0$ has probability

$$(1 - \mu)^{lu}(1 - (1 - \mu)^l)\frac{\mu(1 - \mu)^k}{1 - (1 - \mu)^l} = \mu(1 - \mu)^j$$

which is identical to the probability that the first bit to be flipped is the $j + 1$st. Hence choosing the two integers u and k as above will identify the number j of positions to skip over to reach the next bit which should be flipped. The parameter l may be chosen in whatever manner makes the random choice of u and k convenient. In particular, choosing l equal to the population size r implies that u can be restricted to $0 \leq u \leq \ell$ since skipping over $r\ell$ bits means that nothing in the population will be mutated. Therefore choosing $0 \leq u \leq \ell$ with probability

$$(1 - \mu)^{ru}(1 - (1 - \mu)^r)^{[u < \ell]}$$

where the event $u = \ell$ signifies that no mutation takes place, avoids the initial problem of sampling unbounded u.

Exercises

1. Write an efficient computer implementation of the mutation function.

2. Repeat the previous problem for the general cardinality case. *Hint:* See exercise 6 of section 4.3.

3. Assuming uniform selection and mutation determined by a rate, compute the fixed points of $\mathcal{F}_{\mu}$. *Hint:* see exercise 3 of section 4.3.

5.3 Crossover

Crossover is allowed using any crossover type $c \in \Lambda$. At that level of generality, an efficient implementation of the crossover function is impossible (though the methods of section 5.5 may be helpful to some extent). This section therefore considers 1-point and uniform crossover. Considering crossover types already defined by efficient procedures (like n-point and $2n$-point crossover) is not necessary; the purpose of this section is to show efficient procedural definitions exist for the previously introduced crossover types. Because 1-point and uniform crossover were defined in functional terms, it is appropriate to consider them here. Consider the following procedures:

Given parents x and y, let their children be x and y with probability $1 - \chi$. Taking the children to be identical to the parents is referred to as *cloning*. With probability χ obtain the children as follows:

For 1-point crossover, uniformly choose a position $0 < l < \ell$ and interchange components 0 through $l - 1$ of the parents. That is, the children are $x \otimes i \oplus \bar{i} \otimes y$ and $y \otimes i \oplus \bar{i} \otimes x$ where $i = 2^l - 1$.

For uniform crossover, independently at each bit position interchange bits of the parents with probability $1/2$. In other words, the children are $x \otimes i \oplus \bar{i} \otimes y$ and $y \otimes i \oplus \bar{i} \otimes x$ where i is chosen uniformly from Ω (each i has probability $2^{-\ell}$).

In either case (1-point or uniform), choose uniformly one of the children to be the child. The crossover function defined in the previous chapter is consistent with requiring the children to be $x \otimes i \oplus \bar{i} \otimes y$ and $y \otimes i \oplus \bar{i} \otimes x$ with partial probability χ_i. Note that $i = 0$ implies cloning. For the procedures given above, the corresponding χ_i are

$$\text{1-point: } \chi_i = \begin{cases} \chi/(\ell - 1) & \text{if } i = 2^l - 1 \text{ for some } 0 < l < \ell \\ 1 - \chi & \text{if } i = 0 \\ 0 & \text{otherwise} \end{cases}$$

$$\text{uniform: } \chi_i = \begin{cases} \chi 2^{-\ell} & \text{if } i > 0 \\ 1 - \chi + \chi 2^{-\ell} & \text{if } i = 0 \end{cases}$$

It follows that the procedures given above implement 1-point and uniform crossover if these χ_i are as specified in the previous chapter. That is, provided that

$$\chi_i = \begin{cases} \chi c_i & \text{if } i > 0 \\ 1 - \chi + \chi c_0 & \text{if } i = 0 \end{cases}$$

where the crossover type $c \in \Lambda$ is given by

$$\text{1-point: } c_i = \begin{cases} 1/(\ell - 1) & \text{if } \exists k \in (0, \ell) \,.\, i = 2^k - 1 \\ 0 & \text{otherwise} \end{cases}$$

$$\text{uniform: } c_i = 2^{-\ell}$$

It is easily checked that the required conditions hold (this is exercise 2 below).

Exercises

1. Write an efficient computer implementation of the 1-point, n-point, $2n$-point, and uniform crossover functions for the general cardinality case.

2. Verify the correctness conditions (stated at the end of this section) for the procedures implementing 1-point and uniform crossover.

5.4   The Classical SGA

Finally the selection, crossover, and mutation functions are combined to implement τ. Given the current population, obtain the next generation as follows:

1. Obtain two parents by the selection function.

2. Mutate the parents by the mutation function.

3. Produce the (mutated) parents' child by the crossover function.

4. Put the child into the next generation.

5. If the next generation contains less than r members, go to step 1.

The reader already familiar with genetic algorithms will no doubt recognize the procedure outlined above. Since the mutation function described in the previous section is affected by a rate, it may be performed either before or after crossover (but mutating the child kept is more efficient than mutation before crossover). For the procedure given above to implement τ, it suffices that i is chosen for the next generation with probability $\mathcal{G}(p)_i$, where p is the current population. The probability that i occurs at step 4 is

$$\Pr\{i = \mathcal{X}(\mu(s(p)), \mu(s(p)))\}$$

$$= \sum_{x,y} \Pr\{\langle x, y\rangle = \langle s(p), s(p)\rangle\} \Pr\{i = \mathcal{X}(\mu(x), \mu(y))\}$$

$$= \sum_{x,y} \mathcal{F}(p)_x \mathcal{F}(p)_y \sum_{u,v} \mu_{x\oplus u}\mu_{y\oplus v} \Pr\{i = \mathcal{X}(u, v)\}$$

$$= \sum_{x,y} \mathcal{F}(p)_x \mathcal{F}(p)_y \sum_{u,v} \mu_{x\oplus u}\mu_{y\oplus v} \sum_{k} \frac{\mathcal{X}_k + \mathcal{X}_{\bar{k}}}{2}[u \otimes k \oplus \bar{k} \otimes v = i]$$

Making the change of variable $u \mapsto x \oplus u$ and $v \mapsto y \oplus v$ yields

$$\sum_{x,y} \mathcal{F}(p)_x \mathcal{F}(p)_y \sum_{u,v,k} \mu_u \mu_v \frac{\mathcal{X}_k + \mathcal{X}_{\bar{k}}}{2}[(x \oplus u) \otimes k \oplus \bar{k} \otimes (y \oplus v) = i]$$

Applying theorems 4.3 and 4.4 to the last sum gives

$$\sum_{x,y} \mathcal{F}(p)_x \mathcal{F}(p)_y M_{x\oplus i, y\oplus i}$$

which equals $(\mathcal{M} \circ \mathcal{F}(p))_i$ as required.

The map τ has now a procedural definition, independent of $\mathcal{G}$, for which the following diagram commutes:

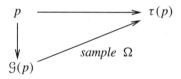

As will be shown in a later chapter, the bottom path in the diagram takes time $O(r + 3^\ell)$ (in the special case where mixing is via a mutation rate and one-point crossover, this can be improved to $O(\ell 2^\ell)$). In contrast, the upper path is $O(\ell r + r \log r)$ provided the parameter k of tournament selection is bounded. This bound holds for any combination of selection, crossover, and mutation functions discussed in this chapter. To complete the computational picture, random sampling is considered in the next section.

Exercises

1. Write a computer program implementing the SGA using τ as described in this section. Include the following options:

- arbitrary fitness function f.
- proportional, ranking, or tournament selection.
- 1-point, n-point, $2n$-point, or uniform crossover (with rate).
- arbitrary mutation rate.

Your code should use the optimized sampling algorithm described in the next section.

2. Extend the computer code of the previous exercise to the general cardinality case.

3. Verify the $O(\ell r + r \log r)$ bound stated at the end of this section. Can it be improved in the case of proportional or tournament selection?

4. Give the procedural implementation of τ for the general cardinality case and modify the derivation of this section to establish that it correctly implements RHS.

5.5   Random Sampling

Let ξ be a random variable distributed over the ordered set $\{a_0, \ldots, a_{n-1}\}$ with corresponding probabilities $\{p_0, \ldots, p_{n-1}\}$. Two algorithms will be described, *init* and *rand*, which share state and satisfy:

- The input to *init* is an array p of size n representing the probability distribution.
- The effect of *init* is the initialization of *rand* to a function of no arguments (the behavior of *rand* depends only on internal state) which returns an integer j from $\{0, \ldots, n-1\}$ with probability p_j.

If the array a contains the range of ξ such that the probability of $\xi = a_j$ is p_j, then a sample value for ξ is obtained by a_{rand}. Since *rand* executes in constant time, sample values for ξ are obtained in constant time. The initialization time taken by *init* is $O(n)$.

Let the function $uniform(n)$ return a real number chosen uniformly from the real interval $[0, n)$. Let *prob* and *alias* be arrays which are initialized by *init*. The body of *rand* is

```
u = uniform(n)
j = ⌊u⌋
If (u − j) ≤ prob_j then return j
                    else return alias_j
```

The function *init* proceeds in two stages. The first stage divides the indices of the input into two arrays, *small* and *large*. The second stage uses the probability distribution p together with *small* and *large* to initialize the arrays *prob* and *alias*. The body of *init* is

$l = 0$, $s = 0$
For $j = 0$ to $n - 1$ If $p_j > \frac{1}{n}$ then $large_l = j$, $l = l + 1$
$\qquad\qquad\qquad\qquad$ else $small_s = j$, $s = s + 1$
While $s \neq 0$ and $l \neq 0$
$\qquad s = s - 1$, $j = small_s$
$\qquad l = l - 1$, $k = large_l$
$\qquad prob_j = n * p_j$
$\qquad alias_j = k$
$\qquad p_k = p_k + (p_j - \frac{1}{n})$
$\qquad$ If $p_k > \frac{1}{n}$ then $large_l = k$, $l = l + 1$
$\qquad\qquad\qquad$ else $small_s = k$, $s = s + 1$
While $s > 0$
$\qquad s = s - 1$, $prob_{small_s} = 1$
While $l > 0$
$\qquad l = l - 1$, $prob_{large_l} = 1$

The reason for including in *init* the (theoretically unnecessary) termination condition $s = 0$ and the third while loop (which theoretically is never entered), is that floating point rounding errors may lead to the misclassification of indices onto *small* or *large*.

Exercises

1. Explain why the random sampling algorithm works.

2. Subtractive or linear congruental methods for random number generation are fastest when the modulus is $2^{\text{word size}}$. In some applications, a resolution of what typically is 32 bits in the random number generator is not sufficient. In this case, several calls to a 32 bit random integer generator may be used to obtain the required precision. Given this situation, the body of *rand* becomes

obtain the required number of random bits
$v = $ (some of the bits) $* \, constant_1$
$j = \lfloor$ (the rest of the bits) $* \, constant_2 \rfloor$
If $v \leq prob_j$ then return j
$\qquad\qquad\qquad$ else return $alias_j$

Here $constant_1$ and $constant_2$ are chosen so that v is uniformly distributed over $[0, 1)$ and j is uniformly distributed in $\{0, \ldots, n - 1\}$. The reader is cautioned to exercise care in choosing random bits; for example, linear congruential methods yield low order bits with small cycle times. Note that, according to *init* and *rand*, the comparison $v \le prob_j$ above has the form

$$(\text{some of the bits}) * constant_1 \le (prob_j = n * p_j)$$

where the assignment takes place in *init*. Show that redefining $constant_1$ (dividing it by n) makes the assignment $prob_j = n * p_j$ unnecessary and allows *prob* and *p* to be the same array! Show the appropriate adjustment to the last two while loops (of *init*) is to assign $1/n$ instead of 1.

3. Suppose q is an array satisfying

$$p_j = \frac{q_j}{\sum q_j}$$

Note that

$$p_k = p_k + (p_j - \frac{1}{n}) \iff q_k = q_k + (q_j - \frac{\sum q_j}{n})$$

and

$$p_k > \frac{1}{n} \iff q_k > \frac{\sum q_j}{n}$$

Show that if the constant $1/n$ in *init* is replaced by $n^{-1} \sum p_j$, and if $constant_1$ is redefined (multiply it by $\sum p_j$), then the array p need not sum to one. This is significant because it is usually faster to compute the direction of p than it is to determine its components (which are subject to the additional constraint that they sum to one).

4. A final optimization is to eliminate the stacks *small*, *large*, and their associated variables s, ℓ which are used by *init*, and hence to also eliminate the initial sorting of indices of p. This is accomplished by letting j and k be indices into p such that p_j would be classified as small (less than $n^{-1} \sum p_j$) and p_k would be classified as large (simply increment j and k until they point at appropriate objects). Work out the details involved (there are a few to consider, and a temporary variable is needed for what was previously the top of *small*).

5. Obtain an implementation of random sampling which incorporates all of the optimizations above.

6 The Walsh Transform

At this point, the definition of the simple genetic algorithm is complete. However, first principles have not yet been laid out. This chapter develops fundamental properties of the mixing scheme. The ability of the Walsh transform to unravel the intricacies of mixing is spectacular. Perhaps its most profound influence is to triangulate the differential $d\mathcal{M}$ of the mixing scheme. While several consequences will be explored later on, this chapter is primarily concerned with underlying results.

The first section defines the Walsh transform and notes some of its fundamental properties. The twist is also defined and simple relationships between the twist and transform are noted. The second section is devoted to the twist and transform of the mixing matrix. The third section determines the spectrum of $d\mathcal{M}$. The final section introduces the Walsh basis and considers how $\mathcal{M}$ transforms in those coordinates.

6.1 Basic Properties

The *Walsh matrix* is defined by

$$W_{i,j} = n^{-1/2}(-1)^{i^T j}$$

It is symmetric, and has entries satisfying

$$W_{i,j\oplus k} = n^{1/2} W_{i,j} W_{i,k}$$

This expresses the fact that

$$(-1)^{(j\oplus k)^T i} = (-1)^{i^T j\oplus k} = (-1)^{i^T j + i^T k} = (-1)^{i^T j}(-1)^{i^T k}$$

Another identity valuable when working with expressions involving components of W is

$$n\delta_{j,0} = \sum(-1)^{i^T j}$$

These equalities form the underpinnings of this chapter; they are pervasive and will be used without comment. The latter identity may be verified as follows. When $j = 0$ it is trivial. If $j > 0$, let k of the form 2^l be such that $k \otimes j = k$. Then $j = k \oplus j \otimes \bar{k}$ and

$$\sum_i (-1)^{i^T j} = \sum_i (-1)^{i^T k}(-1)^{i^T j\otimes\bar{k}}$$

Expressing i as $u \oplus v$ where $u \in \Omega_k$ and $v \in \Omega_{\bar{k}}$ gives $i^T k = \mathbf{1}^T u$ and $i^T j \otimes \bar{k} = v^T j$. The sum is therefore

$$\sum_{u \in \Omega_k} \sum_{v \in \Omega_{\bar{k}}} (-1)^{\mathbf{1}^T u}(-1)^{v^T j} = \sum_{v \in \Omega_{\bar{k}}} (-1)^{v^T j} \sum_{u \in \{0,1\}} (-1)^u$$

and the inner sum is zero.

Theorem 6.1 $W = W^{-1}$

Proof   The i,jth component of WW is

$$n^{-1} \sum_u (-1)^{i^T u}(-1)^{u^T j}$$

$$= n^{-1} \sum_u (-1)^{u^T i \oplus j}$$

$$= \delta_{i \oplus j, 0} \qquad\qquad\qquad\qquad\qquad\qquad\qquad\qquad\qquad\qquad \blacksquare$$

In order to keep formulas simple, it is helpful, for matrix A and vector v, to represent WAW and Wv concisely. The former is denoted by $\hat{A}$ and the latter by $\hat{v}$. If y is a row vector, then $\hat{y}$ denotes yW. The map $u \mapsto \hat{u}$ is referred to as the *Walsh transform*. The following theorem, a straightforward application of the definitions and theorem 6.1, records some useful properties of the Walsh transform.

Theorem 6.2   Let x be a column vector, y a row vector, and A a square matrix. If u and v are any of these, then $\widehat{\hat{u}} = u$, $\widehat{u+v} = \hat{u} + \hat{v}$, $\widehat{uv} = \hat{u}\hat{v}$, $\widehat{u^T} = \hat{u}^T$, $\widehat{u^{-1}} = \hat{u}^{-1}$, $\operatorname{spec}(\hat{u}) = \operatorname{spec}(u)$ whenever operations are defined.

The first application of the Walsh transform is to the set $\{\sigma_k\}$ of permutations. It simultaneously diagonalizes them.

Theorem 6.3 $\widehat{\sigma_k} = \sqrt{n}\,\operatorname{diag}(\widehat{e_k})$ (in particular, the diagonal entries are ± 1).

Proof   The i,jth component of $\widehat{\sigma_k}$ is

$$n^{-1} \sum_{u,v} (-1)^{i^T u + v^T j}[k = u \oplus v]$$

$$= n^{-1} \sum_u (-1)^{u^T i \oplus j}(-1)^{j^T k}$$

$$= (-1)^{j^T k}\delta_{i \oplus j, 0} \qquad\qquad\qquad\qquad\qquad\qquad\qquad\qquad \blacksquare$$

Define the *twist* A^* of a matrix A to have i,jth entry $A_{i \oplus j, i}$. The operator group generated by twist, transpose, and Walsh transform contains 12 elements. Its Cayley diagram is given by the following figure. In this commutative diagram (see plate I for the color version), transitions are straight edges of a single color connecting two nodes; nodes are vertices meeting transitions of three colors. Blue and violet transitions correspond to twist ($*$), red corresponds to transpose (T), and green corresponds to transform ($\wedge$). Blue edges are followed clockwise, violet edges are followed counterclockwise, red and green edges may be traversed in any direction.

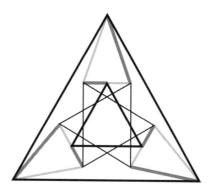

Cayley diagram

For example, beginning at the top node, the paths *green, violet, red, blue* and *red, green* end at the same place. This represents the fact that $A^{\wedge *T*} = A^{T\wedge}$ (indicating the application of several operators with a tower of superscripts is cumbersome; the standard notation is therefore abbreviated by a single superscript containing a string of operators). The Cayley diagram is quite useful for simplifying or rearranging operators in this way. It will be used without comment when dealing with expressions involving combinations of twist, transpose, or transform.

This section closes with a relationship between twist and transform which will be the key to obtaining the spectrum of $d\mathcal{M}$.

A matrix A is called *separative* when $A_{i,j} \neq 0 \implies i^T j = 0$. Note that when A is separative,

$$A^T_{i,j} \neq 0 \implies A_{j,i} \neq 0 \implies i^T j = 0$$

Therefore A is separative if and only if A^T is. Moreover, in this case

$$A^*_{i,j} \neq 0 \implies (i \oplus j) \otimes i = 0 \implies i = j \otimes i \implies i \leq j$$

hence A^* is upper triangular. Because A^{T*} must also be upper triangular, $A^{**} = A^{T*T}$ is lower triangular. This gives partial insight into how the twist rearranges a matrix. It is easy to check that twist cyclicly permutes: first column $\to$ first row $\to$ diagonal. This is illustrated in the following diagram.

Theorem 6.4   If $\hat{A}$ is separative, then its first column is the spectrum of A^*. Moreover, $\mathbf{1}^T$ is a left eigenvector of A^* with corresponding eigenvalue $\hat{A}_{0,0}$.

Proof   By the remarks above, $A^{\wedge**}$ is lower triangular. Thus its spectrum is its diagonal, which is the first column of $\hat{A}$. Note that $\mathrm{spec}(A^{\wedge**}) = \mathrm{spec}(A^{*\wedge}) = \mathrm{spec}(A^*)$. Because $A^{\wedge**}$ is lower triangular,

$$e_0^T A^{\wedge**} = e_0^T (A^{\wedge**})_{0,0}$$

Taking the transform of both sides completes the proof.   ∎

Exercises

1. Verify the equalities which were described as the underpinnings of this chapter.

2. Verify theorem 6.2.

3. Show that $x \in \Lambda \Longrightarrow \hat{x}_0 = n^{-1/2}$.

4. Show the only element of A fixed by twist is $A_{0,0}$.

5. Show that twist cyclicly permutes: first column $\to$ first row $\to$ diagonal.

6. Verify that $x \cdot y = (xy^T)^* e_0$.

7. Prove that if $A = \hat{A}$ or $A = A^T$ then $\mathrm{spec}(A^*) = \mathrm{spec}(A^{**})$.

8. Define the *convolution* $x * y$ of column vectors x and y by $x * y = (xy^T)^{**} \widehat{e_0}$. Use the Cayley diagram to verify that

$$\widehat{x \cdot y} = \hat{x} * \hat{y}$$

$$\widehat{x * y} = \hat{x} \cdot \hat{y}$$

9. Prove that convolution is commutative and associative.

10. Show the mutation scheme is simply convolution with the mutation distribution.

11. Verify the Cayley diagram.

12. Show the following, for general A and B.

(a) Twist is linear, that is, $(\alpha A + \beta B)^* = \alpha A^* + \beta B^*$.

(b) There do not exist fixed matrices U and V (independent of A and B) for which $UAV = A^*$ or $UB^T V = B^*$.

(c) There exists a matrix U (depending on x) such that $Uy = (xy^T)^{**}\widehat{e_0}$.

13. In the general cardinality case, the Walsh transform generalizes to the Fourier transform with matrix

$$W_{i,j} = n^{-1/2} \exp\left(2\pi \sqrt{-1}\, i^T j/c\right)$$

(recall that $n = c^\ell$). Let superscript C denote complex conjugate. The Fourier transform $\hat{u}$ of u is defined as Wu^C when u is a column vector, $u^C W^C$ when u is a row vector, and $Wu^C W^C$ when u is a matrix. Show, with respect to the Fourier transform, that

(a) $W = W^T$

(b) $WW^C = W^C W = I$

(c) $W_{i,j\oplus k} = n^{-1/2} W_{i,j} W_{i,k}$

(d) Theorem 6.2 remains valid provided superscript T is interpreted as conjugate transpose and $\text{spec}(u)$ is replaced by $\text{spec}(u)^C$.

(e) Theorem 6.3 remains valid, except for the parenthetic remark, if $\widehat{e_k}$ is replaced by $\widehat{e_{0\ominus k}}$.

(f) If the twist is extended to $A^*_{i,j} = A_{j\ominus i, 0\ominus i}$ then the Cayley diagram remains valid provided superscript T is interpreted as conjugate transpose.

(g) Theorem 6.4 and the remarks preceding it remain valid provided superscript T is interpreted as conjugate transpose and $\text{spec}(A^*)$ is replaced by $\text{spec}(A^*)^C$.

14. Does the result of exercise 10 carry over to the general cardinality case?

6.2 The Twist and Transform of Mixing

The first result shows the transform of the mixing matrix is separative.

Theorem 6.5 For arbitrary mutation and arbitrary crossover,

$$\hat{M}_{x,y} = \frac{n}{2}[x^T y = 0]\hat{\mu}_x \hat{\mu}_y \sum_{k \in \Omega_{\overline{x} \otimes \overline{y}}} \chi_{k\oplus x} + \chi_{k\oplus y}$$

Proof

$\hat{M}_{x,y}$

$$= n^{-1} \sum_{u,v} (-1)^{x^T u + v^T y} \sum_{i,j,k} \mu_i \mu_j \frac{\chi_k + \chi_{\bar{k}}}{2} [(u \oplus i) \otimes k \oplus \bar{k} \otimes (v \oplus j) = 0]$$

$$= n^{-1} \sum_{i,j,k} \mu_i \mu_j \frac{\chi_k + \chi_{\bar{k}}}{2} \sum_{u,v} (-1)^{x^T u + y^T v} [(u \oplus i) \otimes k = \bar{k} \otimes (v \oplus j)]$$

The condition of the indicator function is equivalent to $k \otimes (u \oplus i) = 0 \wedge \bar{k} \otimes (v \oplus j) = 0$. Hence the last sum is

$$\sum_{k \otimes u = 0} (-1)^{x^T u \oplus i} \sum_{\bar{k} \otimes v = 0} (-1)^{y^T v \oplus j}$$

$$= (-1)^{x^T i + y^T j} \sum_{u \in \Omega_{\bar{k}}} (-1)^{x^T u} \sum_{v \in \Omega_k} (-1)^{y^T v}$$

$$= n(-1)^{x^T i + y^T j} [x \otimes \bar{k} = 0][y \otimes k = 0]$$

This is nonzero only when $x \in \Omega_k \wedge y \in \Omega_{\bar{k}}$, which implies $x \otimes y = 0$. Assume therefore this relation between x and y. Incorporating these simplifications yields

$\hat{M}_{x,y}$

$$= \sum_{i,j} \mu_i \mu_j (-1)^{x^T i + y^T j} \sum_k \frac{\chi_k + \chi_{\bar{k}}}{2} [x \in \Omega_k \wedge y \in \Omega_{\bar{k}}]$$

$$= n \hat{\mu}_x \hat{\mu}_y \frac{1}{2} \sum_k \chi_k ([x \in \Omega_k \wedge y \in \Omega_{\bar{k}}] + [x \in \Omega_{\bar{k}} \wedge y \in \Omega_k])$$

The condition $x \in \Omega_k \wedge y \in \Omega_{\bar{k}}$ is equivalent to $k \oplus x \in \Omega_{\bar{x}} \wedge k \in \Omega_{\bar{y}}$. But $x \otimes y = 0$ implies $x \in \Omega_{\bar{y}}$. Hence $k \oplus x \in \Omega_{\bar{y}}$. Therefore $k \in x \oplus \Omega_{\bar{x} \otimes y}$. By symmetry, $x \in \Omega_{\bar{k}} \wedge y \in \Omega_k$ is equivalent to $k \in y \oplus \Omega_{\bar{x} \otimes y}$. Splitting the last sum across "+", summing k over these ranges, and recombining completes the proof. ∎

The following result, discovered empirically by Alden Wright, is an easy consequence.

Theorem 6.6   If mutation is zero, then $\hat{M} = M$.

Proof   Since mutation is zero, $\mu_i = \delta_{i,0}$. It follows from theorem 6.5 that the left hand side is

$$\sum_{k \in \Omega_{\overline{x} \otimes \overline{y}}} \frac{\chi_{k \oplus x} + \chi_{k \oplus y}}{2} [x \otimes y = 0]$$

The right hand side is

$$\sum_{k} \frac{\chi_k + \chi_{\overline{k}}}{2} [x \otimes k \oplus \overline{k} \otimes y = 0]$$

Note that the indicator function $[x \otimes k \oplus \overline{k} \otimes y = 0]$ is zero unless $x \otimes y = 0$ and it is equivalent to $[x \in \Omega_k \wedge y \in \Omega_{\overline{k}}]$. The proof is finished by rearranging, as in the proof of theorem 6.5.   ∎

Since $\hat{M}$ is separative, theorem 6.4 shows the spectrum of M^* is the first column of $\hat{M}$ and $\mathbf{1}^T$ is a left eigenvector of M^* with corresponding eigenvalue $\hat{M}_{0,0}$. These facts lead to

Theorem 6.7   The spectrum of M^* is given by

$$\hat{M}_{x,0} = \sqrt{n}\,\hat{\mu}_x \frac{1}{2} \sum_{k \in \Omega_{\overline{x}}} \chi_{k \oplus x} + \chi_k$$

for $x \in \Omega$. In particular, the maximal eigenvalue of M^* is 1 with corresponding left eigenvector $\mathbf{1}^T$. If mutation is positive, then all other eigenvalues have modulus less than $1/2$.

Proof   The expression for the spectrum above follows from theorem 6.5 and exercise three of the previous section. Since it is 1 when $x = 0$, 1 is the eigenvalue with corresponding left eigenvector $\mathbf{1}^T$. If μ is positive and $x > 0$, cancellation occurs in the sum defining $\sqrt{n}\,\hat{\mu}_x$ and so it must have absolute value less than 1. Note that the subscripts in the sum above are of the form u and $v \oplus x$ where $u, v \in \Omega_{\overline{x}}$. Since $\Omega_{\overline{x}}$ is a group, $u = v \oplus x$ is impossible; it would lead to the contradiction $u \oplus v = x \in \Omega_{\overline{x}}$. The sum can therefore have no repeated terms and is at most 1.   ∎

To summarize what has been said regarding triangular forms:

- $M^{\wedge *}$ is upper triangular.
- $M^{* \wedge}$ is lower triangular.
- M^* is upper triangular when mutation is zero.
- $\widehat{\sigma_k}$ is diagonal.

The first two points above follow from the separativity of $\hat{M}$ (theorem 6.5), the third follows from theorem 6.6 and the first, the last was shown in the previous section.

In addition to being a means of computing spectrum and establishing triangular forms, theorem 6.5 can greatly simplify the formulas which represent mixing. To illustrate this phenomenon, the remainder of this section considers its application to the mixing matrix corresponding to one point crossover and mutation rate μ. Towards that end, the following preliminary results will be useful.

Lemma 6.8

$$\sum_j (-1)^{x^T j} \alpha^{1^T j} = (1-\alpha)^{1^T x}(1+\alpha)^{1^T \overline{x}}$$

Proof Inducting on $1^T x$, the base case is trivial. Let $\overline{k} = 2^i$ be such that $\overline{k} \otimes x > 0$. Write x as $x = k \otimes x \oplus \overline{k} = (KK^T x) \oplus \overline{k} = (Ky) \oplus \overline{k}$ (i.e., $y = K^T x$ where K is the injection corresponding to k), and write j as $j = u \oplus v$ where $u \in \Omega_{\overline{k}} = \{0, \overline{k}\}$ and $v \in \Omega_k$.

$$\sum_{j \in {}^\ell \Omega} (-1)^{x^T j} \alpha^{1^T j}$$

$$= \sum_{u \in \{0, \overline{k}\}} (-1)^{x^T u} \alpha^{1^T u} \sum_{v \in \Omega_k} (-1)^{x^T v} \alpha^{1^T v}$$

$$= (1-\alpha) \sum_{v \in K({}^{\ell-1}\Omega)} (-1)^{y^T K^T v} \alpha^{v^T 1}$$

$$= (1-\alpha) \sum_{w \in {}^{\ell-1}\Omega} (-1)^{y^T K^T K w} \alpha^{w^T K^T 1}$$

$$= (1-\alpha) \sum_{w \in {}^{\ell-1}\Omega} (-1)^{y^T w} \alpha^{w^T 1}$$

Applying the inductive hypothesis to the last sum completes the proof.   ∎

Theorem 6.9   If mutation is given by a rate, then $\hat{\mu}_x = n^{-1/2}(1-2\mu)^{1^T x}$

Proof

$$n^{1/2} \hat{\mu}_x = \sum_j (-1)^{x^T j} \mu^{1^T j}(1-\mu)^{\ell - 1^T j} = (1-\mu)^\ell \sum_j (-1)^{x^T j}\Big(\frac{\mu}{1-\mu}\Big)^{1^T j}$$

Applying lemma 6.8 to the right hand side completes the proof. ∎

The next lemma, which handles the sum in theorem 6.5, relies on the following auxiliary functions

$$\text{hi}(x) = \begin{cases} 0 & \text{if } x = 0 \\ \sup\{i : 2^i \otimes x > 0\} & \text{otherwise} \end{cases}$$

$$\text{lo}(x) = \begin{cases} \ell - 1 & \text{if } x = 0 \\ \inf\{i : 2^i \otimes x > 0\} & \text{otherwise} \end{cases}$$

Intuitively, the function $\text{hi}(x)$ returns the index of the high order bit of x, and $\text{lo}(x)$ returns the index of the low order bit.

Lemma 6.10 For 1-point crossover, if $x \otimes y = 0$ then

$$\sum_{k \in \Omega_{\overline{x} \otimes \overline{y}}} \chi_{k \oplus x} = (1 - \chi)\delta_{x,0} + \frac{\chi}{\ell - 1}(\text{lo}(y) - \text{hi}(x))^+$$

Proof Let m denote a variable over the domain $\{2^i - 1 : 0 < i < \ell\}$. It follows from the definition of the 1-point crossover type that the left hand side above is

$$\sum_{k \in \Omega_{\overline{x} \otimes \overline{y}}} (1 - \chi)[x = k] + \frac{\chi}{\ell - 1}[\exists m . x \oplus k = m]$$

$$= (1 - \chi)\delta_{x,0} + \frac{\chi}{\ell - 1} \sum_{m,k}[x \oplus k = m \wedge k \otimes (1 \oplus \overline{x} \otimes \overline{y}) = 0]$$

Note that $x \otimes y = 0 \wedge x \oplus k = m \implies k \otimes (1 \oplus \overline{x} \otimes \overline{y}) = x \otimes \overline{m} \oplus m \otimes y$. Hence the indicator function in the sum above simplifies to $[x \in \Omega_m \wedge y \in \Omega_{\overline{m}}]$. Observing that

$$\sum_{m}[x \in \Omega_m \wedge y \in \Omega_{\overline{m}}] = \sum_{\text{hi}(x) < i}[y \in \Omega_{\overline{m}}] = (\text{lo}(y) - \text{hi}(x))^+$$

completes the proof. ∎

Collecting the previous results together yields

Theorem 6.11 For 1-point crossover (with rate χ) and mutation rate μ, $\hat{M}_{i,j}$ is given by

$$\delta_{i \otimes j, 0}(1 - 2\mu)^{\mathbf{1}^T i + \mathbf{1}^T j}\left((1 - \chi)\frac{\delta_{i,0} + \delta_{j,0}}{2} + \chi\frac{(\text{lo}(j) - \text{hi}(i))^+ + (\text{lo}(i) - \text{hi}(j))^+}{2(\ell - 1)}\right)$$

The special case of theorem 6.11 corresponding to $j = 0$ was first proved by Gary J. Koehler. He computed it directly (theorem 6.5 was at that time unknown) to obtain the spectrum of M^*. Theorem 6.9 is also due to him (though by a more complicated argument). Theorem 6.11 and related results were also independently obtained by J. N. Kok and P. Floreen.

Exercises

1. Does $\{M^*\} \cup \{\sigma_k : k \in \Omega\}$ have a common eigenvector?

2. Prove theorem 6.11.

3. What is the analogue of theorem 6.11 for uniform crossover?

4. What is the analogue of theorem 6.11 for n-point crossover?

5. What is the analogue of theorem 6.11 for $2n$-point crossover?

6. What is the spectrum of M^* for zero mutation? What is the multiplicity of the eigenvalue $1/2$ in that case?

7. Show that $\hat{M}$ contains at most 3^ℓ nonzero entries. For 1-point crossover with mutation rate μ, show $\hat{M}$ contains at most $\ell 2^\ell + 1$ nonzero entries.

8. Show the analogue of theorem 6.5 in the general cardinality case is

$$\hat{M}_{-x,y} = \frac{n}{2}[x^T y = 0]\hat{\mu}_x \hat{\mu}_y \sum_k (\chi_k + \chi_{\bar{k}})[x \otimes \bar{k} = y \otimes k = 0]$$

Note that $\hat{M}$ is separative and $\hat{M}_{-x,y} = \hat{M}_{-y,x}$.

9. Show theorem 6.6 carries over to the general cardinality case.

10. What is the analogue of theorem 6.7 in the general cardinality case? *Hint:* See exercise 8 (above) and exercise g of section 6.1.

11. Show in the general cardinality case that

(a) $M^{\wedge *}$ is upper triangular.

(b) $M^{*\wedge}$ is lower triangular.

(c) M^* is upper triangular when mutation is zero.

(d) $\hat{\sigma}_k$ is diagonal.

(e) $\hat{M}$ contains at most $c^\ell (2 - 1/c)^\ell$ nonzero entries.

12. What is the analogue of theorem 6.9 in the general cardinality case?

13. What is the analogue of theorem 6.11 in the general cardinality case?

6.3   The Spectrum of $d\mathcal{M}$

The importance of the spectrum of $d\mathcal{M}$ will become clear later on. For now, the focus is on obtaining it. A first step is the following theorem.

Theorem 6.12   Suppose $Ax = \lambda x$. Then

$$\operatorname{spec}(A) = \operatorname{spec}(A^T\Big|_{x^\perp}) \cup \{\lambda\}$$

Proof   Since x is an eigenvector of A, it follows that $A^T : x^\perp \to x^\perp$. Without loss of generality it may be assumed that x is a unit vector. Let $\{b_1, \ldots, b_n\}$ be an orthonormal basis with $b_n = x$, and let these vectors form the columns of matrix B. Observe that if $j < n$ then $B^T A^T B e_j = B^{-1} A^T b_j \subset B^{-1}(x^\perp) \subset e_n^\perp$. Hence $B^T A^T B$ has the form

$$\begin{pmatrix} C & * \\ 0 & * \end{pmatrix}$$

Note that $e_n^T B^T A^T B = (B^T A x)^T = \lambda (B^{-1} b_n)^T = \lambda e_n^T$. Thus the last diagonal element in the matrix above is λ. Since, with respect to the chosen basis, elements of $x^\perp$ have the form

$$\begin{pmatrix} * \\ 0 \end{pmatrix}$$

it follows that C represents A^T on $x^\perp$. Since the spectrum is invariant under change of basis, it follows from the representation for $B^T A^T B$ that $\operatorname{spec}(A^T) = \operatorname{spec}(C) \cup \{\lambda\}$.   ∎

Theorem 6.12 is useful because $\mathcal{M}$ was defined with respect to an ambient space ($\mathfrak{R}^n$) having dimension larger than the dimension of Λ. However, $\mathcal{M}$ is polynomial and so is actually defined throughout $\mathfrak{R}^n$. With respect to this larger domain, the differential $d\mathcal{M}_x$ of $\mathcal{M}$ at x is the unique linear transformation satisfying

$$\mathcal{M}(x + y) = \mathcal{M}(x) + d\mathcal{M}_x y + o(y)$$

where $o(y)$ is a function of y satisfying $o(y)/\|y\| \to 0$ as $\|y\| \to 0$. Restricting the relation above to Λ requires that $x + y$ and x are in Λ. Hence $\mathbf{1}^T(x + y) = \mathbf{1}^T x = 1$. Hence $y \in \mathbf{1}^\perp$. Therefore, $d\mathcal{M}_x\big|_{\mathbf{1}^\perp}$ is the relevant linear map (unless a domain larger than Λ for $\mathcal{M}$ is being considered). Theorem 6.12 helps clarify what happens when $d\mathcal{M}$ is restricted to $\mathbf{1}^\perp$.

The matrix of $d\mathcal{M}$ is easily computed by partial derivatives. Its i, jth entry is

$$\frac{\partial}{\partial x_j} \sum_{u,v} x_u x_v M_{u \oplus i, v \oplus i}$$

$$= \sum_{u,v} (\delta_{u,j} x_v + \delta_{v,j} x_u) M_{u \oplus i, v \oplus i}$$

$$= \sum_{v} x_v M_{j \oplus i, v \oplus i} + \sum_{u} x_u M_{u \oplus i, j \oplus i}$$

$$= 2 \sum_{u} x_u M_{i \oplus j, u \oplus i}$$

Lurking in the background is M^*. Note that $M_{i \oplus j, u \oplus i} = M^*_{i \oplus u, j \oplus u} = (\sigma_u M^* \sigma_u)_{i,j}$. Therefore

$$d\mathcal{M}_x = 2 \sum \sigma_u M^* \sigma_u x_u$$

Transforming both sides yields the lower triangular form

$$\widehat{d\mathcal{M}_x} = 2 \sum \widehat{\sigma_u} \widehat{M^*} \widehat{\sigma_u} x_u$$

Appealing to theorem 6.3, every matrix in this sum has identical diagonal: premultiplication by $\widehat{\sigma_u}$ scales rows by ± 1, while post multiplication scales columns by ± 1. Hence pre and post multiplication scales the diagonal of M^* by $(\pm 1)^2$. Therefore, taking the diagonal of both sides shows $\mathrm{spec}(\widehat{d\mathcal{M}_x})$ to be

$$2 \sum \mathrm{spec}(\widehat{M^*}) x_u$$

$$= 2 \, \mathrm{spec}(\widehat{M^*}) \sum x_u$$

$$= 2(\mathbf{1}^T x) \, \mathrm{spec}(\widehat{M^*})$$

This leads to:

Theorem 6.13   Considered as a map $\mathcal{M} : \mathfrak{R}^N \longrightarrow \mathfrak{R}^N$,

$$d\mathcal{M}_x = 2 \sum \sigma_u^T M^* \sigma_u x_u$$

Moreover, $\mathrm{spec}(d\mathcal{M}_x) = 2(\mathbf{1}^T x) \, \mathrm{spec}(M^*)$. In particular, $d\mathcal{M}_x$ is linear in x and has maximal eigenvalue $2(\mathbf{1}^T x)$ with corresponding left eigenvector $\mathbf{1}^T$. The largest eigenvalue should be omitted when restricting $d\mathcal{M}$ to $\mathbf{1}^\perp$, and $d\mathcal{M}_x$ has spectrum independent of x when $\mathcal{M}$ is considered as a map on the simplex.

Proof   Linearity follows from the formula for $d\mathcal{M}_x$. Applying theorem 6.7, $\mathbf{1}^T d\mathcal{M}_x$ is

$$2 \sum \mathbf{1}^T \sigma_u M^* \sigma_u x_u$$

$$= 2 \sum \mathbf{1}^T x_u$$

$$= 2(\sum x_u) \mathbf{1}^T$$

Appealing to theorem 6.12,

$$\mathrm{spec}(d\mathcal{M}_x) = \mathrm{spec}((d\mathcal{M}_x)^T) = \mathrm{spec}(\mathcal{M}_x \Big|_{\mathbf{1}^\perp}) \cup \{2(\mathbf{1}^T x)\}$$

Since $\mathbf{1}^T x = 1$ for $x \in \Lambda$, the spectrum of $d\mathcal{M}_x$ is independent of $x \in \Lambda$.   ∎

Exercises

The following exercises develop an application of the basic theoretical results developed in this and previous sections. The conclusion implies that if mutation is positive, then $\mathcal{M}$ is a focused heuristic.

1. Define $\upsilon(x) = \|\hat{x}\|_1$. Prove that $\upsilon(\cdot)$ is a norm.

2. Given the norm $\upsilon(\cdot)$, define the norm of a matrix A by $\upsilon(A) = \sup_{\upsilon(x)=1} \upsilon(Ax)$. Prove that $\upsilon(A) = \|\hat{A}\|_1$.

3. Let $M_\varepsilon = M^*/(\rho + \varepsilon)$ where ρ is the spectral radius of M^* and $\varepsilon > 0$. For matrix A, define $|A|$ to be the matrix with i, jth entry $|A_{i,j}|$. Show that the spectral radius of $|\widehat{M_\varepsilon}|$ is $\rho/(\rho + \varepsilon) < 1$. *Hint:* What can you say about the diagonal of the triangular matrix $M^{*\wedge}$?

4. Consider the semigroup S generated by $\{M_\epsilon\} \cup \{\sigma_k : k \in \Omega\}$. Prove that for a typical element,

$$\upsilon(\sigma_{n_0} M_\varepsilon^{m_0} \sigma_{n_1} M_\varepsilon^{m_1} \cdots \sigma_{n_k})$$

$$\leq \||W\sigma_{n_0}W| \, |WM_\varepsilon^{m_0}W| \cdots |W\sigma_{n_k}W|\|_1$$

$$\leq \||\widehat{M_\varepsilon}|^{\sum m_j}\|_1$$

Conclude that S is bounded with respect to υ, and hence the norm

$$\upsilon_S(x) = \sup_{A \in S} \upsilon(Ax)$$

exists (see appendix).

5. Show $\mathbf{1}^T$ is a left eigenvector for the semigroup S, and hence the construction of the norm υ_S can be carried out within the space $\mathbf{1}^\perp$. Conclude that if mutation is positive, then

$2(\rho + \varepsilon) < 1$ for some $\varepsilon > 0$ when S is restricted to $\mathbf{1}^{\perp}$.

6. Assume positive mutation and let $x \in \Lambda$. Verify the chain of inequalities

$$\upsilon_S(d\mathcal{M}_x \big|_{\mathbf{1}^{\perp}})$$

$$\leq 2(\rho + \varepsilon) \sum \upsilon_S(\sigma_k M_\varepsilon \sigma_k \big|_{\mathbf{1}^{\perp}})x_k$$

$$\leq 2(\rho + \varepsilon) \sum x_k$$

$$< 1$$

Conclude that $\mathcal{M} : \Lambda \to \Lambda$ is a *uniform contraction* (see appendix) with respect to υ_S.

7. When mutation is positive, what is the unique fixed point to which orbits under $\mathcal{M}$ converge?

8. Extend the previous exercises to the general cardinality case. *Hint:* Show theorem 6.13 carries over to the general cardinality case.

6.4   The Walsh Basis

The affine space containing Λ is a translate in the direction of the first column of W of the linear span of the remaining columns. This, and the simplifying influence of the transform demonstrated in previous sections, suggests an appropriate choice of basis is the Walsh basis $\mathcal{W} = \{\widehat{e_0}, \ldots, \widehat{e_{n-1}}\}$. How $\mathcal{M}$ transforms in these coordinates is derived in this section. Applications are postponed to later chapters. The approach to $\mathcal{M}$ is through its differential.

Theorem 6.14

$$(\widehat{d\mathcal{M}_x})_{i,j} = 2\sqrt{n}(\widehat{M^*})_{i,j}\hat{x}_{i \oplus j}$$

Proof   Appealing to theorems 6.13 and 6.3, the left hand side is

$$2 \sum_k (\widehat{\sigma_k}\widehat{M^*}\widehat{\sigma_k})_{i,j}x_k$$

$$= 2 \sum_k x_k \sum_{u,v}(-1)^{u^T k}\delta_{i,u}(\widehat{M^*})_{u,v}(-1)^{j^T k}\delta_{v,j}$$

$$= 2 \sum_k x_k(-1)^{k^T(i \oplus j)}(\widehat{M^*})_{i,j}$$

$$= 2\sqrt{n}(\widehat{M^*})_{i,j}(Wx)_{i\oplus j} \qquad\qquad \blacksquare$$

Theorem 6.15

- $d\mathcal{M}_{\widehat{e_j}}\widehat{e_i} = 2\sqrt{n}\hat{M}_{i,j}\widehat{e_{i\oplus j}}$
- $\widehat{e_i}^T d\mathcal{M}_{\widehat{e_j}} = 2\sqrt{n}(\widehat{M^*})_{i,j}\widehat{e_{i\oplus j}}^T$

Proof   By theorem 6.14 and theorem 6.1,

$$d\mathcal{M}_{\widehat{e_j}}\widehat{e_i}$$

$$= W(\sum e_k e_k^T)(Wd\mathcal{M}_{\widehat{e_j}}W)e_i$$

$$= W\sum e_k(e_k^T d\mathcal{M}_{\widehat{e_j}}e_i)$$

$$= 2\sqrt{n}W\sum(\widehat{M^*})_{k,i}\delta_{k\oplus i,j}e_k$$

$$= 2\sqrt{n}(\widehat{M^*})_{i\oplus j,i}We_{i\oplus j}$$

$$= 2\sqrt{n}(M^{*\wedge *})_{i,j}\widehat{e_{i\oplus j}}$$

The second identity follows from the first and the symmetry of M:

$$\widehat{e_i}^T d\mathcal{M}_{\widehat{e_j}}$$

$$= \widehat{e_i}^T d\mathcal{M}_{\widehat{e_j}}W(\sum e_k e_k^T)W$$

$$= \sum \widehat{e_i}^T(d\mathcal{M}_{\widehat{e_j}}\widehat{e_k})\widehat{e_k}^T$$

$$= 2\sqrt{n}\sum \hat{M}_{k,j}(\widehat{e_i}^T\widehat{e_{k\oplus j}})\widehat{e_k}^T$$

$$= 2\sqrt{n}\hat{M}_{i\oplus j,j}\widehat{e_{i\oplus j}}^T$$

$$= 2\sqrt{n}(M^{\wedge T**})_{i,j}\widehat{e_{i\oplus j}}^T \qquad\qquad \blacksquare$$

Theorem 6.16 $d\mathcal{M}_x y$ is symmetric and linear in x and y. Moreover,

- $\mathcal{M}(x) = \frac{1}{2}d\mathcal{M}_x x$
- $\mathcal{M}(x) - \mathcal{M}(y) = d\mathcal{M}_{\frac{x+y}{2}}(x-y)$
- $\mathbf{1}^T\mathcal{M}(x) = (\mathbf{1}^T x)^2$

Proof Linearity follows from theorem 6.13. Symmetry in x and y is a consequence of linearity and the fact that symmetry holds on a basis (theorem 6.15). The second formula is a consequence of symmetry, linearity, and the first. The third formula follows from the first and theorem 6.13. The first formula is a simple calculation:

$$\mathcal{M}(x)$$

$$= \sum_i e_i \sum_k x_k \sum_j M_{i \oplus j, i \oplus k} x_j$$

$$= \sum_k x_k \sum_i e_i \sum_j (\sigma_k M^* \sigma_k)_{i,j} x_j$$

$$= \sum_k x_k \sum_i e_i (e_i^T \sigma_k M^* \sigma_k) x$$

$$= \sum_i e_i e_i^T \sum_k \sigma_k M^* \sigma_k x_k x$$

$$= \frac{1}{2} d\mathcal{M}_x x \qquad\qquad\qquad \blacksquare$$

How $\mathcal{M}$ transforms with respect to $\mathcal{W}$ is easily derived given this background. First, taking the Walsh transform of the following standard representation

$$x = \sum x_j e_j$$

and then replacing x with $\hat{x}$ yields

$$x = \sum \hat{x}_j \widehat{e_j}$$

Passing between these equivalent representations for x will be useful. In particular, the second representation shows the coordinates of x with respect to the basis $\mathcal{W}$ are given by the vector $\hat{x}$. By theorem 6.16, $\mathcal{M}(x)$ is

$$\frac{1}{2} d\mathcal{M}_x x$$

Using the second representation for x given above and expanding by the bilinearity of $d\mathcal{M}_{(\cdot)}(\cdot)$ allows this to be written as

$$\frac{1}{2} \sum_{i,j} \hat{x}_i \hat{x}_j d\mathcal{M}_{\widehat{e_i}} \widehat{e_j}$$

Appealing to the first formula of theorem 6.15 and making the change of variables $i \oplus j = k$ leads to

$$\mathcal{M}(x) = \sqrt{n} \sum_k \widehat{e_k} \sum_i \hat{x}_i \hat{x}_{i \oplus k} \hat{M}_{i, i \oplus k}$$

This derivation together with the fact that $\hat{M}_{i, i \oplus k} \neq 0 \Longrightarrow i \in \Omega_k$ ($\hat{M}$ is separative) establishes

Theorem 6.17   The kth component of $\mathcal{M}(x)$ with respect to $\mathcal{W}$ is

$$\sqrt{n} \sum_{i \in \Omega_k} \hat{x}_i \hat{x}_{i \oplus k} \hat{M}_{i, i \oplus k}$$

Exercises

1. Contrast computation of $\mathcal{M}$ in the standard basis vs in the basis $\mathcal{W}$ in terms of speed.

2. Repeat the previous exercise, but contrast in terms of computational stability.

3. Use theorem 6.16 to show that the only solutions to $\mathcal{M}(x) = x$ in the positive mutation case are 0 and $1/\sqrt{n}$. *Hint:* Use the second formula and knowledge about the spectrum of the differential.

4. Compare the previous exercise with exercise 7 of section 6.3.

5. Show theorem 6.14 carries over to the general cardinality case provided $i \oplus j$ is replaced by $i \ominus j$.

6. Show theorem 6.15 carries over to the general cardinality case provided the double subscript i, j is replaced by $i, 0 \ominus j$.

7. Show theorem 6.16 carries over to the general cardinality case.

8. Show the analogue of theorem 6.17 in the general cardinality case is

$$\sqrt{n} \sum_i \overline{\hat{x}_i \hat{x}_{k \ominus i}} \hat{M}_{i, i \ominus k}$$

where the overline indicates complex conjugation. *Hint:* In general, the kth component of x with respect to the transformed basis is the *complex conjugate* of $\hat{x}_k$.

9. As an "alternative" to using theorem 6.17 for the computation of $\mathcal{M}(x)$, one might exploit the fact that the transform of the scalor $\mathcal{M}(x)_k$ is itself. Therefore, by theorems 6.2 and 6.3,

$$\mathcal{M}(x)_k = n\hat{x}^T \mathrm{diag}(\widehat{e_k}) \hat{M} \mathrm{diag}(\widehat{e_k}) \hat{x}$$

Show, using the separativity of $\hat{M}$, that this leads to

$$\mathcal{M}(x)_k = \sum_i \sum_{j \in \Omega_i} \hat{x}_i \hat{x}_{i \oplus j} (-1)^{k^T i} \hat{M}_{j, j \oplus i}$$

10. According to theorem 6.17,

$$\widehat{e}_k{}^T \mathcal{M}(x) = \sqrt{n} \sum_{i \in \Omega_k} \hat{x}_i \hat{x}_{i \oplus k} \hat{M}_{i, i \oplus k}$$

Using the representation above, take the Walsh transform to obtain the result of the previous exercise.

11. Repeat the previous two exercises for the general cardinality case, making appropriate modifications. *Hint:* Use exercise 8.

12. Which is faster, using theorem 6.17 for the computation of $\mathcal{M}(x)$, or the method suggested by problem 9?

7 Computing with the Heuristic

At this point the Simple Genetic Algorithm has been defined and a minimal collection of basic results pertaining to its component parts are in place. Before moving on to examples and theoretical results, computational issues are briefly considered.

This chapter is devoted to efficient computation related to $\mathcal{G}$. The first section is devoted to computing $\mathcal{F}$, the second is devoted to computing $\mathcal{M}$. The concluding section touches upon the computation of fixed points of $\mathcal{G}$.

The key to quickly computing $\mathcal{M}$ is the Walsh transform, but $\mathcal{F}$ is best computed in standard coordinates. When computing $\mathcal{G} = \mathcal{M} \circ \mathcal{F}$, it would be nice to have it both ways, which is precisely what the Fast Walsh Transform allows; switching between coordinate systems is a relatively inexpensive $O(n \log n)$.

The *Fast Walsh Transform* (FWT) implementing $x \mapsto \sqrt{n}\,\hat{x}$ is defined by the following algorithm:

```
s = 1
While s < n
        t = s + s
        i = 0
        While i < n
                j = i + s
                For k = i to j − 1
                        l = k + s
                        w = x_k
                        x_k = w + x_l
                        x_l = w − x_l
                i = i + t
        s = t
```

7.1 Selection

The obvious implementation of the proportional selection scheme

$$\mathcal{F}(x) = f \cdot x / f^T x$$

takes time $O(n)$. The following theorem is an easy exercise.

Theorem 7.1 For proportional selection,

$$d\mathcal{F}_x = \frac{f^T x \,\mathrm{diag}(f) - f \cdot x \, f^T}{(f^T x)^2}$$

Like proportional selection, the ranking selection distribution may also be computed in time $O(n)$. Let ψ be a permutation of $0, \ldots, n-1$ such that $i < j \iff f(\psi_i) < f(\psi_j)$. Consider the vector η defined recursively by

$$\eta_{\psi_0} = 0$$

$$\eta_{\psi_{i+1}} = \eta_{\psi_i} + x_{\psi_i}$$

Note that computation of η takes time $O(n)$. The cost of obtaining ψ is irrelevant if it is amortized over arbitrarily many calls to $\mathcal{F}$. The vectors ψ and η defined above will be used throughout the remainder of the text.

Theorem 7.2   The ranking selection scheme satisfies

$$\mathcal{F}(x)_i = \int_{\eta_i}^{\eta_i + x_i} \varrho(y)\,dy$$

Proof   It suffices to show

$$\eta_i = \sum [f(j) < f(i)] x_j$$

note that

$$\sum [f(j) < f(\psi_0)] x_j = 0$$

Moreover,

$$\sum [f(j) < f(\psi_{i+1})] x_j$$

$$= \sum ([f(j) < f(\psi_i)] + [f(\psi_i) \le f(j) < f(\psi_{i+1})]) x_j$$

$$= \sum [f(j) < f(\psi_i)] x_j + x_{\psi_i}$$

Since η_i and $\sum [f(j) < f(i)] x_j$ satisfy the same recursion, they are identical.   ∎

Assuming integration in constant time, computing the ranking selection distribution is therefore $O(n)$. The following theorem is an easy exercise.

Theorem 7.3   The differential of the ranking selection scheme has i, jth component

$$\varrho(\eta_i + x_i)[f_j \le f_i] - \varrho(\eta_i)[f_j < f_i]$$

The tournament selection scheme is

$$\mathcal{F}(x)_i = k! \sum_{v \in X_n^k} \mathcal{F}'(v/k)_i \prod_j \frac{x_j^{v_j}}{v_j!}$$

where $k > 1$ is an integer parameter and $\mathcal{F}'$ is any ranking selection scheme. It is easy to see that $\mathcal{F}'(v/k)_{\psi_i}$ depends only on $\{v_{\psi_j} : j \le i\}$. Thus it makes sense to define the function $\mathcal{F}'_\psi(\langle y_0, \ldots, y_i \rangle)_i$ as $\mathcal{F}'(z)_{\psi_i}$ where z satisfies $0 \le j \le i \implies z_{\psi_j} = y_j$. Therefore

$\mathcal{F}(x)_{\psi_i}$

$$= k! \sum_{u=0}^{k} \sum_{w \in X_{i+1}^u} \mathcal{F}'_\psi(w/k)_i \sum_{v \in X_n^k} \prod_{j \le i} [v_{\psi_j} = w_j] \prod_{j < n} \frac{x_j^{v_j}}{v_j!}$$

$$= k! \sum_{u=0}^{k} \sum_{w \in X_{i+1}^u} \mathcal{F}'_\psi(w/k)_i \prod_{j \le i} \frac{x_{\psi_j}^{w_j}}{w_j!} \sum_{v \in X_{n-i-1}^{k-u}} \prod_{j > i} \frac{x_{\psi_j}^{v_j}}{v_j!}$$

Applying the multinomial theorem (lemma 3.2) in the last sum and rearranging yields

$$\sum_{u=0}^{k} \binom{k}{u} (1 - \sum_{j \le i} x_{\psi_j})^{k-u} u! \sum_{w \in X_{i+1}^u} \mathcal{F}'_\psi(w/k)_i \prod_{j \le i} \frac{x_{\psi_j}^{w_j}}{w_j!}$$

Next let $w_{\psi_i} = v$ and $\sum_{j<i} w_{\psi_j} = u - v$. Then $\mathcal{F}'_\psi(w/k)_i = \sum_{j<v} t_{j+u-v}$ where the t_j are as defined in section 5.1, for the choice $\mathcal{F} = \mathcal{F}'$ and $r = k$. The sum above becomes

$$\sum_{u=0}^{k} \binom{k}{u} (1 - \sum_{j \le i} x_{\psi_j})^{k-u} \sum_{v=0}^{u} u! \sum_{w \in X_i^{u-v}} \sum_{j<v} t_{j+u-v} \frac{x_{\psi_i}^v}{v!} \prod_{j<i} \frac{x_{\psi_j}^{w_j}}{w_j!}$$

$$= \sum_{u=0}^{k} \binom{k}{u} (1 - \sum_{j \le i} x_{\psi_j})^{k-u} \sum_{v=0}^{u} \binom{u}{v} x_{\psi_i}^v \sum_{j<v} t_{j+u-v} (u-v)! \sum_{w \in X_i^{u-v}} \prod_{j<i} \frac{x_{\psi_j}^{w_j}}{w_j!}$$

Applying the multinomial theorem in the last sum and rearranging proves the following.

Theorem 7.4   The tournament selection scheme satisfies

$$\mathcal{F}(x)_{\psi_i} = \sum_{u=0}^{k} \binom{k}{u} (1 - \sum_{j \le i} x_{\psi_j})^{k-u} \sum_{v=0}^{u} \binom{u}{v} x_{\psi_i}^v (\sum_{j<i} x_{\psi_j})^{u-v} \sum_{j<v} t_{j+u-v}$$

where the t_j are as defined in section 5.1, for the choice $\mathcal{F} = \mathcal{F}'$ and $r = k$.

Given $\sum_{j<i} x_{\psi_j}$, the formula given in theorem 7.4 for $\mathcal{F}(x)_{\psi_i}$ can be computed in constant time since k is assumed to be bounded. But x_{ψ_j} can be summed incrementally as the components $\mathcal{F}(x)_{\psi_i}$ are calculated. Therefore computation of $\mathcal{F}$ takes $O(n)$ time. The following theorem is an easy exercise.

Theorem 7.5   The differential of the tournament selection scheme has i, jth component

$$\sum_{u \leq k} \sum_{v \leq u} \sum_{h < v} \binom{k}{u}\binom{u}{v} t_{h+u-v}\big((u-k)(1-x_i-\eta_i)^{k-u-1}[f_j \leq f_i]x_i^v\eta_i^{u-v}+$$

$$(1-x_i-\eta_i)^{k-u}vx_i^{v-1}[i=j]\eta_i^{u-v} + (1-x_i-\eta_i)^{k-u}x_i^v(u-v)\eta_i^{u-v-1}[f_j < f_i]\big)$$

The next section will show $\mathcal{M}$ is computable in time $O(3^\ell)$. Therefore the expense of $\mathcal{G}$ is also $O(3^\ell)$ with arbitrary mutation, arbitrary crossover, and any of proportional, ranking, or tournament selection. In the special case where mixing is via a mutation rate and one-point crossover, this can be improved to $O(\ell 2^\ell)$.

Exercises

1. Explain why the algorithm given for the fast Walsh transform works.

2. Prove the execution time of the fast Walsh transform is $O(n \log n)$.

3. Implement proportional, ranking, and tournament selection as indicated above.

4. Show that

$$\eta_{\psi_i} = \sum_{j<i} x_{\psi_j}$$

5. Prove theorems 7.1, 7.3, and 7.5.

6. What happens to the results of theorems 7.2 through 7.5 as the probability measure corresponding to ϱ converges to point mass at 1? Interpret the limits in terms of selecting the most fit among a uniform choice of k population members.

7. Are any modifications to this section appropriate for the general cardinality case?

7.2   Mixing

The components of the mixing function are best computed via theorem 6.17 by the formula

$$\widehat{\mathcal{M}(x)}_k = \sqrt{n} \sum_{i \in \Omega_k} \hat{x}_i \hat{x}_{i \oplus k} \hat{M}_{i, i \oplus k}$$

after which the FWT can be used to recover $\mathcal{M}(x)$. Given $\hat{x}$, the cost of the sum above is the size of Ω_k. The expense of $\mathcal{M}(x)$ is therefore bounded by the order of

$$\sum_k 2^{\mathbf{1}^T k}$$

$$= \sum_u 2^u \sum_k [\mathbf{1}^T k = u]$$

$$= \sum_u 2^u \binom{\ell}{u}$$

$$= 3^\ell$$

It is important to be able to quickly compute $d\mathcal{M}_x y$ and $y^T d\mathcal{M}_x$. These expressions are related to finding solutions of $\mathcal{G}(x) = x$, a topic touched on in the next section. Like $\mathcal{M}(x)$, the next theorem shows they are computable in time $O(3^\ell)$.

Theorem 7.6 The coefficient of $\widehat{e_k}$ in $d\mathcal{M}_x y$ is

$$2\sqrt{n} \sum_{i \in \Omega_k} \hat{x}_i \hat{y}_{i \oplus k} \hat{M}_{i, i \oplus k}$$

The coefficient of $\widehat{e_k}^T$ in $y^T d\mathcal{M}_x$ is

$$2\sqrt{n} \sum_{i \in \Omega_{\bar{k}}} \hat{x}_i \hat{y}_{i \oplus k} \hat{M}_{i, k}$$

Proof The formulas follow from theorems 6.16 and 6.15. The first is an exercise, the second is

$$\sum \hat{y}_i \widehat{e_i}^T d\mathcal{M}_{\sum \hat{x}_j \widehat{e_j}}$$

$$= 2\sqrt{n} \sum_{i,j} \hat{y}_i \hat{x}_j \widehat{M^*}_{i,j} \widehat{e_{i \oplus j}}^T$$

$$= 2\sqrt{n} \sum_{k,j} \hat{x}_j \hat{y}_{j \oplus k} (M^{\wedge **})_{j \oplus k, j} \widehat{e_k}^T$$

$$= 2\sqrt{n} \sum_k \widehat{e_k}^T \sum_j \hat{x}_j \hat{y}_{j \oplus k}, \hat{M}_{j,k}$$

Restricting the summation to nonzero terms ($\hat{M}$ is separative) completes the proof. ■

Exercises

1. Write a computer program implementing $\mathcal{M}$ as indicated above. Take advantage of the fact that, except for the case $k = 0$, every term in the sum defining $\widehat{\mathcal{M}(x)}_k$ occurs twice.

2. Write a computer program implementing the formulas in theorem 7.6.

3. Complete the proof of theorem 7.6.

4. Show when mixing is via a mutation rate and one-point crossover that $\mathcal{M}(x)$, $d\mathcal{M}_x y$, and $y^T d\mathcal{M}_x$ can be computed in time $O(\ell 2^\ell)$. *Hint:* Use theorem 6.11 to show $\hat{M}$ is significantly more sparse than indicated by its separativity.

5. The use of the FWT to pass between standard and Walsh coordinates has an analogue: the Fast Fourier Transform (FFT). Show the spirit of this section carries over to the general cardinality case via the FFT. *Hint:* If generalizing the FWT to the FFT is problematical, consider a visit to the library.

6. Show the analogue of theorem 7.6 in the general cardinality case involves the formulas

$$2\sqrt{n} \sum_i \overline{\hat{x}_i \hat{y}_{k \ominus i}} \hat{M}_{i, i \ominus k}$$

$$2\sqrt{n} \sum_i \overline{\hat{x}_i \hat{y}_{k \ominus i}} \hat{M}_{i, k}$$

where the overline indicates complex conjugation.

7.3 Fixed Points

As will become apparent, an important equation in the theory of the SGA is the fixed point equation $\mathcal{G}(x) = x$. The next chapter presents examples making use of the techniques in this section to illustrate how fixed points explain some aspects of the simple genetic algorithm's behavior.

As is by now obvious, direct computation with objects related to the heuristic quickly becomes infeasible. In fact, it rapidly becomes impossible to obtain the solution to even a simple linear system involving n equations and n unknowns, since that is typically an $O(n^3)$ affair (i.e., $O(8^\ell)$).

One method of obtaining fixed points is iteration, since $\mathcal{G}(x)$ is typically focused. This can be one of the least expensive options, costing $O(3^\ell)$ per iteration.

Another approach is *Newton's method*. Letting $x = y + \delta$ and approximating $\mathcal{G}$ by its differential[1] gives the equation

$$\mathcal{G}(y) + d\mathcal{G}_y \delta = y + \delta$$

which leads to the solution $x = y + \delta = y + (d\mathcal{G}_y - I)^{-1}(y - \mathcal{G}(y))$. Naturally, the differential was only an approximation, so the process has to be regarded as an iterative one which given an initial y produces an improved x. The main problem here is the solution of the linear system, which takes time $O(n^3)$. Convergence is also a concern, though a lesser one.

The final possibility which will be mentioned is to turn the problem into one of minimization. The function

$$h(x) = (\mathcal{G}(x) - x)^T (\mathcal{G}(x) - x)$$

has global minima (of zero) at fixed points and is positive elsewhere. Approximate h by the quadratic

$$h(y + \delta) \approx h(y) + dh_y \delta + \frac{1}{2} \delta^T A \delta$$

where A is the *Hessian matrix*

$$A_{i,j} = \left. \frac{\partial^2 h}{\partial x_i \partial x_j} \right|_y$$

The differential of the right hand side of this approximation (with respect to δ) is easily calculated as $dh_y + \delta^T A$. But this differential must vanish for δ minimizing h; thus $0 = dh_y + \delta^T A$. It follows that the solution is $x = y + \delta = y - A^{-1} dh_y^T$ (since A is symmetric).

An obvious problem with this approach is the possibility of becoming trapped at local minima. In the case of proportional selection, the solution of the linear system can be obtained faster than $O(8^\ell)$; δ can be obtained in $O(6^\ell)$ time. The reasons for this are that A is positive definite near a fixed point, and the basis $\mathcal{W}$ and fast Walsh transform allow Az to be computed in time $O(3^\ell)$ for any z. The details of how and why will be more fully explained shortly.

As before, this process is an iterative one which given an initial y produces an improved x, but when the method works $O(\ell)$ iterations typically suffice. Compared to calculating

---

1. The differential may be calculated via the chain rule $(d\mathcal{G}_y = d\mathcal{M}_{\mathcal{F}_y} \circ d\mathcal{F}_y)$ using formulas from previous sections.

$\mathcal{G}$, it is a factor of $O(\ell 2^\ell)$ worse; it is superior to iterating $\mathcal{G}$ to a fixed point when $\mathcal{G}$ has not converged in $O(\ell 2^\ell)$ steps. A virtue of finding fixed points by the minimization method is that it will converge to any fixed point provided it is started sufficiently close.

Each of the three methods above searches for fixed points differently. As a byproduct of computing the Hessian (below) it will be shown that the last two methods are essentially equivalent if the initial point y is close to a fixed point. Note that dh_x is

$$d\big(\mathcal{G}(x) - x\big)^T\big(\mathcal{G}(x) - x\big)\big)_x = 2(\mathcal{G}(x) - x)^T(d\mathcal{G}_x - I)$$

On the other hand, this is the *gradient* ∇h of h and has ith component $\partial h/\partial x_i$. Thus $\partial^2 h/\partial x_j \partial x_i$ is the jth entry of the gradient of the function $\nabla h e_i$, which is

$$d\big(2(\mathcal{G}(x) - x)^T(d\mathcal{G}_x - I)e_i\big)_x e_j$$
$$= 2e_i^T(d\mathcal{G}_x - I)^T(d\mathcal{G}_x - I)e_j + 2(\mathcal{G}(x) - x)^T d\big(d\mathcal{G}_x e_i\big)_x e_j$$

Note that if x is near a fixed point, then $\mathcal{G}(x) - x$ is small, and the second term above may be negligible. In that case

$$A \approx 2(d\mathcal{G}_x - I)^T(d\mathcal{G}_x - I)$$

and the solution $y - A^{-1}dh_y^T$ is

$$y - (d\mathcal{G}_y - I)^{-1}(d\mathcal{G}_y - I)^{-T}(d\mathcal{G}_y - I)^T(\mathcal{G}(y) - y)$$
$$= y + (d\mathcal{G}_y - I)^{-1}(y - \mathcal{G}(y))$$

which is Newton's method. The term $(\mathcal{G}(x) - x)^T d\big(d\mathcal{G}_x e_i\big)_x e_j$ presents no difficulty from a computational standpoint (exercise 2 below). On the other hand, since speed is at issue, neglecting it generally improves performance; it will be disregarded for the remainder of this section. Moreover, unless this term is omitted, the matrix A need not be positive definite.

In the case of proportional selection, the fixed point equation $\mathcal{M} \circ \mathcal{F}(x) = x$ is equivalent to $\mathcal{M}(f \cdot x) = x$, since, if such an x can be found, it is then a simple matter of scaling x to obtain a solution of the original equation. This avoids the complications of division in $\mathcal{F}(x)$. The change of variables $z = f \cdot x$ yields $f \cdot \mathcal{M}(z) = z$, which is a particularly convenient form to work with. Therefore, $\mathcal{G}$ may without loss of generality be regarded as $f \cdot \mathcal{M}$. This simplification is used throughout the exercises.

Evaluating Az rests on computing expressions of the form $d\mathcal{G}_x z$ and $(w^T d\mathcal{G}_x)^T$, both of which are $O(3^\ell)$ by theorem 7.6. It follows that Az can be computed in time $O(3^\ell)$ for any $z, \ldots$ but how is the linear system $A\delta = -dh_y^T$ to be solved? The answer is to regard δ as the solution to minimizing $k(x) = x^T A x / 2 + b^T x$ where $b = dh_y^T$. As above, the minimum occurs at $0 = dk_x = x^T A + b^T$, so the minimizing δ is $-A^{-1}b$ as desired. A simple conjugate gradient algorithm will minimize k—and hence produce the solution δ— in n iterations (the reader is referred to a text on unconstrained nonlinear minimization for the details and implementation of conjugate gradient methods). In conclusion, this technique allows the linear system $A\delta = -dh_y^T$ to be solved in time $O(n3^\ell) = O(6^\ell)$.

Exercises

1. A function $\mathcal{G}$ is called *hyperbolic*[2] if, at every fixed point x, the differential $d\mathcal{G}_x$ has no eigenvalue of modulus 1. In the discussion above, $d\mathcal{G}_y - I$ was treated as invertible. How does hyperbolicity (of $\mathcal{G}$) relate to this?

2. In the case of proportional selection, how can the "discarded" second term's contribution to Az be computed in $O(3^\ell)$ time? *Hint:* Show it is $2d\mathcal{M}_z^T \operatorname{diag}(f)(\mathcal{G}(x) - x)$ by using theorem 6.16 before and after the outer differential.

3. Write computer code to implement the minimization of $h(x) = (\mathcal{G}(x) - x)^T (\mathcal{G}(x) - x)$ as described above.

4. Both Newton's method and the minimization method have the following general form: given approximation y, produce a better approximation of the form $y + tv$, where v is a direction to move from y, and t is a scalar which may be regarded as how far to move in that direction. For h as in the previous exercise, show that in the case of proportional selection, $h(y + tv)$ is a polynomial in t with derivative

$$t^3 \, 4\mathcal{G}(v)^T \mathcal{G}(v) +$$

$$t^2 \, 6\mathcal{G}(v)^T (f \cdot d\mathcal{M}_y v - v) +$$

$$t \, 2((f \cdot d\mathcal{M}_y v - v)^T (f \cdot d\mathcal{M}_y v - v) + 2\mathcal{G}(v)^T (\mathcal{G}(y) - y)) +$$

$$2(\mathcal{G}(y) - y)^T (f \cdot d\mathcal{M}_y v - v)$$

Hence the optimal value of t with respect to minimization of $h(y + tv)$ is a root of this cubic.

5. The form $f \cdot \mathcal{M}(x)$ is linear in f, quadratic in x, and has as natural domain complex space. Thus when using proportional selection, the fixed point equation $f \cdot \mathcal{M}(x) = x$ need

---

2. "Hyperbolic" is later introduced (section 10.4) as a technical term in the theory of random heuristic search to describe a focused heuristic all of whose fixed points are hyperbolic. A fixed point of $\mathcal{G}$ is hyperbolic if the differential $d\mathcal{G}_x$ has no eigenvalue of modulus 1.

not be constrained to real x within the simplex. Generalize the code produced for exercise 3 to handle the case of arbitrary complex x.

6. Discussion of the minimization method focused on proportional selection. Extend the discussion to include the ranking and tournament selection schemes.

7. How do things change in the general cardinality case?

8 Basic Examples

8.1 Transient Population Trajectories

Now that first principles have been laid out, some basic examples will be considered. Emergent behavior is of interest here; the SGA is viewed with the aim of discerning what patterns of behavior are exhibited. Perhaps the most fundamental question is: Where in Λ is the SGA at time t? Since the state space Λ has dimensionality too large for direct visualization, except in the case $\ell = 2$, alternate means of monitoring the progression from one generation to the next are required.

A primitive means of reducing dimensionality is by measuring distance from populations to a reference point, say to the center $1/n$ of Λ. The following graph shows what this looks like for string length 4, random fitness function, (one-point) crossover rate 0.8, and mutation rate 0.01. Motivated by theoretical observations following theorem 3.4, the vertical axis measures distance as discrepancy,

$$\text{distance}(x, y) = \sum x_j \log \frac{x_j}{y_j}$$

and the horizontal axis spans $1,000$ generations. This example has population size 4 and corresponding state space of 3,876 populations in a simplex of dimension 15. The initial population p is random, and subsequent generations are produced by τ.

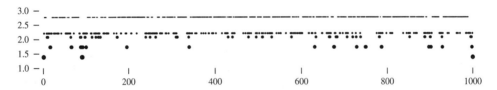

Distance to $1/n$

The size of the points in the graph reflects *entropy*, which is $-\sum x_j \log x_j$. Here larger points correspond to higher entropy, and smaller points correspond to lower entropy. Measuring distance to $1/n$ is equivalent to plotting the difference between $\log n$ and entropy, which explains why large points have lower ordinates; maximum entropy is at the center of Λ. This graph indicates the SGA prefers low entropy states.

Certainly populations equidistant from $1/n$ (i.e., with equal entropy) need not be near each other, but nevertheless there may be relatively few regions where the SGA is spending most of its time. One natural way to explore this is to locate regions where it seems reasonable that the SGA could be spending time, and then plot distance from the current population to such a place. The result should be essentially flat since at a typical generation (abscissa), the distance to one of these regions (ordinate) should be small.

Candidate regions are suggested by the discussion following theorem 3.4. Likely next generations are strongly related to the expected next generation. Near a fixed point, expected behavior is for the next generation to be near the current one, so fixed points of $\mathcal{G}$ may indicate areas where there is little pressure for change. It is plausible that the SGA could spend more time near such regions of Λ.

Fixed points come in various sorts, however. The following figure illustrates an *unstable fixed point*.

Dynamics near unstable fixed point.

The following discussion of the color version (see plate II) assumes continuous differentiability of $\mathcal{G}$. The intersection of the red, green, yellow, and blue curves is the fixed point ω. The red line represents the *unstable space*, the largest invariant space of the differential such that the spectrum is exterior to the unit disk. The green line represents the *stable space*, the largest invariant space of the differential such that the spectrum is interior to the unit disk. Here ω is assumed to be *hyperbolic*, which means $d\mathcal{G}_\omega$ has no eigenvalue of unit modulus (a later chapter is devoted to the issue of hyperbolicity). In the hyperbolic case, it follows from the Jordan canonical form (of $d\mathcal{G}_\omega$) that for suitable choice of inner product, space is the direct sum of the stable and unstable spaces.

Since $d\mathcal{G}$ approximates $\mathcal{G}$ near a fixed point (by choosing the coordinate system with ω as the origin), the trajectory of expected populations, shown by black curves, approximates the behavior indicated by the red and green lines. The blue curve is the *stable manifold*. It is the set V of points which remain near ω under iteration of $\mathcal{G}$. Since the image under $\mathcal{G}$ of points near ω is approximately their image under $d\mathcal{G}_\omega$, and since iterating $d\mathcal{G}_\omega$ sends points either to ω or ∞, it follows that iterates of $\mathcal{G}$

send V towards ω. In fact, $\mathcal{G}$ is a contraction mapping on V with unique fixed point ω. The *basin of attraction* of ω is the set U of points converging to ω under iteration of $\mathcal{G}$,

$$U = \bigcup_{k=0}^{\infty} \mathcal{G}^{-k}(V)$$

The yellow curve is the *unstable manifold*, the set of points which remain near ω under iteration of $\mathcal{G}^{-1}$. A *stable fixed point* (assuming hyperbolicity) has a trivial unstable space, that is, all eigenvalues have modulus less than 1. Hence the stable space is all of space. A diagram depicting this situation is

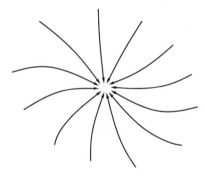

Dynamics near stable fixed point.

The expected behavior of all nearby populations is to converge towards a stable fixed point. Fixed points with this property are called *attractors*. A natural hypothesis is that attractors indicate locations within Λ where the SGA may be predisposed to be near.

One method of locating attracting fixed points is to iterate $\mathcal{G}$ (this is not the only method; recall the last section of the previous chapter). The series of graphs presented on the following page shows generations (horizontal) versus distance to the stable fixed point to which iterates of $\mathcal{G}$ converge (vertical). The initial population p is random, and subsequent generations are produced by τ. The fitness function is random, a (one-point) crossover rate of 0.8 and mutation rate of 0.01 is used, and 1000 generations are spanned. The string length ℓ begins at 4, increasing by 2 with each graph. The population size is approximately $\sqrt{n}$. Points are colored (see plate III for the color version) according to which basin of attraction the current population is in.

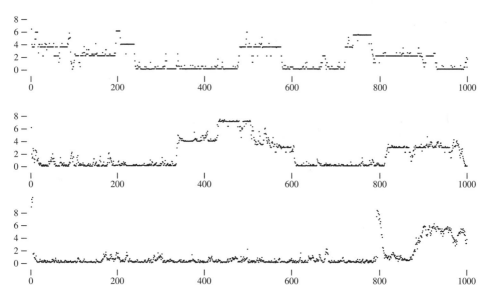

Series 1: Distance to real attracting fixed points in Λ.

Given the complexity of these graphs, one might question the ability of fixed points to explain emergent behavior. However, it is possible that the SGA is particularly adept at seeking out fixed points, more so than is the method of iterating $\mathcal{G}$ to locate them. The plateaus in the graphs above suggest populations might be concentrated in localized regions of Λ.

Extending $\mathcal{G}$ to the real affine space containing Λ (i.e., to $\{x \in \Re^n : \mathbf{1}^T x = 1\}$), using the method of minimization (as discussed in the previous chapter) to locate fixed points—whether stable or not and whether within Λ or not—and then measuring distance to the nearest fixed point results in the next series of graphs (see plate IV for the color version; colors indicate from which fixed point distance is measured: red corresponds to the first fixed point a population trajectory approached, blue to the last, and rainbow colors inbetween).

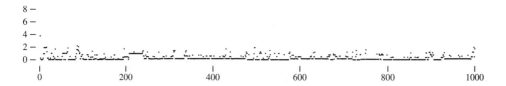

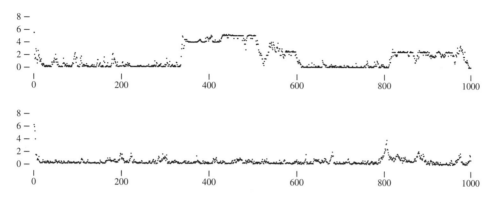

Series 2: Distance to real fixed points.

Correlation between the colors in series 2 and the plateaus in series 1 (see plate IV for the color versions) supports the hypothesis that plateaus correspond to fixed points of $\mathcal{G}$. Although in some graphs the same color appears to correspond to distinct plateaus, that is a consequence of slightly different colors not being separated enough in hue to look distinct.

Even though overall the height of the graphs in the second series is much lower, indicating a typical population's proximity to some fixed point, a few regions remain far from any fixed point. The possibility remains, however, that the SGA is seeking out and spending time near complex as well as real fixed points.

The following graphs consider that possibility. The third series is as the previous, except the fixed point equations were considered over complex space. See plate V for color versions.

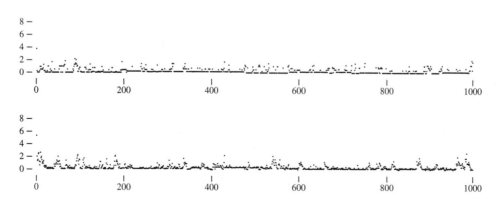

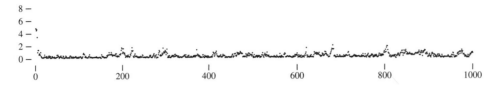

Series 3: Distance to complex fixed points.

All graphs exhibit small height now that complex fixed points are included. The majority of fixed points are unstable and outside the simplex, but near a vertex. The principles at work have been encountered before (see chapter 3). At a fixed point, the expected next generation is the same as the current population. That is, the signal (as given by $\mathcal{G}$) accounts for no change. By continuity, regions within Λ but near fixed points—including unstable and complex fixed points whether within Λ or not—have a signal contributing weakly to change. Discrepancy favors the lattice point nearest the fixed point as the next generation. In addition, sampling effects contribute to counterbalance the instability of the dynamical system corresponding to $\mathcal{G}$ in regions near vertices of Λ. Random heuristic search has a preference for low dispersion states, and in such reagons the variance is small, further contributing to stasis.

As illustrated by the previous graphs, these mechanisms give rise to temporary stability near fixed points which are not attractors, which are not within Λ, and which are not even real. Given a random initial population, this phenomenon—the relative importance of unstable and complex fixed points—typically diminishes as the population size increases.

Even though these examples are anecdotal, they are representative of several hundreds of cases. It should not be supposed that irregularities in the graphs indicate an inability of fixed points to typically explain behavior. Finding fixed points is a difficult task exacerbated by high dimensionality which increases exponentially with ℓ. It is unlikely that all relevant fixed points have been found.

On the other hand, it has not been proven that fixed points will in most cases explain emergent behavior as well as these examples suggest. Uncertainty principally revolves around the linkage between population size and string length (these graphs have $r \approx \sqrt{n}$). Whereas the large population case is fairly well understood (there the answer is yes), the small population case is not well understood in terms of proven analytical results, and that case is the more interesting one from the point of view of search/optimization. The conjecture that the behavior presented above would emerge for a wide class of objective functions given a logarithmic coupling (or some power of a log) between search space size and population size is not incompatible with the empirical evidence.

From an analytic perspective, what complicates the small population case is threefold. First, as r decreases, the noise component increases. Second, the relative influence of dispersion grows. Third, the lattice of points available to populations becomes increasingly coarse as fewer points, located in lower dimensional faces of Λ, become available for occupation. Genetic search is conducted in a low dimensional "skeleton" of Λ which constrains the system's ability to follow the signal.

A natural question is whether the graphs presented in this section would retain their general appearance if, while leaving the fitness functions unchanged, alternate initial populations or different seeds for the random number generator were used. The answer is typically yes; sufficiently many fixed points corresponding to each fitness function were found so that populations are generally nearby. This begs the question of whether, with many fixed points available, a random point in Λ with the same entropy as a population would be near one of them. Were that the case, these graphs would have little meaning.

The fourth series of graphs presented below (see plate VI for color versions) address this issue. Distance is measured to the nearest fixed point from random points having the same entropy distribution as the populations in the previous graphs.

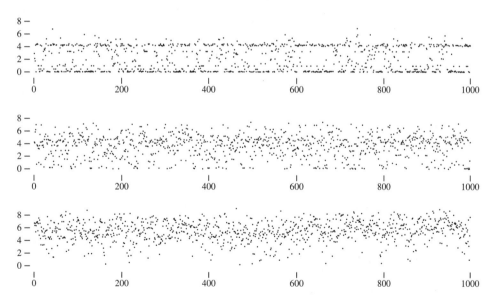

Series 4: Random populations (distance to complex fixed points).

As one might expect, these graphs support the conclusion that the emergent behavior as characterized above is genuine and is not a simple artifact of a plethora of fixed points.

Moreover, the mechanisms responsible are not operational only in the restricted context of the simple genetic algorithm; they apply in far greater generality to arbitrary instances of random heuristic search (a point relevant to the material in chapters 17 and 18).

Revisiting those graphs in which distance to fixed points is measured along population trajectories—the second and third series—a correlation can be seen between increasing string length and a tendency for stretches of blue to occur in later generations. Since population size is approximately the square root of search space size, which grows exponentially with string length, this may have more to do with increasing r than ℓ. In any case, a later chapter shows that when string length is kept fixed, exploration of Λ slows as $r \to \infty$. Transient behavior takes infinitely long in the limit, and the blue regions migrate towards infinity. This raises the question of what behavior is beyond the 1000 generations these graphs span. That question is touched upon in the next section.

8.2   Long Term Probabilities

Long term behavior, in a statistical sense, is provided by the left eigenvector π^T of Q corresponding to the eigenvalue 1 where Q is the transition matrix corresponding to the Markov chain which represents RHS. Recall from section 3.3 that the probability of $\tau^k(p) = q$ is the qth component of $v^T Q^k$ where the tth component of v is the probability of $p = t$. In the positive mutation case, Q is a positive matrix (theorem 4.7) and the limit

$$\pi^T = \lim_{k \to \infty} v^T Q^k$$

exists (see appendix). Therefore

$$\pi^T = (\lim_{k \to \infty} v^T Q^{k-1})Q = \pi^T Q$$

For large k, the qth component of π is approximately the probability that $\tau^k(p) = q$. The influence of initial conditions diminishes with increasing k since π is independent of the initial population distribution v.

Direct computation of π from Q quickly becomes impossible. For example, string length 5 with population size 6 corresponds to a matrix Q containing over 10^{12} entries. For this reason, only examples corresponding to string lengths 2,3, and 4 are considered in this section. Like before, the examples are anecdotal, $r = \sqrt{n}$, and crossover and mutation are as in the previous section.

Sorting components of π by magnitude, the three most probable populations account for approximately 60% of the probability. They are given in the following table for each of $\ell = 2, 3, 4$.

ℓ	n	r	Populations	Vector	Probability	Cumulative
2	4	2	10	$\langle 0, 0, 0, 1 \rangle$	0.330	0.330
				$\langle 1, 0, 0, 0 \rangle$	0.228	0.558
				$\langle 0, 1, 0, 0 \rangle$	0.207	0.765
3	8	3	120	$\langle 0, 0, 0, 1, 0, 0, 0, 0 \rangle$	0.277	0.277
				$\langle 0, 0, 0, 0, 0, 0, 0, 1 \rangle$	0.173	0.450
				$\langle 1, 0, 0, 0, 0, 0, 0, 0 \rangle$	0.133	0.583
4	16	4	3,876	$\langle 0, 0, 0, 0, 0, 0, 0, 0,$ $1, 0, 0, 0, 0, 0, 0, 0 \rangle$	0.333	0.333
				$\langle 0, 0, 0, 0, 0, 0, 0, 0,$ $0, 0, 1, 0, 0, 0, 0, 0 \rangle$	0.208	0.541
				$\langle 0, 0, 0, 0, 0, 0, 0, 0,$ $0, 0, 0, 1, 0, 0, 0, 0 \rangle$	0.054	0.595

As might be expected, fixed points of $\mathcal{G}$ are near the population vectors above. For $\ell = 2$ they are

$$\langle .002, .045, .031, .922 \rangle$$

$$\langle .728, .201, .065, .006 \rangle + \sqrt{-1} \, \langle -.192, .133, .034, .025 \rangle$$

$$\langle -.180, 1.210, .004, -.034 \rangle$$

Note that the first fixed point is contained in Λ, the third is real but exterior to Λ, and the second is complex. This is not surprising, being consistent with the behavior observed in the previous section. While certainly related, this phenomenon of nearby fixed points is not identical to that evidenced in the previous section. Here the focus is on asymptotic behavior, whereas previously it was the relationship of fixed points to transient behavior that was being considered.

For $\ell = 3$ the nearby fixed points of $\mathcal{G}$ are

$$\langle .002, .038, .027, .863, .000, .002, .002, .066 \rangle$$

$$\langle .000, -.002, -.001, -.077, .000, .012, .012, 1.056 \rangle$$

$$\langle .780, .133, .055, .002, .024, .004, .002, .000 \rangle +$$

$$\sqrt{-1} \, \langle -.166, .110, .035, .027, -.010, .002, .001, .001 \rangle$$

For $\ell = 4$ the nearby fixed points are

$\langle.017, .001, .002, .000, .000, .000, .000, .000, .833, .026,$

$\quad .105, .004, .010, .000, .002, .000\rangle$

$\langle-.002, .000, .017, .001, .000, .000, .000, .000, -.123, -.005, 1.042,$

$\quad .053, -.001, .000, .016, .002\rangle$

$\langle-.001, .003, -.001, .062, .000, .000, .000, .001, -.013, .051, -.020,$

$\quad .907, .000, .001, .000, .010\rangle$

In each case, the most probable population accounts for approximately 30% of the probability and is near a stable fixed point of $\mathcal{G}$. As string length increases, the persistence of this trend is unlikely however. Theorem 3.1 shows populations become dense in Λ as $r \to \infty$, independent of ℓ. With $r = \sqrt{n} = 2^{\ell/2}$, increasing ℓ will make available many states for RHS to occupy. The probability of the most likely population will diminish as it shares probability with the many other states nearby a fixed point.

In color plates VII to IX, asymptotic probabilities (vertical) are plotted against distance from a fixed point (horizontal) in a series of three bar graphs for the last example above (corresponding to $\ell = 4$). This gives a view of the distribution of probability around the three fixed points of $\mathcal{G}$ given above. Bars, corresponding to populations, are colored red if closest to the first fixed point, green if closest to the second fixed point, and blue if closest to the third fixed point. The graphs include all 3,876 populations. The series is partially reproduced below, but only the red bars are shown for the first graph, only the green bars are shown for the second graph, and only the blue bars are shown for the third graph.

Distance measured from the first fixed point.

Distance measured from the second fixed point.

Distance measured from the third fixed point.

Restricting consideration to populations having sizable probability, the graphs indicate an inverse correlation between probability and distance to the nearest fixed point. It is interesting to observe in the first graph, however, that the closest lattice point has probability only one tenth that of a population located further away.

When interpreting these graphs, it is important to keep in mind that the distance measured is not a metric; it is not symmetric (the distance from a to b is not the same as from b to a) nor does it satisfy the triangle inequality. Hence the first graph is most easily interpreted with respect to the red group of states, the second with respect to the green group, and the third with respect to the blue group.

So far, examples have involved extremely small string lengths. Locating fixed points was a difficulty in the previous section. Here, the sheer size of the state space is an obstacle.

The next section pushes a bit further by focusing on iterates of $\mathcal{G}$. Although size quickly becomes unmanageable for computation, it should be appreciated that computation and analysis are often orthogonal pursuits; difficulty with one does not preclude progress with the other.

8.3   Trajectory of Expectations

This section contrasts the behavior of τ and $\mathcal{G}$. In color plate X, a series of graphs begins with string length 8, increasing by one with each graph. As before, the examples are anecdotal, $r = \sqrt{n}$, and crossover and mutation have not been changed.

Each graph is a composite of five separate subgraphs, one each of color red, gold, green, light blue, and dark blue. The separate subgraphs were drawn in that order; thus later colors may overlay (obscure) earlier ones. In general, the i th subgraph has 2^i parts, corresponding to sampling the SGA's population trajectory at generations $\{j2^{10-i} : 0 \le j < 2^i\}$. The j th part graphs the discrepancy between the SGA's behavior, given by $\tau^k(p)$, and the trajectory of expectations, given by $\mathcal{G}^{k-j2^{10-i}}(\tau^{j2^{10-i}}(p))$, for $j2^{10-i} \le k < (j+1)2^{10-i}$. In other words, the path traced by iterates of $\mathcal{G}$ is reset to the population trajectory (as determined by τ) at the beginning of a part; the remainder of a part measures discrepancy between the trajectories determined by τ and $\mathcal{G}$.

The first graph (for string length 8) is discussed to review its structure and general features.

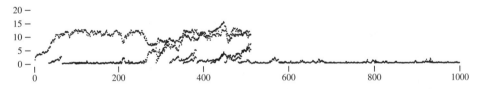

Distance between τ and $\mathcal{G}$ (string length 8).

Note how the last subgraph (dark blue) begins at the origin by increasing. This indicates divergent paths from initial population p are followed by $\tau^k(p)$ and $\mathcal{G}^k(p)$. The discontinuity at generation 32 is the beginning of the second part of the last subgraph (it has 32 parts). Another discontinuity at the start of its third part (generation 64) is visible. Discrepancy is 0 every 32 generations (dark blue parts span 32 generations). When the trajectories determined by τ and $\mathcal{G}$ do not diverge, the beginning of a part will not appear as a jump to 0 since the height of the graph is already small. Divergence of τ and $\mathcal{G}$ are also visible at generations 256, 288, 320, 352, and 448. The first subgraph of the first graph (red) also begins at the origin by increasing, but it is not visible until generation 256 because later subgraphs (gold, green, light blue, dark blue) overlay it. In general, the graph of an early color is identical to that of a later color where the early color cannot be seen. The red subgraph is not reset to correspond to a point on the population trajectory until generation 512, while later colors are reset sooner (gold is reset every 256 generations, green every 128, and light blue every 64). Earlier colors are therefore uncovered if divergent paths are followed by τ and $\mathcal{G}$. In particular, the dominance of dark blue beginning at generation 512 speaks to the ability of $\mathcal{G}$ to indicate the population trajectory for 512 consecutive generations beginning from $\tau^{512}(p)$.

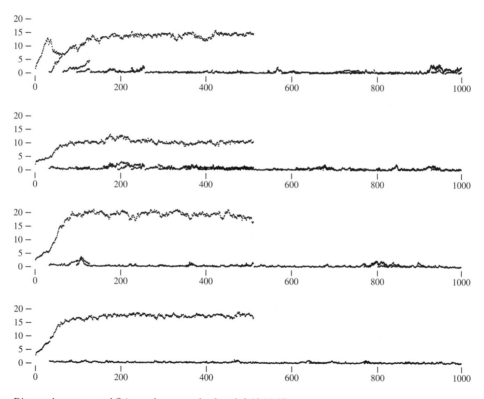

Distance between τ and $\mathcal{G}$ (top to bottom: string length 9,10,11,12).

Note the change in character between the first graphs in the series and the later ones. For example, when $\ell = 9$ (the second graph in the series), the dark blue subgraph indicates frequent divergence between the behavior of τ and $\mathcal{G}$ early on (at generations 0, 32, 64, 96 for example). It is not until around generation 256 that general agreement between τ and $\mathcal{G}$ is observed. In contrast, the last graph (corresponding to $\ell = 12$) shows sustained agreement between τ and $\mathcal{G}$ beginning from generation 32.

Assuming positive mutation and that $\mathcal{G}$ is focused, it is plausible that the path followed by $\mathcal{G}^k(p)$ converges to a stable fixed point (positive mutation guarantees $\mathcal{G}^k(p)$ moves into the interior of Λ where basins of attraction of unstable fixed points have low dimension). In that case, general agreement between τ and $\mathcal{G}$ speaks to the asymptotic behavior of random heuristic search by indicating that population trajectories shadow the movement towards stable fixed points of $\mathcal{G}$ by spending time nearby. This possibility will be explored in some detail in a later chapter.

Exercises

1. As pointed out by Jonathan Rowe, fixed points are not the only regions which RHS has a predisposition for. He has given an example where $\mathcal{G}$ is nearly the identity within the unstable manifold of an unstable fixed point. Since the flow has therefore stalled at lattice points near that manifold, it is the *entire manifold*—not just the fixed point—which impacts the behavior of RHS. Give examples to illustrate this phenomenon. *Hint:* Consider a "linear" heuristic, i.e., one of the form

$$\mathcal{G}(x) = \frac{Ax}{\mathbf{1}^T x}$$

for suitable matrix A.

2. As the population size decreases, the lattice $\frac{1}{r} X_n^r$ of allowable values for population vectors becomes increasingly coarse, as fewer points become available for occupation. Search is conducted in lower dimensional faces of Λ, which constrains the system's ability to follow the signal. Ergodic random heuristic search is adept at locating regions in low dimensional faces where the flow has stalled near lattice points, and that may occur in areas not necessarily associated with fixed points or with stable/unstable manifolds. Give examples which illustrate this.

3. Looking at the series of graphs plotting distance to fixed points, there is a tendency for graphs associated with larger string lengths to have a fuzzy appearance. Explain this.

4. Explain the observation made about the first graph which plots asymptotic probability vs distance from the first fixed point. In particular, what role does discrepancy play in explaining the fact that the closest lattice point has probability only one tenth that of a population located further away? Is it relevant that the graph represents *asymptotic* probability? How?

5. The examples presented in this chapter were randomly chosen. Write computer code to generate random examples corresponding to each type of example shown. Obtain several sets of examples to supplement those given in this chapter.

6. Repeat the previous exercise for the general cardinality case.

9 The Inverse Heuristic

The previous chapter raised the prospect that a domain larger than Λ could be relevant to SGA behavior. When mutation is positive, $\mathcal{G}$ maps Λ into its interior and $\mathcal{G}^{-1}$ maps $\Lambda \setminus \mathcal{G}(\Lambda)$ to the exterior of Λ (provided $\mathcal{G}$ is defined there). It is natural to regard Λ as an attractor and to consider its basin of attraction to be

$$\bigcup_{k \geq 0} \mathcal{G}^{-k}(\Lambda)$$

This chapter presents preliminary and anecdotal results concerning this basin.

Section one is devoted to the inverse of $\mathcal{F}$. Section two derives a formula for $\mathcal{M}^{-1}$. The final section concerns $\mathcal{G}^{-1}$ and the visualization of some aspects of the dynamical system corresponding to $\mathcal{G}$ near what appears to be $\mathcal{G}^{-\infty}(\Lambda)$.

9.1 Selection

First consider the problem of recovering $x \in \Lambda$ from $\mathcal{F}(x)$. In the case of proportional selection,

$$\mathcal{F}^{-1}(x) = \frac{\mathrm{diag}(f)^{-1}x}{1^T \mathrm{diag}(f)^{-1}x}$$

Verification of this is left as an exercise. For ranking selection, theorem 7.2 gives $\mathcal{F}(x)_i$ as

$$\int_{\eta_i}^{\eta_i + x_i} \varrho(y)\, dy$$

Since ϱ is positive, $\mathcal{F}(x)_i$ is an increasing function of x_i given η_i. Hence the zero of

$$h_i(z) = \int_{\eta_i}^{\eta_i + z} \varrho(y)\, dy - \mathcal{F}(x)_i$$

is at $z = x_i$ and can be found numerically provided η_i is known. Because ϱ is increasing, h_i has positive second derivative and is concave up. The graph of h_i is qualitatively like the following

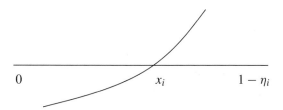

Using Newton's method, an acceptable initial guess is $z = 1 - \eta_i$, and an improved guess z' can be obtained by

$$z' = z - \frac{h_i(z)}{\varrho(\eta_i + z)}$$

For this method, convergence is assured, and the components of x may be solved in the order $x_{\psi_0}, x_{\psi_1}, \ldots$ since then the η_i are known:

$$\eta_{\psi_0} = 0$$

$$\eta_{\psi_{i+1}} = \eta_{\psi_i} + x_{\psi_i}$$

The case of tournament selection is similar. By theorem 7.4,

$$\mathcal{F}(x)_{\psi_i} = \sum_{u=0}^{k} \binom{k}{u}(1 - \sum_{j \leq i} x_{\psi_j})^{k-u} \sum_{v=0}^{u} \binom{u}{v} x_{\psi_i}^v (\sum_{j < i} x_{\psi_j})^{u-v} \sum_{j < v} t_{j+u-v}$$

where the t_j are as defined in section 5.1. Let x_{ψ_i} be abbreviated by z, and let $\sum_{j < v} t_{j+u-v}$ be abbreviated by $w(u, v)$. It follows that

$$\frac{\partial}{\partial z} \mathcal{F}(x)_{\psi_i}$$

$$= \sum_{u=0}^{k} \sum_{v=0}^{u} \frac{k! \eta_{\psi_i}^{u-v} w(u, v)}{(k-u)!(u-v)!v!}\left((1 - z - \eta_{\psi_i})^{k-u} v z^{v-1} - (k-u)(1 - z - \eta_{\psi_i})^{k-u-1}z^v\right)$$

$$= \sum_{u=0}^{k} \sum_{v=1}^{u} \frac{k! \eta_{\psi_i}^{u-v} w(u, v)(1 - z - \eta_{\psi_i})^{k-u} z^{v-1}}{(k-u)!(u-v)!(v-1)!}$$

$$- \sum_{u=0}^{k-1} \sum_{v=0}^{u} \frac{k! \eta_{\psi_i}^{u-v} w(u, v)(1 - z - \eta_{\psi_i})^{k-u-1} z^v}{(k-u-1)!(u-v)!v!}$$

Making the change of variables $u = u' + 1$, $v = v'$ in the first sum (of the right hand side above), and $u = u'$, $v = v' - 1$ in the second sum, and then recombining them yields

$$\sum_{u'=0}^{k-1} \sum_{v'=1}^{u'+1} \frac{k! \eta_{\psi_i}^{u'-v'+1}(1 - z - \eta_{\psi_i})^{k-u'-1} z^{v'-1}}{(k-u'-1)!(u'-v'+1)!(v'-1)!}\left(w(u'+1, v') - w(u', v'-1)\right)$$

$$= \sum_{u=0}^{k-1} \sum_{v=1}^{u+1} \frac{k! \eta_{\psi_i}^{u-v+1}(1 - z - \eta_{\psi_i})^{k-u-1} z^{v-1}}{(k-u-1)!(u-v+1)!(v-1)!} t_u$$

$$= \sum_{u=0}^{k-1} \binom{k}{u} t_u (k-u)(1 - z - \eta_{\psi_i})^{k-u-1} \sum_{v=1}^{u+1} \binom{u}{v-1} z^{v-1} \eta_{\psi_i}^{u-v+1}$$

$$= \sum_{u=0}^{k-1} \binom{k}{u} t_u (k-u)(1 - z - \eta_{\psi_i})^{k-u-1} (z + \eta_{\psi_i})^u$$

The second derivative is computed similarly,

$$\frac{\partial^2}{\partial z^2} \mathcal{F}(x)_{\psi_i}$$

$$= \sum_{u=0}^{k-1} \binom{k}{u} t_u (k-u) \big((1 - z - \eta_{\psi_i})^{k-u-1} u (z + \eta_{\psi_i})^{u-1}$$

$$- (k-u-1)(1 - z - \eta_{\psi_i})^{k-u-2} (z + \eta_{\psi_i})^u \big)$$

$$= \sum_{u=1}^{k-1} \frac{k!(1 - z - \eta_{\psi_i})^{k-u-1}(z + \eta_{\psi_i})^{u-1}}{(u-1)!(k-u-1)!} t_u - \sum_{u=0}^{k-2} \frac{k!(1 - z - \eta_{\psi_i})^{k-u-2}(z + \eta_{\psi_i})^u}{u!(k-u-2)!} t_u$$

Making the change of variables $u = u' + 1$ in the first sum (of the right hand side above), replacing u' with u and then recombining the sums yields

$$\sum_{u=0}^{k-2} \frac{k!(1 - z - \eta_{\psi_i})^{k-u-2}(z + \eta_{\psi_i})^u}{u!(k-u-2)!} (t_{u+1} - t_u)$$

Note that the first derivative is positive when $0 \leq z + \eta_{\psi_i} \leq 1$, and since ϱ is increasing (i.e., $t_{u+1} - t_u > 0$) the second derivative is also positive in this case. As in the case of ranking selection, the zero of the function

$$h_i(z) = \sum_{u=0}^{k} \binom{k}{u} (1 - \eta_i - z)^{k-u} \sum_{v=0}^{u} \binom{u}{v} z^v \eta_i^{u-v} \sum_{j<v} t_{j+u-v} - \mathcal{F}(x)_i$$

can be found numerically provided η_i is known. Like before, h_i is increasing and concave up with root $z = x_i$ in the interval $[0, 1 - \eta_i]$. Using Newton's method, an acceptable initial guess is $z = 1 - \eta_i$, and an improved guess z' can be obtained by

$$z' = z - h_i(z) / \sum_{u=0}^{k-1} \binom{k}{u} t_u (k-u)(1 - z - \eta_i)^{k-u-1} (z + \eta_i)^u$$

For this method, convergence is assured, and the components of x may be solved in the order $x_{\psi_0}, x_{\psi_1}, \ldots$ since then the η_i are known:

$$\eta_{\psi_0} = 0$$

$$\eta_{\psi_{i+1}} = \eta_{\psi_i} + x_{\psi_i}$$

Theorem 9.1 $\mathcal{F}^{-1} : \Lambda \to \Lambda$ is continuously differentiable in the interior of Λ (provided, in the case of ranking selection, that ϱ is positive).

Proof   In the case of proportional selection, since f is positive, $\mathcal{F}^{-1}$ is the same as $\mathcal{F}$ but with alternate choice of f (invert each component).

For ranking selection, any $v \in \Lambda$ satisfies $v_i \geq 0$ and $\mathbf{1}^T v = 1$. Since ϱ is a probability density on $[0, 1]$, there exists corresponding ξ_i such that $0 = \xi_0 \leq \xi_1 \leq \ldots \leq \xi_n = 1$ and

$$\int_{\xi_i}^{\xi_{i+1}} \varrho(y) \, dy = v_i$$

It follows that the equations which are solved numerically to compute $\mathcal{F}^{-1}(v)$ have non-negative solutions which sum to 1 (the root x_{ψ_i} of h_{ψ_i} is $\xi_{i+1} - \xi_i$).

Finally consider tournament selection. That the equations

$$v_i = \sum_{u=0}^{k} \binom{k}{u} (1 - \eta_i - z)^{k-u} \sum_{v=0}^{u} \binom{u}{v} z^v \eta_i^{u-v} \sum_{j<v} t_{j+u-v}$$

have solutions x_i follows from the fact that the right hand side varies from 0 to $1 - \sum_{j<i} v_j$ for $z \in [0, 1 - \eta_i]$. To see this, induct on i. First note that the case $z = 0$ is trivial. Next regard v_i as being defined by the right hand side for the choice of $z = x_i$ and set $x_j = 0$ for $j > h$. To establish the claim at $i = h$, let $z = x_h = 1 - \eta_h$ so that what needs to be proved is $\mathbf{1}^T v = 1$ (since $v_j = 0$ for $j > h$ by choice of x_j). By exercise 1 of section 4.2,

$$\mathbf{1}^T v = \mathbf{1}^T \mathcal{F}(x) = 1$$

According to the inverse function theorem, continuous differentiability would follow from the invertibility of $d\mathcal{F}$. Since, for both ranking and tournament selection, $\mathcal{F}(x)_{\psi_i}$ depends only on $\{x_{\psi_j} : j \leq i\}$, it follows that the differential is triangular in a suitable basis with general diagonal element given by the partial of $\mathcal{F}(x)_{\psi_i}$ with respect to x_{ψ_i}. By the discussion preceding theorem 9.1, these partials are positive in the interior of Λ and hence the differential has positive determinant. Continuous differentiability, in the case of proportional selection, is an easy exercise.   ∎

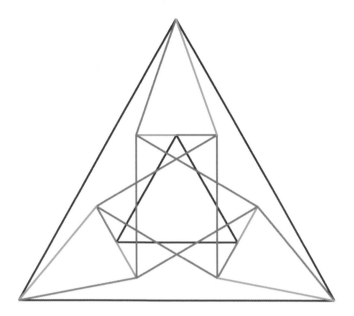

Plate I. Cayley diagram.

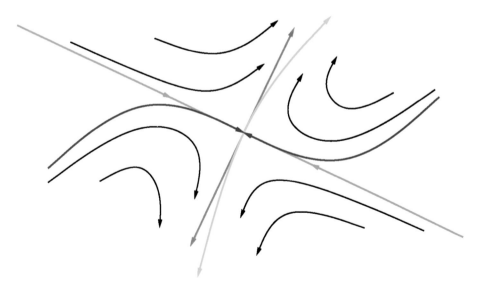

Plate II. Dynamics near unstable fixed point.

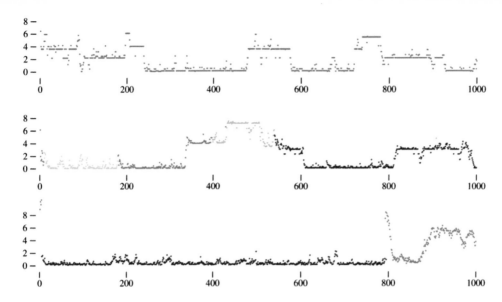

Plate III. Series 1: Distance to real attracting fixed points in Λ.

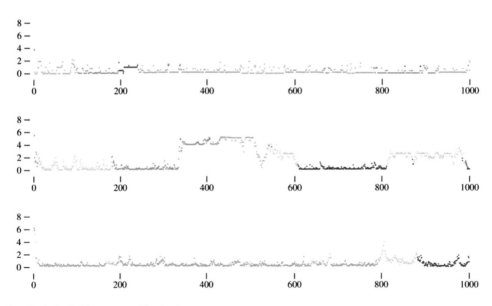

Plate IV. Series 2: Distance to real fixed points.

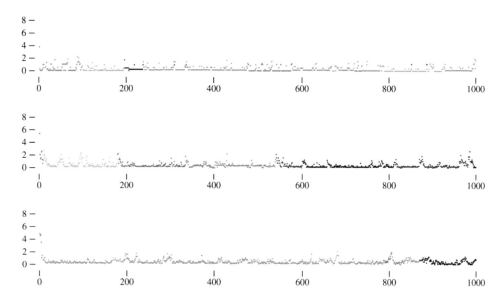

Plate V. Series 3: Distance to complex fixed points.

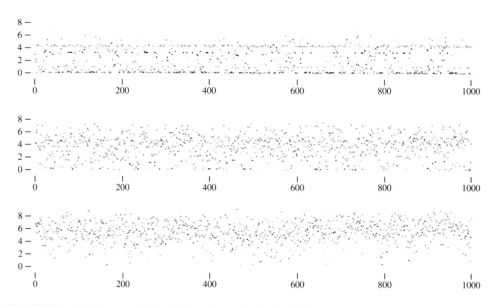

Plate VI. Series 4: Random populations (distance to complex fixed points).

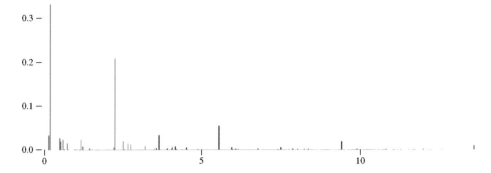

Plate VII. Distance measured from the first fixed point.

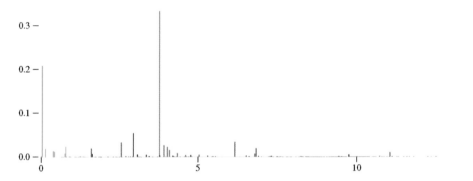

Plate VIII. Distance measured from the second fixed point.

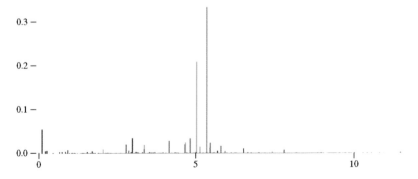

Plate IX. Distance measured from the third fixed point.

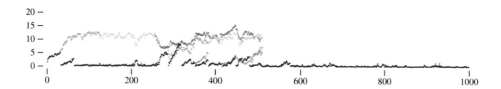

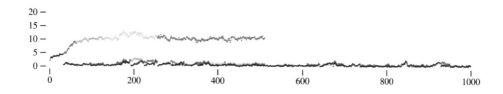

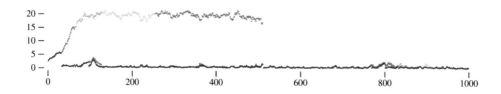

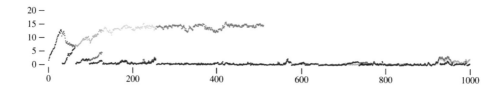

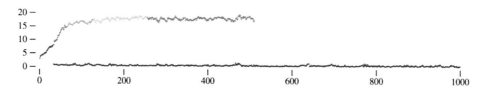

Plate X. Distance between τ and $\mathcal{G}$ (top to bottom: string length 8,9,10,11,12).

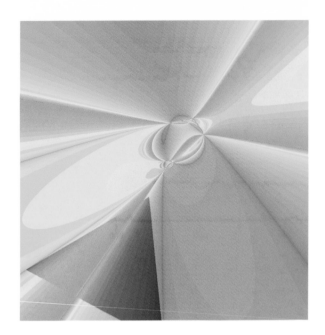

Plate XI. Figure 9.1.

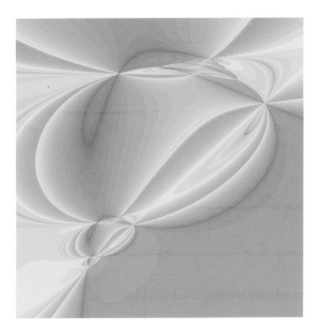

Plate XII. Figure 9.2.

Plate XIII. Figure 9.3.

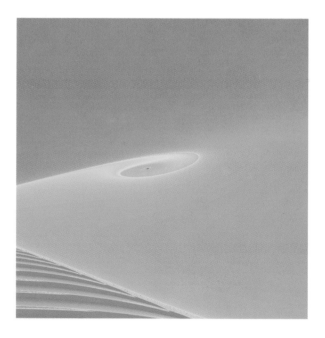

Plate XIV. Figure 9.4.

Plate XV. Figure 9.5.

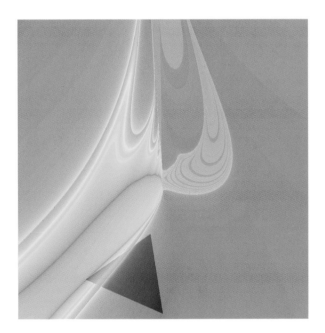

Plate XVI. Figure 9.6.

Exercises

1. Verify the inverse for proportional selection.

2. Prove theorem 9.1.

3. Write a computer program implementing $\mathcal{F}^{-1}$ on Λ for proportional, ranking, and tournament selection.

4. Let D be the complement of $\{x : \mathbf{1}^T \text{diag}(f)^{-1}x = 0\}$. Show, for proportional selection, that the function $\mathcal{F}^{-1}$ is defined on D but does not necessarily map into D. Notice that nothing requires x to be real; it may be a vector in complex space.

5. Show that requiring ϱ to be an entire function of a complex variable extends ranking selection to complex space such that the invariance of the affine space containing Λ (i.e., $\{x : \mathbf{1}^T x = 1\}$) is preserved.

6. Show that requiring ϱ to be an increasing function on the real line extends ranking selection to an injective function on $\mathfrak{R}^n$.

7. For ranking selection, show that requiring ϱ to be a positive increasing function on the real line makes the algorithm given in this section for recovering x from $\mathcal{F}(x)$ valid (except for the location of the root and the "initial guess").

8. Show how, in the process of computing $\mathcal{F}^{-1}(x)$ for ranking selection, it may be determined whether x lies in the domain.

9. Show any continuous increasing probability density ϱ on $[0, 1]$ can be uniformly approximated by a probability density ϱ' on $[0, 1]$ which is an entire function and is positive and increasing on the real line. *Hint:* Any increasing function on $[0, 1]$ can be uniformly approximated by a positive linear combination of Heavyside functions function (a Heavyside function is a nondecreasing step function mapping $\mathfrak{R}$ onto $\{0, 1\}$). Hence it suffices to integrate a positive linear combination of approximations to Dirac delta functions (the derivatives of Heavyside functions . . . you may want to visit the library for the full story; although they are widely used, Dirac delta functions do not, technically speaking, exist). Use normal densities (with appropriate means and variances) to approximate the Dirac delta functions.

10. Reconsider the previous exercises in the general cardinality case.

9.2 Mixing

The Walsh basis will be used throughout this section. Theorem 6.17 triangulates the equations which relate x to $\mathcal{M}(x)$. Alden Wright first noticed this could be used to invert $\mathcal{M}$. Let Ω_k' denote $\Omega_k \setminus \{0, k\}$. The vector $y = \mathcal{M}(x)$ satisfies

$$y_k = \begin{cases} x_k & \text{if } k = 0 \\ 2\hat{M}_{k,0}x_k + \sqrt{n} \sum_{i \in \Omega'_k} x_i x_{i \oplus k} \hat{M}_{i,i \oplus k} & \text{if } k > 0 \end{cases}$$

This relationship follows from Theorem 6.17 and the observation that $x_0 = 1/\sqrt{n}$ for all $x \in \Lambda$. Solving for x_k gives the equations

$$x_k = \begin{cases} y_k & \text{if } k = 0 \\ (2\hat{M}_{k,0})^{-1}(y_k - \sqrt{n} \sum_{i \in \Omega'_k} x_i x_{i \oplus k} \hat{M}_{i,i \oplus k}) & \text{if } k > 0 \end{cases}$$

These equations serve to define x_k recursively in terms of x_i for $i \in \Omega'_k$. Therefore the polynomial map

$$y \mapsto x$$

determined by this recursive definition is the inverse function to $\mathcal{M}$ on Λ. The inverse is defined provided division by zero is avoided, that is, provided $\hat{M}_{k,0} \neq 0$ for $k \in \Omega$. By Theorem 6.7, this is equivalent to the invertibility of M^*. These remarks establish the "if" part of the following theorem, the "only if" is left as an exercise.

Theorem 9.2   The function $\mathcal{M} : \Lambda \to \mathcal{M}(\Lambda)$ is invertible if and only if M^* is. The inverse, when it exists, is infinitely differentiable.

Exercises

1. Write a computer program implementing $\mathcal{M}^{-1}$ in standard coordinates. *Hint:* Use the FWT.

2. Show that $\mathcal{M}$ is defined on and maps the affine space containing Λ (i.e., $\{x : \mathbf{1}^T x = 1\}$) into itself. Notice that nothing requires x to be real; it may be a vector in complex space.

3. Prove that $\mathcal{M}$ is invertible on $\{x : \mathbf{1}^T x \neq 0\}$ when M^* is invertible. Notice that nothing requires x to be real; it may be a vector in complex space. What is the inverse?

4. Prove theorem 9.2.

5. Show that if mutation is positive, then $\mathcal{M}^{-1}(\Lambda)$ is not contained in Λ.

6. Show the definition of the polynomial map giving the inverse of $\mathcal{M}$ extends to the general cardinality case provided the single subscript $i \oplus k$ is replaced with $i \ominus k$ and the double subscript $i, i \oplus k$ is replaced with $i, i \ominus k$.

7. Show theorem 9.2 carries over to the general cardinality case.

9.3 $\mathcal{G}$

The following theorem is a straightforward consequence of previous results.

Theorem 9.3 For either proportional, ranking, or tournament selection, $\mathcal{G} : \Lambda \to \mathcal{G}(\Lambda)$ is invertible if and only if M^* is. In particular, $\mathcal{G}$ is invertible if the crossover rate is less than 1 and the mutation rate satisfies $0 < \mu < 1/2$. The inverse, when it exists, is continuously differentiable in $\mathcal{G}(\Lambda^o)$, where Λ^o denotes the interior of Λ (provided, in the case of ranking selection, that ϱ is positive).

Although the methods for computing $\mathcal{F}^{-1}$ and $\mathcal{M}^{-1}$ may be valid in larger domains (see the exercises of sections 9.1 and 9.2 for example), tournament selection has not been completely analyzed. While injective on Λ, it is in general a polynomial of arbitrary degree in several variables. Questions concerning when and where it is injective outside of Λ have not been addressed.

Although one would like to regard $\mathcal{G}^{-1}$ as a function of a complex variable, with the exception of proportional selection $\mathcal{F}^{-1}$ is not understood in the complex case. Of course, formulating the inverse problem as the numerical solution to an equation $h = 0$ (a method used in section 9.1) is an applicable technique. However, if ϱ is entire then neither ranking nor tournament selection are invertible functions of complex variables. This is because of the triangular form of the equations involved. When solved in the order $x_{\psi_0}, x_{\psi_1}, \ldots$ (see section 9.1), each equation has the form $h(z) = 0$ where h is an entire function of z. Such equations cannot have unique solutions unless h is linear.

The remainder of this section concerns the visualization of some aspects of the dynamical system corresponding to $\mathcal{G}(x)$ on $\{x : \mathbf{1}^T x = 1\}$. That this is the natural region containing the basin of attraction of Λ follows from the following considerations. First, it is desirable that ϱ be increasing on the real line so that the methods of section 9.1 apply to ranking selection outside of Λ. In particular,

$$\mathbf{1}^T \mathcal{F}(x) = \int_0^{\mathbf{1}^T x} \varrho(y) \, dy$$

is an increasing function of $\mathbf{1}^T x$ which is 1 only when $\mathbf{1}^T x = 1$. Since by theorem 6.16

$$\mathbf{1}^T \mathcal{G}(x) = \mathbf{1}^T \mathcal{M} \circ \mathcal{F}(x) = (\mathbf{1}^T \mathcal{F}(x))^2$$

it follows that the sequence $x, \mathcal{G}(x), \mathcal{G}^2(x), \ldots$ can never enter Λ unless $\mathbf{1}^T x = 1$. These latter remarks apply to tournament selection as well; there $\mathbf{1}^T \mathcal{F}(x) = (\mathbf{1}^T x)^k$ is also an increasing function of $\mathbf{1}^T x$ which is 1 only when $\mathbf{1}^T x = 1$. As far as proportional selection is concerned, the division in

$$\mathfrak{F}(x) = \frac{f \cdot x}{f^T x}$$

can be thought of as a retraction of x to $\{x : \mathbf{1}^T x = 1\}$ since it makes $\mathfrak{F}$, and hence $\mathcal{G}$, a function of only the direction of x, so that $x/\mathbf{1}^T x$ may serve as a representative. The division also forces the image to be in $\{x : \mathbf{1}^T x = 1\}$. Thus $\{x : \mathbf{1}^T x = 1\}$ is in every case (proportional, ranking, and tournament selection) the natural region containing the basin of attraction of Λ.

Empirically, for the case $\ell = 2$ and proportional selection, the examples below suggest (by way of computer calculation) that every $x \in \Lambda$ has a backwards time trajectory (via iterates of $\mathcal{G}^{-1}$) ending in a point $\alpha = \mathcal{G}^{-\infty}(\Lambda)$. Conversely, every x near α appears to have a forward time evolutionary trajectory (via iterates of $\mathcal{G}$) ending in a fixed point of $\mathcal{G}$ in Λ. Computations therefore suggest that every point in Λ lies on a path from near α to Λ.

Although this scenario is too simplistic (see the exercises), it nevertheless represents typical behavior for the examples presented below. As an application of the invertibility of $\mathcal{G}$, some aspects of its dynamical system will be visualized near α. The pictures presented below depict the speed of convergence to a fixed point in Λ of $\mathcal{G}^k(x)$ as $k \to \infty$. This method of visualizing the dynamics of $\mathcal{G}$ was first suggested by Jenny Juliany. The fitness functions used to generate the graphics are

$$f_1 = \{(0, 0.823359), (1, 0.439341), (2, 0.256464), (3, 0.723834)\}$$

$$f_2 = \{(0, 0.723359), (1, 0.639341), (2, 0.256464), (3, 0.583834)\}$$

$$f_3 = \{(0, 0.723359), (1, 0.639341), (2, 0.583834), (3, 0.256464)\}$$

The selection schemes are proportional and ranking; tournament selection is not used. The string length is 2 ($\ell = 2$), and mixing is one point crossover with rate 0.6 and mutation rate 0.00505.

Since $n = 4$, the set $\{x : \mathbf{1}^T x = 1\}$ is characterized by the equation $x_0 + x_1 + x_2 + x_3 = 1$. This is a flat Euclidean 3-space embedded in $\mathfrak{R}^4$. Because only two dimensions fit on a page, three points of this space were chosen to describe a slicing plane. The behavior exhibited within this slicing plane is mapped to the page (projections are not considered). Most of the pictures are generated with α being one of these three points, where α is located at or near the center of the picture.

Points on the slicing plane are colored as follows: Point x is red if it is close in time to its destiny (relatively few iterations of $\mathcal{G}$ were required from x to approach a fixed point), blue if far away in time (many iterations of $\mathcal{G}$ required), and through rainbow colors inbetween. The computer code producing the graphics defines "few generations" as the minimum number, over the collection of points to be colored, of iterations of $\mathcal{G}$ required to converge. The definition of "many generations" is the analogous maximum. The definition of convergence is a small change from x to $\mathcal{G}(x)$.

The exception to this description of the coloring scheme is that points inside Λ are in reverse color so they can be visually identified. One need not wonder if the reverse of red is blue (it is) or in that case how to tell if a blue area is really blue or reverse red. In the case where Λ does not occur in a picture, no colors are reversed. When Λ does occur, it is clearly visible as containing points which seem out of color-context. In that case, only the colors within Λ have been reversed. Moreover, each picture has an accompanying description explaining whether Λ is present and if so where it is. In general, Λ looks like a triangle.

The first picture (figure 9.1) is for f_1 (see plate XI). The reverse color (blue) triangle located below and left of center is Λ. Its lower corner is out of view, being below the bottom of the picture. There are two attracting fixed points of $\mathcal{G}$ contained in Λ. One is near the lower corner of Λ (out of view), the other is near the left corner ("near" means within a few pixels of resolution). Note how Λ is divided by a yellow line. This represents the common boundary of the basins of attraction for the two attracting fixed points in Λ. The negative time fixed point α is at the center of the picture.

Figure 9.2 (see plate XII) is a closeup of the smallest visible oval in the center of figure 9.1. Note the oval beneath it, which has an oval beneath it, which has . . . The limit of this sequence is α. Note the overall regularity. This picture does not intersect Λ. Note how figure 9.2 is roughly divided into two regions differentiated by tint or shade of color; one has a redish hue and other is tinted yellow. The first (redish) region is the basin of attraction for one of the two attractors in Λ, the other region is the basin corresponding to the remaining attractor in Λ. These same remarks apply to figure 9.1.

The next picture, figure 9.3, corresponds to f_2 (see plate XIII). Here $\mathcal{G}$ has only a single attracting fixed point in Λ. As before, α is at the center of the picture. The big blue piece of triangle below and left of center (its lower and left corners are out of view) is Λ. The attracting fixed point is near the lower corner (out of view) of Λ.

Figure 9.4 is a closeup near the smallest visible egg shape towards the center of figure 9.3 (see plate XIV). There are other spirals near both larger and smaller egg shapes. This picture does not intersect Λ. The spiral suggests a complex eigenvalue of the differential of $\mathcal{G}$. Since the color gradient is towards red as the spiral unfolds, the modulus of the eigenvalue is greater than one.

The next picture (figure 9.5) is for f_3 (see plate XV). Like the previous function, it has a single associated attractor in Λ. Figure 9.5 is a closeup of an area below and to the left of α. The blue triangle in the upper right corner (only its left most vertex is in view) is Λ. Note the extreme sensitivity on initial conditions indicated by the interleaved blue and yellow curves.

The final picture (figure 9.6, see plate XVI) revisits f_1. The blue triangle below and left of center is Λ. There are two attracting fixed points of $\mathcal{G}$ contained in Λ, located in the same corners as before. The yellow line dividing Λ is the boundary between their basins of attraction, and the negative time fixed point α is at the center of the picture. What accounts for the difference in appearance between figures 9.1 and 9.6 is the selection scheme. Whereas the former was computed using proportional selection, the latter corresponds to ranking selection. Note how the change in selection scheme has shifted the boundary between the attracting fixed points to the left.

The "convergence portraits" presented here are fascinating. They are a charming and beautiful aspect of $\mathcal{G}$ which as yet is not understood. The task of computing accurate convergence portraits can be expensive, requiring extended precision floating point routines when overflow/underflow would otherwise occur during the computation of orbits.

Exercises

1. Prove theorem 9.3.

2. Prove $\mathcal{G}$ maps the affine space containing Λ into itself provided $\mathcal{F}$ corresponds to proportional, ranking, or tournament selection.

3. In the proportional selection case, $\mathcal{G}$ is a fraction and division by zero is possible. Show the set

$$\bigcup_{k \geq 0} \mathcal{G}^{-k}(\{x : \mathbf{1}^T x = 1 \text{ and } x \in f^\perp\})$$

is on a forward time trajectory to division by 0.

4. Assuming nonzero mutation, show the set

$$\bigcap_{k \geq 0} \mathcal{G}^k(\Lambda)$$

is compact, connected, and invariant under $\mathcal{G}^{-1}$. Conclude that if x_1 and x_2 are two distinct fixed points of $\mathcal{G}$ in Λ, then there is an uncountable subset of Λ connecting them which is invariant under $\mathcal{G}^{-1}$.

5. Compute graphics like those presented in this section for alternate choices of dimension (n), crossover rate ($\mathcal{X}$), mutation rate (μ), and fitness (f).

6. Compute graphics like those presented in this section for alternate choices of mutation and crossover schemes.

7. Except for possible difficulty in locating α, convergence portraits of $\mathcal{G}$ using tournament selection are straightforward to obtain. Compute several, and contrast them with those corresponding to proportional and ranking selection.

8. Investigate convergence portraits for the general cardinality case.

10 Focused Heuristics

What is currently known concerning general conditions under which $\mathcal{F}$, $\mathcal{M}$, and $\mathcal{G}$ are focused is broken into three chapters. This chapter presents the first part, which is principally concerned with selection and mixing.

A basic technique for establishing convergence of iterates is presented in section one. The following section shows the selection schemes defined in section 4.2 are focused. Necessary and sufficient conditions under which mixing is focused are developed in section three. The final section presents a brief summary and foreshadows the results to be presented in the following two chapters.

10.1   Lyapunov's Criterion

There do not seem to be many techniques for establishing that iterates of a function must converge. When there is a single fixed point, the contraction mapping theorem is a natural candidate. But in the case of several fixed points, that method is not as easily applied. The following discrete analogue of Lyapunov's stability theorem is often useful in situations where the contraction mapping theorem is not.

Theorem 10.1   If continuously differentiable $g : \Lambda \to \Lambda$ has finitely many fixed points, and if there is a continuous function ϕ satisfying

$$x \neq g(x) \Longrightarrow \phi(x) > \phi(g(x))$$

then g is focused.

Proof   For fixed point ω_j, let U_j be the open ball $\mathcal{B}_\varepsilon(\omega_j)$, with $\varepsilon > 0$ chosen sufficiently small that $x \in U_j \Rightarrow g(x) \notin U_k$ for $k \neq j$. The proof proceeds by contradiction; thus the sequence $g(x), g^2(x), g^3(x), \ldots$ lies in the complement of $\bigcup U_j$ infinitely often. By compactness, let z be a limit point in this complement. Hence $\phi(z) > \phi(g(z))$. By continuity, let V be a closed neighborhood of z such that $\phi(z) > \phi(g(V))$. Since z is the limit of a sequence of points in $\bigcup_k g^k(V)$, this leads to the contradiction $\phi(z) > \phi(z)$.   ■

The function ϕ occurring above is called a *Lyapunov function* for g on Λ. The condition on ϕ given in theorem 10.1 may just as well be taken as

$$x \neq g(x) \Longrightarrow \phi(x) < \phi(g(x))$$

since it is actually the monotone behavior of ϕ along trajectories that matters. This alternate condition on ϕ will be used throughout the rest of this book. When ϕ assigns distinct values to distinct fixed points, it will be called a *complete Lyapunov function*. Note that theorem 10.1 is valid when Λ is replaced by a closed set invariant under $\mathcal{G}$ (this is left as an exercise).

Exercises

1. Show theorem 10.1 is valid when Λ is replaced by a closed set invariant under $\mathcal{G}$.

2. Theorem 10.1 required g continuously differentiable so that a focused heuristic could be obtained. Show a much weaker hypothesis suffices to conclude that iterates of g converge.

3. A *periodic point* ω of g is a fixed point of g^k where the minimal such k is greater than 1. Show that if g has a Lyapunov function then it has no periodic points.

10.2   Selection

The first result is that the selection schemes are focused heuristics.

Theorem 10.2   Given population vector p, let j be such that $f_j = \max\{f_i : p_i \neq 0\}$. Then $\phi(x) = x_j$ is a Lyapunov function for the proportional, ranking, and tournament selection schemes beginning from initial population p (i.e., on the closure of the orbit of p). In particular, the selection schemes are focused.

Proof   First consider proportional selection. By choice of j, $f_i > f_j \Longrightarrow p_i = 0$. Hence

$$\phi(\mathcal{F}(p))$$

$$= \frac{f_j p_j}{\sum f_i p_i}$$

$$= \frac{p_j}{\sum (f_i/f_j) p_i}$$

$$\geq \frac{p_j}{\sum p_i}$$

$$= p_j$$

The inequality is strict unless the implication $p_i \neq 0 \Longrightarrow f_i = f_j$ holds. Hence equality implies $p = e_j$ since f is assumed injective. Since the standard basis vectors are the fixed points of $\mathcal{F}$, theorem 10.1 applies to show $\mathcal{F}$ is focused.

Next suppose $\mathcal{F}$ is the ranking selection scheme. By theorem 7.2,

$$\mathcal{F}(p)_i = \int_{\eta_i}^{\eta_i + p_i} \varrho(y) \, dy$$

where ψ is a permutation of $\langle 0, 1, \ldots, n-1 \rangle$ such that $i < j \Longrightarrow f(\psi_i) < f(\psi_j)$ and η is defined recursively by

$$\eta_{\psi_0} = 0$$

$$\eta_{\psi_{i+1}} = \eta_{\psi_i} + p_{\psi_i}$$

Appealing to the mean value theorem, $\mathcal{F}(p)_i = \varrho(\xi_i)p_i$ where $\eta_i < \xi_i < \eta_i + p_i$. Now choose j such that $\varrho(\xi_j) = \max\{\varrho(\xi_i) : p_i \neq 0\}$. Because ϱ is increasing, this choice is equivalent to $\eta_j = \max\{\eta_i : p_i \neq 0\}$. By the definitions of ψ and η, this is equivalent to $f_j = \max\{f_i : p_i \neq 0\}$ as before. It follows that

$$\phi(\mathcal{F}(p))$$

$$= \varrho(\xi_j)p_j$$

$$= \frac{\varrho(\xi_j)p_j}{\sum \varrho(\xi_i)p_i}$$

$$= \frac{p_j}{\sum (\varrho(\xi_i)/\varrho(\xi_j))p_i}$$

$$\geq \frac{p_j}{\sum p_i}$$

$$= p_j$$

The inequality is strict unless the implication $p_i \neq 0 \implies \varrho(\xi_i) = \varrho(\xi_j)$ holds. Because ϱ is increasing, equality implies $p = e_j$. Theorem 10.1 shows $\mathcal{F}$ is focused as before.

Finally, consider the tournament selection scheme with ϕ and j as above,

$$\mathcal{F}(p)_j = \sum_{q \in \frac{1}{k}X_n^k} \mathcal{F}'(q)_j k! \prod_i \frac{p_i^{kq_i}}{(kq_i)!}$$

Note that if $q_j = 0$, then $\mathcal{F}'(q)_j = 0$. If there exists i such that $q_i > 0$ and $p_i = 0$, then the product is zero. Hence by considering only nonzero terms, it may be assumed that $q_j > 0$ and $q_i > 0 \implies p_i > 0$. It follows from the analysis of ranking selection that $\mathcal{F}'(q)_j \geq q_j$ with equality only when $q = e_j$. Therefore

$$\phi(\mathcal{F}(p))$$

$$= \sum_{q \in \frac{1}{k}X_n^k} \mathcal{F}'(q)_j k! \prod_i \frac{p_i^{kq_i}}{(kq_i)!}$$

$$\geq \sum_{q \in \frac{1}{k}X_n^k} q_j k! \prod_i \frac{p_i^{kq_i}}{(kq_i)!}$$

The right hand side was seen in the proof of theorem 3.3 to be p_j. Thus $\phi(\mathcal{F}(p)) \geq p_j$. Equality holds only if in every nonzero term $q = e_j$, which implies $p = e_j$ since $k > 1$. Theorem 10.1 applies as before. ∎

According to theorem 10.2, the proportion of the most fit element in the population increases under the influence of selection. A consequence is that fixed points are easily classified; p_j must attain a maximal value. Hence the only possible fixed points are the standard basis vectors (that they are in fact fixed points is exercise 3 of section 5.1). By computing the differentials of the selection schemes, issues such as stability and hyperbolicity can be addressed. In the following theorem, the selection schemes are considered as maps from the simplex to the simplex.

Theorem 10.3   The spectrum of $d\mathcal{F}_{e_v}$ is

$\{f_i/f_v : 0 \leq i < n, i \neq v\}$ if selection is proportional,

$\{\varrho([f_v < f_{\psi_i}]) : 0 < i < n\}$ if selection is ranking,

$$\left\{k[f_v > f_i]\int_0^{1/k}\varrho(y)\,dy + k[f_v < f_i]\int_{1-1/k}^1 \varrho(y)\,dy : 0 \leq i < n, i \neq v\right\}$$

if selection is tournament.

Proof   The differential of the proportional selection scheme (theorem 7.1) is

$$(I - \frac{f \cdot x \mathbf{1}^T}{f^T x})\frac{\operatorname{diag}(f)}{f^T x}$$

Substituting $x = e_v$ gives

$$(\operatorname{diag}(f) - e_v f^T)/f_v$$

If $i \neq v$, a left eigenvector is e_i^T with corresponding eigenvalue f_i/f_v. Since $\mathbf{1}^T$ is a left eigenvector (with eigenvalue 0), it follows from theorem 6.12 that the differential leaves $\mathbf{1}^\perp$ invariant and the spectrum on that space is $\{f_i/f_v : 0 \leq i < n, i \neq v\}$.

The differential of the ranking selection scheme at x (theorem 7.3) has i, jth entry

$$\varrho(\eta_i + x_i)[f_j \leq f_i] - \varrho(\eta_i)[f_j < f_i]$$

Define the permutation matrix A by $A_{i,j} = \delta_{i,\psi_j}$. It follows that

$$(A^{-1}d\mathcal{F}_x A)_{i,j} = \varrho(\eta_{\psi_i} + x_{\psi_i})[j < i+1] - \varrho(\eta_{\psi_i})[j < i]$$

This triangular matrix has diagonal $\{\varrho(\eta_{\psi_i} + x_{\psi_i}) : 0 \leq i < n\}$. Note that $\eta_{\psi_i} + x_{\psi_i} = \eta_{\psi_{i+1}}$. Since $\mathbf{1}^T$ is a left eigenvector (with eigenvalue $\varrho(1)$), the differential leaves $\mathbf{1}^\perp$ invariant and the spectrum on that space is the diagonal with one copy of $\varrho(1)$ omitted. Hence the spectrum is $\{\varrho(\eta_{\psi_i}) : 0 < i < n\}$. When $x = e_v$, then $\eta_{\psi_i} = [f_v < f_{\psi_i}]$.

The differential of the tournament selection scheme at x has i, jth entry

$$k! \sum_{q \in X_n^k} \mathcal{F}'(q/k)_i \frac{q_j x_j^{q_j-1}}{q_j!} \prod_{u \neq j} \frac{x_u^{q_u}}{q_u!}$$

Note that with $x = e_v$, the second factor is zero if $j \neq v$ and $q_j \neq 1$. If $j = v$, then the third factor (the product) is zero unless $q/k = e_v$. Moreover when $j \neq v$, the third factor is zero unless $q/k = \alpha e_j + (1 - \alpha)e_v$. It follows from the remarks concerning the second factor that we may assume $\alpha = 1/k$. Thus substituting $x = e_v$ gives rise to two cases:

Case I, $j = v$. The i, jth entry of $d\mathcal{F}_{e_v}$ is

$$k!\mathcal{F}'(e_v)_i \frac{1}{(k-1)!} 1 = k(e_v)_i = k\delta_{v,i}$$

Case II, $j \neq v$. The i, jth entry of $d\mathcal{F}_{e_v}$ is

$$k!\mathcal{F}'((1/k)e_j + (1 - 1/k)e_v)_i 1 \frac{1}{(k-1)!} = k(\beta_j \delta_{j,i} + \gamma_j \delta_{v,i})$$

where $\mathcal{F}'((1/k)e_j + (1 - 1/k)e_v) = \beta_j e_j + \gamma_j e_v$. Combining these two cases yields

$$(d\mathcal{F}_{e_v})_{i,j} = k(\delta_{j,v}\delta_{v,i} + (1 - \delta_{j,v})(\beta_j \delta_{j,i} + \gamma_j \delta_{v,i}))$$

If $i \neq v$, a left eigenvector is e_i^T with corresponding eigenvalue $k\beta_i$. Since $\mathbf{1}^T$ is a left eigenvector with eigenvalue k, it follows that the differential leaves $\mathbf{1}^\perp$ invariant and the spectrum on that space is $\{k\beta_i : 0 \leq i < n, i \neq v\}$.   ∎

Theorem 10.4   The unique stable fixed point of proportional, ranking, and tournament selection is e_v where $f_v = \max\{f_j : 0 \leq j < n\}$. Moreover, all fixed points are hyperbolic.

Proof   For proportional selection, the ratios f_i/f_v of theorem 10.3 are less than 1. In the case of ranking selection, the spectrum is $\varrho(0)$. But

$$\varrho(0) < \int_0^1 \varrho(y)\,dy = 1$$

since ϱ is continuous and increasing. For tournament selection, the spectrum is

$$k \int_0^{1/k} \varrho(y)\,dy < \int_0^1 \varrho(y)\,dy$$

Thus e_v is stable as claimed. Consider next a fixed point e_j, $j \neq v$. For proportional selection, no ratio f_i/f_j is 1 (since f is injective), but some ratio is greater than 1 since f_j is not maximal. In the case of ranking selection, the spectrum may consist of $\varrho(0)$ or $\varrho(1)$. The latter possibility occurs because f_j is not maximal. Moreover,

$$\varrho(1) > \int_0^1 \varrho(y)\,dy$$

For tournament selection, the spectrum may consist of $k\int_0^{1/k} \varrho(y)\,dy$ or $k\int_{1-1/k}^1 \varrho(y)\,dy$. The latter possibility occurs because f_j is not maximal. Moreover,

$$k\int_{1-1/k}^1 \varrho(y)\,dy > \int_0^1 \varrho(y)\,dy \qquad\qquad \blacksquare$$

The next theorem notes a property common to all selection schemes.

Theorem 10.5 If $x \in e_j^\perp$ then $d\mathcal{F}_x : e_j^\perp \longrightarrow e_j^\perp$

Proof Arbitrary selection satisfies $p_j = 0 \Rightarrow \mathcal{F}(p)_j = 0$. Hence if $x, \delta \in e_j^\perp$ then both $\mathcal{F}(x)$ and $\mathcal{F}(x + \delta)$ are in $e_j^\perp$. Since $\mathcal{F}(x + \delta) = \mathcal{F}(x) + d\mathcal{F}_x\delta + o(\delta)$ it follows that

$$0 = e_j^T d\mathcal{F}_x\delta + e_j^T o(\delta)$$

Rearranging and dividing through by $\|\delta\|$ gives

$$e_j^T d\mathcal{F}_x \frac{\delta}{\|\delta\|} = -e_j^T \frac{o(\delta)}{\|\delta\|}$$

Letting $\delta \to 0$ finishes the proof. $\qquad\qquad\qquad\qquad\qquad\qquad\qquad\qquad \blacksquare$

Exercises

1. A fixed point is *cyclic* if its unstable manifold intersects its basin of attraction. The discussion in section 8.1 concerning stable/unstable fixed points applies to $\mathcal{F}$ (representing proportional, ranking, or tournament selection) since $\mathcal{F}$ is continuously differentiable and has hyperbolic fixed points (theorem 10.4). Use the Lyapunov function of theorem 10.2 to show that no fixed point of $\mathcal{F}$ is cyclic.

2. Show theorem 10.5 implies that if $i \neq v$ then $(d\mathcal{F}_{e_v}x)_i = x_i(d\mathcal{F}_{e_v})_{i,i}$. Use this fact together with the proof of theorem 10.3 (which gives explicitly the differentials at e_v for the proportional, ranking, and tournament selection schemes) to conclude that there exists constants $0 < \alpha < 1$ and $1 < \beta$ depending on f such that for all v

$$(d\mathcal{F}_{e_v}x)_i \begin{cases} > \beta x_i & \text{if } f_i > f_v \\ < \alpha x_i & \text{if } f_i < f_v \end{cases}$$

3. Show the results of this section carry over to the general cardinality case.

10.3 Mixing

The mixing equations provided by Theorem 6.17 are triangular. This allows the fixed points of $\mathcal{M}$ to be explicitly determined. In fact, the triangular form can be used to determine when

$$\lim_{j \to \infty} \mathcal{M}^j(x)$$

exists. An important preliminary result is

Lemma 10.6   If $z > 0$ then $|\hat{M}_{z,0}| \le 1/2$. When equality holds and $z = x \oplus y$ for nonzero x and y, then $\hat{M}_{x,y} = 0$.

Proof   Assume equality holds and $z = x \oplus y > 0$ for nonzero x and y. By theorem 6.5,

$$\hat{M}_{u,v} = \frac{n}{2} \delta_{u \otimes v, 0} \, \hat{\mu}_u \, \hat{\mu}_v \sum_{k \in \Omega_{\overline{u \otimes v}}} \chi_{k \oplus u} + \chi_{k \oplus v}$$

Since $|n \, \delta_{u \otimes v, 0} \, \hat{\mu}_u \, \hat{\mu}_v| \le 1$, it follows that if $|\hat{M}_{0, x \oplus y}| = 1/2$ then

$$1 \le \sum_{k \in \Omega_{\overline{x \oplus y}}} \chi_k + \chi_{k \oplus x \oplus y}$$

Since k and $k \oplus x \oplus y$ range over disjoint sets, and since the components of χ sum to 1, this lower bound can hold only if the nonzero components of χ are indexed by $\Omega_{\overline{x \oplus y}} \cup \{k \oplus x \oplus y : k \in \Omega_{\overline{x \oplus y}}\}$. (That k and $k \oplus x \oplus y$ range over disjoint sets holds provided $x \oplus y > 0$. In particular, the sum can be at most 1, and hence $|\hat{M}_{0,z}| \le 1/2$). Moreover, the conclusion $\hat{M}_{x,y} = 0$ is trivially satisfied unless $x \otimes y = 0$, and in that case $\Omega_{\overline{x \otimes y}} = \Omega_{\overline{x \oplus y}}$. Thus the proof would be complete if

$$0 = \sum_{k \in \Omega_{\overline{x \oplus y}}} \chi_{k \oplus x} + \chi_{k \oplus y}$$

when $x \otimes y = 0$. Note that each of $k \oplus x$, $k \oplus y$, k, and $k \oplus x \oplus y$ range over disjoint sets for $k \in \Omega_{\overline{x \oplus y}}$. In particular, the subscripts $k \oplus x$ and $k \oplus y$ in the sum above are disjoint from $\Omega_{\overline{x \oplus y}} \cup \{k \oplus x \oplus y : k \in \Omega_{\overline{x \oplus y}}\}$ and therefore index zero components of χ. ∎

That the mixing equation $y = \mathcal{M}(x)$ provided by Theorem 6.17 is triangular was first noticed by Alden Wright. The component equations have the form

$$\hat{y}_k = \begin{cases} \hat{x}_k & \text{if } k = 0 \\ 2\hat{M}_{0,k}\hat{x}_k + \sqrt{n}\sum_{i \in \Omega'_k} \hat{x}_i\hat{x}_{i \oplus k}\hat{M}_{i,i \oplus k} & \text{if } k > 0 \end{cases}$$

where Ω'_k denotes $\Omega_k \setminus \{0, k\}$. This can be put in the abbreviated form

$$\hat{y}_k = \begin{cases} \hat{x}_k & \text{if } k = 0 \\ \alpha_k\hat{x}_k + \beta_k & \text{if } k > 0 \end{cases}$$

It is easy to determine whether $\mathcal{M}$ is focused by considering kth components in order of increasing $\mathbf{1}^T k$. But first note when $\mathbf{1}^T k = 1$ the sum β_k is empty, hence zero. Also, lemma 10.6 implies that $|\alpha_k| \leq 1$ and that $|\alpha_k| = 1 \implies \beta_k = 0$ provided $\mathbf{1}^T k > 1$ (because of the factors $\hat{M}_{i,i \oplus k}$ in the terms of β_k).

Clearly the 0th component of $\lim_j \mathcal{M}^{(j)}(x)$ has already converged since $\hat{y}_0 = \hat{x}_0$. Next, for $\mathbf{1}^T k = 1$, if $\alpha_k = 1$ then $\hat{y}_k = \hat{x}_k$ so the kth component has converged. If $\alpha_k = -1$ then the kth component is periodic, oscillating between $\pm\hat{x}_k$. When $|\alpha_k| < 1$, the kth component converges to 0 because the relation between successive iterations is $\hat{y}_k = \alpha_k\hat{x}_k$.

In the general case of $\mathbf{1}^T k > 1$, the sum β_k may be treated as having already converged because it involves components subscripted by j with $\mathbf{1}^T j < \mathbf{1}^T k$. If for some values of j components are periodic, replacing $\mathcal{M}$ by $\mathcal{M}^2$ restores convergence since oscillations have period 2. If $\alpha_k = 1$ then $\hat{y}_k = \hat{x}_k$ (since $\beta_k = 0$) so the kth component has already converged. If $\alpha_k = -1$ then $\hat{y}_k = -\hat{x}_k$ and the kth component oscillates for $\mathcal{M}$, but has already converged for $\mathcal{M}^2$. When $|\alpha_k| < 1$, the kth component converges to $\beta_k/(1 - \alpha_k)$ since the relation between successive iterations is $\hat{y}_k = \alpha_k\hat{x}_k + \beta_k$.

This discussion is summarized by the following theorem.

Theorem 10.7   The polynomial function $x \mapsto y$ defined recursively by

$$\hat{y}_k = \begin{cases} \hat{x}_k & \text{if } k = 0 \text{ or } |\hat{M}_{0,k}| = 1/2 \\ \sqrt{n}(1 - 2\hat{M}_{k,0})^{-1}\sum_{i \in \Omega'_k} \hat{y}_i\hat{y}_{i \oplus k}\hat{M}_{i,i \oplus k} & \text{otherwise} \end{cases}$$

produces the fixed point $y = \lim_j \mathcal{M}^{2j}(x)$ of $\mathcal{M}^2$. If no $\hat{M}_{k,0}$ equals $-1/2$, then y is also the fixed point $\lim_j \mathcal{M}^j(x)$ of $\mathcal{M}$. Otherwise, $\mathcal{M}^j(x)$ converges to a periodic orbit which oscillates between y and $\mathcal{M}(y)$.

The following theorem summarizes some of the more obvious consequences of theorem 10.7 and the theory preceding it.

Theorem 10.8   The fixed points of $\mathcal{M}^2$ form a surface of dimension equal to the multiplicity that 1/2 has as an eigenvalue of M^*, and is parametrized by those $\hat{x}_j$ for which $|\hat{M}_{0,j}| = 1/2$. When this surface is zero dimensional, $\mathcal{M}$ is a contraction mapping on Λ with unique hyperbolic attractor $\mathbf{1}/n$. Otherwise, the fixed point $\mathbf{1}/n$ is neither an attractor nor is it hyperbolic. In the special case of positive mutation, $\mathbf{1}/n$ is an attractor. In the special case of zero mutation, periodic orbits are not possible.

Proof   A direct calculation verifies $\mathcal{M}(\mathbf{1}/n) = \mathbf{1}/n$. Appealing to theorems 6.13 and 6.7, $|\hat{M}_{0,j}| = 1/2$ for some $j > 0$ if and only if $\mathbf{1}/n$ is not an attractor (Lemma 10.6 implies $|\hat{M}_{j,0}| \leq 1/2$, but if $\mathbf{1}/n$ is not an attractor then $\text{spec}(d\mathcal{M}_{\mathbf{1}/n}) \not\subset \mathcal{B}_1(0)$. Conversely, if $|\hat{M}_{j,0}| = 1/2$ for some $j > 0$, theorem 10.7 shows there are fixed points arbitrarily near $\mathbf{1}/n$; they are produced by varying the jth Walsh coordinate of $x = \mathbf{1}/n$). In this case the fixed point $\mathbf{1}/n$ is not hyperbolic and $\text{spec}(d\mathcal{M}_{\mathbf{1}/n})$ contains 1 with multiplicity equal to the multiplicity that 1/2 has as an eigenvalue of M^*. Moreover, theorem 10.7 shows the fixed points of $\mathcal{M}^2$ form a surface of dimension equal to this multiplicity, parametrized by those $\hat{x}_j$ for which $|\hat{M}_{j,0}| = 1/2$.

When $\mathbf{1}$ is an attractor, $\mathcal{M}$ is focused and has unique fixed point. Appealing to theorems 6.13 and 6.7, the fixed point is hyperbolic, since $\text{spec}(d\mathcal{M}_{\mathbf{1}}) \subset \mathcal{B}_1(0)$. Uniqueness follows from the fact that if $x \in \Lambda$ then $\hat{x}_0 = n^{-1/2}$ (exercise 3 of section 6.1). Hence the function $x \mapsto y$ of theorem 10.7 is independent of x if $j > 0 \implies |\hat{M}_{j,0}| < 1/2$. This holds when mutation is positive, and $\mathcal{M}$ is a contraction mapping when $\mathbf{1}$ is an attractor in any case (since $\text{spec}(d\mathcal{M}_{\mathbf{1}}) \subset \mathcal{B}_1(0)$, the argument outlined in the exercises of section 6.3 applies).

In the special case of zero mutation, -1/2 cannot be an eigenvalue of M^* since $\hat{M}_{k,0} \geq 0$ (it is a sum of nonnegative terms by theorem 6.7). Therefore convergence to a periodic orbit is not possible with zero mutation.   ∎

The following theorem specializes theorem 10.7 to the zero mutation case and considers a situation where the recursion in theorem 10.7 simplifies.

Theorem 10.9   Given zero mutation, $y = \lim_j \mathcal{M}^j(x)$, and $\mathbf{1}^T k > 1 \implies \hat{M}_{k,0} < 1/2$, it follows that

$$\hat{y}_k = 2^{(\mathbf{1}^T k - 1)\ell/2} \prod_{2^u \in \Omega_k} \hat{x}_{2^u}$$

Proof   Induct on $\mathbf{1}^T k$. The base case ($k = 0$) follows from the fact that $y \in \Lambda$ implies $\hat{y}_0 = n^{-1/2}$ (exercise 3 of section 6.1).

For the inductive case, let $i \in \Omega'_k$. Since $\mathbf{1}^T i < \mathbf{1}^T k$ and $\mathbf{1}^T (i \oplus k) < \mathbf{1}^T k$, the induction hypothesis gives

$$\hat{y}_i \hat{y}_{i\oplus k}$$

$$= \left(2^{(\mathbf{1}^T i - 1)\ell/2} \prod_{2^u \in \Omega_i} \hat{x}_{2^u}\right)\left(2^{(\mathbf{1}^T(i\oplus k) - 1)\ell/2} \prod_{2^v \in \Omega_{i\oplus k}} \hat{x}_{2^v}\right)$$

$$= 2^{\mathbf{1}^T(i + i\oplus k)\ell/2 - \ell} \prod_{2^u \in \Omega_k} \hat{x}_{2^u}$$

$$= 2^{(\mathbf{1}^T k - 2)\ell/2} \prod_{2^u \in \Omega_k} \hat{x}_{2^u}$$

Using $M = \hat{M}$ and theorem 10.7 yields

$$\hat{y}_k = \sqrt{n}(1 - 2M_{k,0})^{-1} \sum_{i \in \Omega_k'} 2^{(\mathbf{1}^T k - 2)\ell/2} M_{i,i\oplus k} \prod_{2^u \in \Omega_k} \hat{x}_{2^u}$$

Simplifying by $(1 - 2M_{k,0})^{-1} \sum_{i \in \Omega_k'} M_{i,i\oplus k} = 1$, which follows from exercise 7 of section 4.5 since

$$\sum_{i \in \Omega_k} M_{i,i\oplus k} = 2M_{k,0} + \sum_{i \in \Omega_k'} M_{i,i\oplus k}$$

completes the proof.   ∎

The following lemma, whose proof is an exercise, follows easily from theorem 10.9.

Lemma 10.10   Given zero mutation, $y = \lim_j \mathcal{M}^j(x)$ and $\mathbf{1}^T k > 1 \implies \hat{M}_{k,0} < 1/2$, it follows that $u \otimes v = 0 \implies \hat{y}_{u\oplus v} = \hat{y}_u \hat{y}_v \sqrt{n}$.

Bit positions u and v are said to be *linked* if for all k

$$\chi_k > 0 \implies [2^u \otimes k = 0] = [2^v \otimes k = 0]$$

Crossover is said to be *separating* if bit positions u and v are linked only when $u = v$.

Theorem 10.11   Bit positions u and v are linked if and only if

$$\left(M\bigg|_{\mu=e_0}\right)_{0,2^u \oplus 2^v} = (1 + \delta_{u,v})/2$$

Proof   The case $u = v$ is trivial. In the other case,

$$\left(M\Big|_{\mu=e_0}\right)_{0,2^u\oplus 2^v}$$

$$=\sum_k \chi_k([k\otimes(2^u\oplus 2^v)=0]+[\bar{k}\otimes(2^u\oplus 2^v)=0])/2$$

$$=\frac{1}{2}\sum_k \chi_k([k\otimes(2^u\oplus 2^v)=0\vee \bar{k}\otimes(2^u\oplus 2^v)=0]$$

which is $1/2$ if and only if $\chi_k > 0 \Longrightarrow k\otimes 2^u = k\otimes 2^v = 0 \vee \bar{k}\otimes 2^u = \bar{k}\otimes 2^v = 0$, which is equivalent to bit positions u and v being linked.   ∎

Lemma 10.12   If mutation is zero, then $\mathbf{1}^T k > 1 \Longrightarrow \hat{M}_{k,0} < 1/2$, provided crossover is separating.

Proof   Given $\mathbf{1}^T k > 1$, let 2^u and 2^v be distinct elements of Ω_k. By theorem 6.6, $\hat{M}_{0,k}$ is

$$\sum_i \frac{\chi_i+\chi_{\bar{i}}}{2}[i\otimes k=0]\le \sum_i \frac{\chi_i+\chi_{\bar{i}}}{2}[i\otimes(2^u\oplus 2^v)=0]$$

The right hand side is $M_{0,2^u\oplus 2^v} < 1/2$ (the latter inequality follows from lemma 10.6 and theorem 10.11).   ∎

Fix population $x\in\Lambda$ and define

$$p_i(j)=\sum_k [k\otimes 2^i = j\otimes 2^i]x_k$$

as the proportion of x having i^{th} bit in agreement with j. The following is an easy exercise.

Lemma 10.13   If $u\otimes 2^i = v\otimes 2^i$ then $p_i(u)=p_i(v)$. Moreover,

$$\sqrt{n}\,\hat{x}_{2^i}=2p_i(0)-1=1-2p_i(\mathbf{1})$$

The final result is Geiringer's theorem (though by a different method; the account given here was obtained jointly with Alden Wright).

Theorem 10.14   Let mutation be zero, let $x\in\Lambda$ and let $y=\lim_j \mathcal{M}^j(x)$. If crossover is separating, then

$$y_j=\prod_{i=0}^{\ell-1} p_i(j)$$

Proof   Beginning with the Walsh transform, and using lemmas 10.10 and 10.12

$$\sqrt{n}\, y_k$$

$$= \sum_i (-1)^{k^T i} \hat{y}_i$$

$$= \sum_{u_0 \in \Omega_{2^0}} \cdots \sum_{u_{\ell-1} \in \Omega_{2^{\ell-1}}} (-1)^{k^T (u_0 \oplus \cdots \oplus u_{\ell-1})} \hat{y}_{u_0 \oplus \cdots \oplus u_{\ell-1}}$$

$$= \sum_{u_0 \in \Omega_{2^0}} \cdots \sum_{u_{\ell-1} \in \Omega_{2^{\ell-1}}} (-1)^{k^T u_0} \cdots (-1)^{k^T u_{\ell-1}} \hat{y}_{u_0} \cdots \hat{y}_{u_{\ell-1}} \sqrt{n}^{\ell-1}$$

Therefore

$$n\, y_k = \prod_{j=0}^{\ell-1} \sum_{u_j \in \Omega_{2^j}} \sqrt{n} (-1)^{k^T u_j} \hat{y}_{u_j}$$

If $k \otimes 2^j = 0$, then, by theorem 10.9 and lemma 10.13,

$$\sum_{u_j \in \Omega_{2^j}} (-1)^{k^T u_j} \hat{y}_{u_j}$$

$$= \hat{y}_0 + \hat{y}_{2^j}$$

$$= 2^{-\ell/2} + \hat{x}_{2^j}$$

$$= 2 p_j(k) / \sqrt{n}$$

Similarly, when $k \otimes 2^j = 1$,

$$\sum_{u_j \in \Omega_{2^j}} (-1)^{k^T u_j} \hat{y}_{u_j} = 2 p_j(k) / \sqrt{n}$$

Therefore,

$$y_k = \prod_{j=0}^{\ell-1} p_j(k) \qquad \blacksquare$$

Exercises

1. Give specific examples of periodic orbits under $\mathcal{M}$.

2. Since $\mathcal{M}$ may have periodic fixed points, conclude that it cannot, in general, have a Lyapunov function.

3. In the case where **1** is not hyperbolic, graph all possible fixed point surfaces corresponding to $\ell = 2$.

4. Prove lemma 10.10.

5. Prove lemma 10.13.

6. How should theorem 10.7 and theorem 10.8 be modified for the general cardinality case? *Hint:* Show lemma 10.6 carries over to the general cardinality case provided $x \oplus y$ is replaced by $x \ominus y$, then apply the technique illustrated in this section using the formula given in exercise 8 of section 6.4.

7. Continuing the previous exercise, explicitly compute both cyclic and asymptotically cyclic orbits (of the form $x, \mathcal{M}(x), \mathcal{M}^2(x), \ldots$) in the general cardinality case. *Hint:* Consider choosing k such that $\#k > 1$, choosing χ such that $j \otimes k \neq 0 \Longrightarrow \chi_j = 0$, choosing i such that $i^T k$ is nonzero modulo c, and choosing μ such that $\mu_j > 0 \Longrightarrow j^T k = i^T k$.

8. What is the analogue of theorem 10.9 in the general cardinality case? *Hint:* $\Omega = Z_c^\ell$. Replace 2 with c, $\mathbf{1}^T k$ with $\#k$, and Ω_k with $\{i \epsilon \Omega_k : \#i = 1 \wedge i^T(k \ominus i) = 0\}$.

9. Extend the concepts of *linked positions* and *separating crossover* to the general cardinality case. Extend theorem 10.14 to the general cardinality case. *Hint:* $\Omega = Z_c^\ell$. Define $p_i(j)$ by

$$p_i(j) = \sum_k [k \otimes c^i = j \otimes c^i] x_k$$

10.4   Summary

A focused heuristic having only hyperbolic fixed points is called *hyperbolic*. An instance of random heuristic search is called hyperbolic if its heuristic is. The previous sections characterize when $\mathcal{F}$ and $\mathcal{M}$ are hyperbolic. In particular, $\mathcal{G}$ may be hyperbolic when mixing is cloning (then $\mathcal{G} = \mathcal{F}$), or when mutation is positive and selection is uniform (then $\mathcal{G} = \mathcal{M}$). While these are degenerate cases, a later chapter on perturbation arguments will show every "nearby" case corresponds to a hyperbolic heuristic.

A class of fitness functions for which average population fitness is a Lyapunov function for $\mathcal{G}$ (provided mutation is zero) is discussed in the next chapter. In the generic case, $\mathcal{G}$ is hyperbolic if fitness is in this class and mutation is zero. Thus the perturbation theory is applicable to the results of the next chapter as well.

11 Linear Fitness

This chapter shows average population fitness is a Lyapunov function for $\mathcal{G}$ when mutation is zero and the fitness function is of a special kind (linear fitness).

The first section considers how mixing relates to fitness when the fitness function is linear and mutation is zero. The second section develops some general properties of selection which are useful in establishing average population fitness is a complete Lyapunov function. This, and the final section which considers hyperbolicity issues, is important to applying the perturbation theory presented the next chapter.

11.1 Crossover

A fitness function is called *linear* if it has the form $f(i) = a^T i + b$ for some $a \in \mathfrak{R}^\ell$, $b \in \mathfrak{R}$. In the special case of linear fitness and zero mutation, $\phi(x) = f^T x$ is a Lyapunov function for $\mathcal{G}$. The first step in demonstrating this is to establish $\phi(x) = \phi(\mathcal{M}(x))$. The following lemmas prepare the way.

Lemma 11.1   If mutation is zero, then

$$\sum_i (-1)^{i^T 2^j} M_{u \oplus i, v \oplus i} = (-1)^{u^T 2^j} [u \otimes 2^j = v \otimes 2^j]$$

Proof   Replacing the dummy summation variable i by $i \oplus u$, and using the fact that the summation is symmetric in u and v shows the left hand side is

$$(-1)^{u^T 2^j} \sum_i (-1)^{i^T 2^j} M_{i, u \oplus v \oplus i} = (-1)^{v^T 2^j} \sum_i (-1)^{i^T 2^j} M_{i, u \oplus v \oplus i}$$

Since this equation cannot hold when $u^T 2^j \neq v^T 2^j$ unless both sides are zero, it follows that the sum is

$$(-1)^{u^T 2^j} [u \otimes 2^j = v \otimes 2^j] \sum_i (-1)^{i^T 2^j} M_{i, u \oplus v \oplus i}$$

$$= (-1)^{u^T 2^j} [u \otimes 2^j = v \otimes 2^j] \sum_i (-1)^{i^T 2^j} \sum_k \frac{\chi_k + \chi_{\bar{k}}}{2} [0 = i \otimes k \oplus \bar{k} \otimes (u \oplus v \oplus i)]$$

$$= (-1)^{u^T 2^j} [u \otimes 2^j = v \otimes 2^j] \sum_k \frac{\chi_k + \chi_{\bar{k}}}{2} \sum_i (-1)^{i^T 2^j} [i = \bar{k} \otimes (u \oplus v)]$$

$$= (-1)^{u^T 2^j} \sum_k \frac{\chi_k + \chi_{\bar{k}}}{2} ([u \otimes 2^j = v \otimes 2^j](-1)^{\overline{(\bar{k} \otimes (u \oplus v))}^T 2^j})$$

$$= (-1)^{u^T 2^j} [u \otimes 2^j = v \otimes 2^j] \sum_k \frac{\chi_k + \chi_{\overline{k}}}{2} \qquad \blacksquare$$

Lemma 11.2 If mutation is zero and fitness is linear, then

$$\sum_i f_i M_{u \oplus i, v \oplus i} = \frac{f_u + f_v}{2}$$

Proof   First note that

$$a^T i = \frac{1}{2} \sum a_j (1 - (-1)^{i \otimes 2^j})$$

(for $a \in \Re^\ell$ and $i \in \Omega$), and

$$\sum_i 2M_{u \oplus i, v \oplus i} - \delta_{u,i} - \delta_{v,i} = 0$$

Making use of these identities and lemma 11.1,

$$\sum_i (b + a^T i)(2M_{u \oplus i, v \oplus i} - \delta_{u,i} - \delta_{v,i})$$

$$= \sum_i \frac{1}{2} \sum_j a_j (1 - (-1)^{i^T 2^j})(2M_{u \oplus i, v \oplus i} - \delta_{u,i} - \delta_{v,i})$$

$$= -\frac{1}{2} \sum_i \sum_j a_j (-1)^{i^T 2^j} (2M_{u \oplus i, v \oplus i} - \delta_{u,i} - \delta_{v,i})$$

$$= -\frac{1}{2} \sum_j a_j \sum_i (-1)^{i^T 2^j} (2M_{u \oplus i, v \oplus i} - \delta_{u,i} - \delta_{v,i})$$

$$= -\frac{1}{2} \sum_j a_j (2(-1)^{u^T 2^j} [u \otimes 2^j = v \otimes 2^j] - (-1)^{u^T 2^j} - (-1)^{v^T 2^j})$$

$$= 0$$

Therefore

$$2 \sum_i f_i M_{u \oplus i, v \oplus i} = \sum_i f_i (\delta_{u,i} + \delta_{v,i}) \qquad \blacksquare$$

Theorem 11.3   If fitness is linear and mutation is zero, then $\phi(\mathcal{M}(x)) = \phi(x)$.

Proof   Using lemma 11.2,

$$\phi(\mathcal{M}(x))$$

$$= \sum_i f_i \sum_{u,v} x_u x_v M_{u \oplus i, v \oplus i}$$

$$= \sum_{u,v} x_u x_v \sum_i f_i M_{u \oplus i, v \oplus i}$$

$$= \frac{1}{2} \sum_{u,v} x_u x_v (f_u + f_v)$$

$$= \frac{1}{2} \sum_u x_u f_u + \frac{1}{2} \sum_v x_v f_v \qquad\qquad \blacksquare$$

Note that $\phi(x)$ is *average population fitness*,

$$f^T x = \sum (\text{fitness of } i)\,(\text{proportion of } i \text{ in population } x)$$

The message of theorem 11.3 is that average population fitness is an invariant of crossover, provided the fitness function is linear.

Exercises

1. If average population fitness is an invariant of mixing, does that force mutation to be zero?

2. If average population fitness is an invariant of crossover, does that force the fitness function to be linear?

3. Show lemma 11.2 carries over to the general cardinality case when $M_{u \oplus i, v \oplus i}$ is replaced by $M_{u \ominus i, v \ominus i}$. *Hint:* The proof given in this section relies on symmetries of the transform peculiar to the binary case. Therefore, a direct approach that avoids the transform is recommended.

4. Show theorem 11.3 carries over to the general cardinality case.

11.2 Monotone Selection

The next step is to show ϕ is a Lyapunov function for $\mathcal{F}$. Because the proof relies on a general property of selection which is independent of the fitness function, the material presented here may seem out of place. However, it is a step in showing ϕ is a Lyapunov function for $\mathcal{G}$, and that result does rely on linear fitness.

Theorem 11.4   For proportional, ranking, or tournament selection,

$$\sum_{j<i} \mathcal{F}(x)_{\psi_j} \leq \eta_{\psi_i}$$

where ψ and η are as in section 7.1. Moreover, the inequality is strict unless $\eta_{\psi_i} \in \{0, 1\}$.

Proof   First consider proportional selection. If $f_{\psi_j} \leq f^T x$ for all $j < i$, then

$$\sum_{j<i} \mathcal{F}(x)_{\psi_j}$$

$$= \sum_{j<i} \frac{f_{\psi_j}}{f^T x} x_{\psi_j}$$

$$\leq \sum_{j<i} x_{\psi_j}$$

as desired (see section 7.1, exercise 4). Moreover, if $0 < \eta_{\psi_i} < 1$ then $x_{\psi_j} f_{\psi_j}/f^T x < x_{\psi_j}$ for the first (with respect to j) nonzero term; hence the inequality is strict. Assuming the theorem false therefore entails $f_{\psi_i} > f^T x$ so that

$$\mathbf{1}^T \mathcal{F}(x)$$

$$> \eta_{\psi_i} + \sum_{j \geq i} \frac{f_{\psi_j}}{f^T x} x_{\psi_j}$$

$$\geq \eta_{\psi_i} + \sum_{j \geq i} x_{\psi_j}$$

$$= 1$$

which is a contradiction. Next consider ranking selection. If, for $0 < t < 1$,

$$\int_0^t \varrho(y)\, dy < t$$

then for $0 < \eta_i < 1$,

$$\sum_{j<i} \mathcal{F}(x)_{\psi_j}$$

$$= \int_0^{\eta_{\psi_i}} \varrho(y)\, dy$$

$$< \eta_{\psi_i}$$

as desired. But if $t \in (0, 1)$ were such that

$$\int_0^t \varrho(y)\, dy \geq t$$

then by the mean value theorem, and the fact that ϱ is increasing, $\varrho(t) \geq 1$. Consequently

$$\int_0^1 \varrho(y)\, dy$$

$$> t + \int_t^1 dy$$

$$= 1$$

which is a contradiction. Finally consider tournament selection. By what has already been shown,

$$\sum_{j<i} \mathcal{F}(x)_{\psi_j}$$

$$= k! \sum_{q \in X_n^k} \sum_{j<i} \mathcal{F}'(q/k)_{\psi_j} \prod_h \frac{x_h^{q_h}}{q_h!}$$

$$\leq k! \sum_{q \in X_n^k} \sum_{j<i} (q/k)_{\psi_j} \prod_h \frac{x_h^{q_h}}{q_h!}$$

$$= \sum_{j<i} \left(k! \sum_{q \in X_n^k} \frac{q}{k} \prod_h \frac{x_h^{q_h}}{q_h!} \right)_{\psi_j}$$

$$= \sum_{j<i} x_{\psi_j}$$

where the last equality was established in the proof of theorem 3.3. Moreover, if $0 < \eta_i < 1$ then there exist $u < i \leq v$ for which $0 < x_{\psi_u}$ and $0 < x_{\psi_v}$. It follows that the inequality involving the term $q = e_{\psi_u} + (k-1)e_{\psi_v}$ is sharp. ∎

Any selection scheme satisfying theorem 11.4 is called *monotone* .

Theorem 11.5 Average population fitness is a complete Lyapunov function for any monotone selection scheme. This applies in particular to proportional, ranking, and tournament selection.

Proof Let

$$u_i = \sum_{j<i} \mathcal{F}_{\psi_j} - x_{\psi_j}$$

and note that $u_0 = u_n = 0$ and $u_i \leq 0$ (theorem 11.4). For $x \in \Lambda$ not a vertex, it suffices to prove the positivity of

$$\sum f_{\psi_i}(\mathcal{F}_{\psi_i} - x_{\psi_i})$$

$$= \sum f_{\psi_i}(u_{i+1} - u_i)$$

$$= \sum_{i=0}^{n-1} f_{\psi_i} u_{i+1} - \sum_{i=0}^{n-1} f_{\psi_i} u_i$$

$$= \sum_{i=0}^{n-2} f_{\psi_i} u_{i+1} - \sum_{i=0}^{n-2} f_{\psi_{i+1}} u_{i+1}$$

$$= \sum_{i=0}^{n-2} (f_{\psi_i} - f_{\psi_{i+1}}) u_{i+1}$$

$$\geq 0$$

The last inequality follows from $u_i \leq 0$ and the definition of ψ. Moreover, if x is not a vertex, then some u_i is nonzero. This argument is valid for any selection scheme satisfying theorem 11.4. Since fitness is injective, ϕ maps distinct fixed points to distinct values. ∎

Theorem 11.6 If fitness is linear and mutation is zero, then $\mathcal{G}$ is focused, the only fixed points are vertices of Λ, and average population fitness increases from one generation to the expected next (except at a fixed point).

Proof By theorem 11.3 and theorem 11.5,

$$\phi(\mathcal{G}(x))$$

$$= \phi(\mathcal{F}(x))$$

$$\geq \phi(x)$$

with equality only at vertices of Λ. ∎

Theorem 11.6 has interesting consequences for the SGA. Using theorems 3.3 and 3.4, the expected average fitness of the next generation is given by

$$r! \sum_{q \in X_n^r} f^T q/r \prod_i \frac{\mathcal{G}(x)_i^{q_i}}{q_i!}$$

$$= f^T (r! \sum_{q \in X_n^r} q/r \prod_i \frac{\mathcal{G}(x)_i^{q_i}}{q_i!})$$

$$= f^T \mathcal{G}(x)$$

which is the average fitness of the expected next generation. This observation establishes the following.

Theorem 11.7 The expected average population fitness increases from one generation to the next (except at a fixed point), independent of population size, provided fitness is linear and mutation is zero.

Exercises

1. Do theorems 11.6 and 11.7 require proportional, ranking, or tournament selection, or do they hold for any monotone selection scheme?

2. If theorem 10.2 holds for a selection scheme, then must it be monotone?

3. Show the results of this section carry over to the general cardinality case.

11.3 Hyperbolicity

Throughout this section, fitness is assumed to be linear and mutation is zero.

In order to apply the perturbation theory developed in the next chapter, $\mathcal{G}$ must be hyperbolic. While in general $\mathcal{G}$ is not hyperbolic, it is *generically,* meaning that there is a dense open set of parameters for which it is. The first step towards establishing this is to characterize the spectrum of the differential at fixed points. The following theorem does not require a linear fitness function.

Theorem 11.8   Assuming zero mutation, and regarding $\mathcal{G}$ as a function on Λ,

$$\mathrm{spec}(d\mathcal{G}_{e_v}) = \{2M_{0,i}(d\mathcal{F}_{e_v})_{i\oplus v, i\oplus v} : 0 < i < n\}$$

where, for $i > 0$, $(d\mathcal{F}_{e_v})_{i\oplus v, i\oplus v}$ is

$f_{i\oplus v}/f_v$,   for proportional selection

$\varrho([f_v \le f_{i\oplus v}])$,   for ranking selection

$k[f_v > f_{i\oplus v}] \displaystyle\int_0^{1/k} \varrho(y)\, dy + k[f_v < f_{i\oplus v}] \int_{1-1/k}^1 \varrho(y)\, dy$,   for tournament selection

Proof   By the chain rule, $d\mathcal{G}_{e_v}$ is given by

$$d\mathcal{M}_{\mathcal{F}(e_v)}d\mathcal{F}_{e_v}$$

$$= 2\sum_u \sigma_u M^* \sigma_u(e_v)_u d\mathcal{F}_{e_v}$$

$$= 2\sigma_v M^* \sigma_v d\mathcal{F}_{e_v}$$

Hence the spectrum is $2\,\mathrm{spec}(M^*\sigma_v d\mathcal{F}_{e_v}\sigma_v)$. The matrix M^* is upper triangular (section 6.2), with i, i th entry $M_{0,i}$. The matrix $\sigma_v d\mathcal{F}_{e_v}\sigma_v$ is also upper triangular, as will now be shown. In the case of proportional selection, theorem 7.1 shows $(d\mathcal{F}_{e_v})_{i\oplus v, j\oplus v}$ is

$$\left(\frac{f_v \mathrm{diag}(f) - f_v e_v f^T}{f_v^2}\right)_{i\oplus v, j\oplus v} = \frac{\delta_{i,j} f_{i\oplus v} - \delta_{i,0} f_{j\oplus v}}{f_v}$$

For this case, the i, i th entry of $\sigma_v d\mathcal{F}_{e_v}\sigma_v$ is $[i > 0]f_{i\oplus v}/f_v$. For ranking selection, theorem 7.3 shows $(d\mathcal{F}_{e_v})_{i\oplus v, j\oplus v}$ is

$$\varrho([f_v \le f_{i\oplus v}])[f_{j\oplus v} \le f_{i\oplus v}] - \varrho([f_v < f_{i\oplus v}])[f_{j\oplus v} < f_{i\oplus v}]$$

$$= \delta_{i,j}\varrho([f_v \le f_{i\oplus v}]) + [j \ne i][i = 0](\varrho(1) - \varrho(0))[f_{j\oplus v} < f_v]$$

For this case, the i, i th entry of $\sigma_v d\mathcal{F}_{e_v}\sigma_v$ is $\varrho([f_v \le f_{i\oplus v}])$. For tournament selection, the proof of theorem 10.3 shows $(d\mathcal{F}_{e_v})_{i\oplus v, j\oplus v}$ is

$$k(\delta_{j,0}\delta_{i,0} + (1 - \delta_{j,0})(\beta_{j\oplus v}\delta_{i,j} + \gamma_{j\oplus v}\delta_{i,0}))$$

where

$$\mathcal{F}'((1/k)e_{j\oplus v} + (1 - 1/k)e_v) = \beta_{j\oplus v}e_{j\oplus v} + \gamma_{j\oplus v}e_v$$

For this case, the i, ith entry of $\sigma_v d\mathcal{F}_{e_v}\sigma_v$ is $k[i = 0] + k[i > 0]\beta_{i\oplus v}$.

It is easily checked that $\mathbf{1}^T$ is a left eigenvector (of $\sigma_v d\mathcal{F}_{e_v}\sigma_v$ and hence of $d\mathcal{F}_{e_v}$) in all three cases, with eigenvalue $(d\mathcal{F}_{e_v})_{v,v}$. Thus by theorem 6.13,

$$\mathbf{1}^T d\mathcal{M}_{\mathcal{F}(e_v)}d\mathcal{F}_{e_v}$$

$$= 2(\mathbf{1}^T\mathcal{F}(e_v))\mathbf{1}^T d\mathcal{F}_{e_v}$$

$$= 2(d\mathcal{F}_{e_v})_{v,v}\mathbf{1}^T$$

It follows from the upper triangular forms and theorem 6.12 that

$$\text{spec}(d\mathcal{G}_{e_v}) = \{2M_{0,i}(d\mathcal{F}_{e_v})_{i\oplus v,i\oplus v} : 0 < i < n\} \qquad \blacksquare$$

Theorem 11.9 Assume fitness function $f(i) = a^T i + b$ and zero mutation. Then $\mathcal{G}$ is hyperbolic for a dense open set of b, in the case of proportional selection, and for a dense open set of ϱ, in the case of ranking or tournament selection.

Proof By theorem 11.8, hyperbolicity is obtained by perturbing $(d\mathcal{F}_{e_v})_{i,i}$ away from a finite number of values (those for which $2M_{0,i}(d\mathcal{F}_{e_v})_{i,i} = 1$ for some $0 < i < n$). In the case of proportional selection, $(d\mathcal{F}_{e_v})_{i,i}$ depends continuously on b and takes uncountably many values as b ranges over a small interval. For either ranking or tournament selection, $(d\mathcal{F}_{e_v})_{i,i}$ depends continuously on ϱ and takes uncountably many values as ϱ ranges over a small open set of continuous increasing probability densities. $\blacksquare$

Exercises

1. Use theorem 10.3 to prove theorem 11.8.

2. Proportional selection may be generalized to allow the fitness function to depend on the current population. Given any fitness scheme $\mathcal{F}$, define f depending on x by

$$f_x(i) = \frac{1}{x_i}\mathcal{F}(x)_i$$

Then the proportional selection scheme with fitness function $f_x(\cdot)$ coincides with $\mathcal{F}$. Prove that $\sigma_v d\mathcal{F}_{e_v}\sigma_v$ is upper triangular where $\mathcal{F}$ is generalized proportional selection (this was first noticed by Herbert Dawid).

3. Use the previous exercise to prove theorem 11.8. *Hint:* It may be necessary to calculate $f_{e_v}(i)$ by continuity.

4. Complete the proof of theorem 11.9 by providing suitable definition for "a small open set of continuous increasing probability densities".

5. Show theorem 11.9 holds for a dense open set of a (instead of b).

6. Show theorem 11.8 carries over to the general cardinality case.

7. Show theorem 11.9 carries over to the general cardinality case.

12 Perturbation Arguments

This chapter presents a perturbation theory which generalizes the conditions under which a heuristic is focused. The idea is that a hyperbolic heuristic will remain so if not too greatly perturbed. For example, if the mixing matrix is $M' = (1e_0^T + e_0 1^T)/2$, which corresponds to cloning, then

$$\mathcal{M}(x)_i = \frac{1}{2} \sum_u \sum_v x_{u \oplus i} x_{v \oplus i} (\delta_{u,0} + \delta_{v,0}) = x_i$$

Thus $\mathcal{G} = \mathcal{M} \circ \mathcal{F} = \mathcal{F}$ is hyperbolic provided $\mathcal{F}$ is, and will remain hyperbolic for M in some neighborhood of M'. The same principle can be applied, beginning with a choice of f or ϱ such that $\mathcal{F}$ is the identity, and then perturbing away from hyperbolic $\mathcal{M}$ to obtain hyperbolic $\mathcal{G}$.

A hyperbolic heuristic which has a complete Lyapunov function is called *normal*. An instance of RHS is normal when its heuristic is. Although a more general perturbation theory is possible, the presentation given here makes use of a complete Lyapunov function in an essential way. Thus normal heuristics are the subject of this chapter.

The first section is devoted to general principles, the second concerns their application. Although this material is not difficult, it is more technical than what has come before.

12.1 Small Perturbations

Let M' and f' refer to a mixing matrix and fitness function (respectively) for which the corresponding heuristic $\mathcal{G}'$ is hyperbolic. When $\mathcal{G}'$ is normal, its complete Lyapunov function will be denoted by ϕ. Let the fixed points of $\mathcal{G}'$ be $\{\omega_0, \ldots, \omega_k\}$. This is justified by the following theorem.

Theorem 12.1   A hyperbolic heuristic has only finitely many fixed points in Λ.

Proof   Otherwise, by compactness of Λ, there would be a convergent sequence of them, say $\lim x_i = x$. Without loss of generality, no x_i is x. Since $\mathcal{G}'$ is continuous,

$$\mathcal{G}'(x) = \lim \mathcal{G}'(x_i)$$

Hence x is also a fixed point. By compactness of the unit sphere, let η be a limit of the set

$$\left\{ \frac{x_i - x}{\|x_i - x\|} \right\}$$

and let i_j be a sequence of indices for which $\eta = \lim_j (x_{i_j} - x)/\|x_{i_j} - x\|$. Note that

$$x_{i_j} = \mathcal{G}'(x + (x_{i_j} - x)) = \mathcal{G}'(x) + d\mathcal{G}'_x(x_{i_j} - x) + o(x_{i_j} - x)$$

Subtracting x, dividing by $\|x_{i_j} - x\|$, and taking the limit as $j \to \infty$ yields

$$\eta = \lim_j d\mathcal{G}'_x\left(\frac{x_{i_j} - x}{\|x_{i_j} - x\|}\right) + o\left(\frac{x_{i_j} - x}{\|x_{i_j} - x\|}\right) = d\mathcal{G}'_x\eta$$

which contradicts the hypothesis that the fixed point x is hyperbolic. ■

Throughout this chapter, notation like $\mathcal{B}_\lambda(\mathcal{G}')$ and $\|\mathcal{G} - \mathcal{G}'\| < \lambda$ will be used for the sake of convenience. The latter notation indicates

$$\max\{\|M - M'\|, \|f - f'\|\} < \lambda$$

where $\mathcal{G}$ and $\mathcal{G}'$ have respective mixing matrices M and M', and fitness functions f and f'. The former notation denotes the set of all $\mathcal{G}$ satisfying the latter condition. Note that if $\|\mathcal{G} - \mathcal{G}'\| \to 0$ then

$$\sup_{x \in \Lambda} \|\mathcal{G}(x) - \mathcal{G}'(x)\| \to 0$$

since Λ is compact and $\mathcal{G}$ depends "continuously" on x, M, and f. This requires interpretation in the case of ranking or tournament selection. Because f' is injective, when $\|f - f'\|$ is sufficiently small the rankings induced by f and f' will coincide (at which point the corresponding selection schemes will be identical). Similarly,

$$\sup_{x \in \Lambda} \|d\mathcal{G}_x - d\mathcal{G}'_x\| \to 0$$

as $\|\mathcal{G} - \mathcal{G}'\| \to 0$. The phrase "$\|\mathcal{G} - \mathcal{G}'\|$ is appropriately small" means—among whatever other things are indicated by context—that $\|\mathcal{G} - \mathcal{G}'\| < \lambda$ with λ small enough for the rankings induced by f and f' to coincide.

Lemma 12.2 Suppose $\|\mathcal{G} - \mathcal{G}'\|$ is appropriately small, and consider $\mathcal{G}$ as having domain $\overline{\mathcal{B}}_\varepsilon(\omega_j)$. The function $o(y) = \mathcal{G}(x + y) - \mathcal{G}(x) - d\mathcal{G}_x(y)$ is Lipschitz in y, uniformly in x, M, and f, with Lipschitz constant $o(1)$ as $\varepsilon \to 0$.

Proof Note that $d\mathcal{G}_x$ is a continuous function of x, M, and f for any selection scheme. By hypothesis, both $\|M - M'\|$ and $\|f - f'\|$ are bounded, so x, M, and f range over compact sets. Hence $d\mathcal{G}_x$ is uniformly continuous in x, M and f. Next,

$$\|o(y) - o(z)\|$$

$$= \left\| \int_0^1 \frac{d}{dt} o(ty + (1 - t)z)\, dt \right\|$$

$$= \| \int_0^1 (d\mathcal{G}_{x+ty+(1-t)z} - d\mathcal{G}_x)(y - z)\, dt \|$$

$$\leq \|y - z\| \int_0^1 \|d\mathcal{G}_{x+ty+(1-t)z} - d\mathcal{G}_x\|\, dt$$

$$\leq \|y - z\| \sup_{0 \leq t \leq 1} \|d\mathcal{G}_{x+ty+(1-t)z} - d\mathcal{G}_x\|$$

By the uniform continuity of $d\mathcal{G}_x$, the supremum is arbitrarily small if y and z are arbitrarily small. Moreover, $\{x + y, x + z, x\} \subset \overline{\mathcal{B}}_\varepsilon(\omega_j)$. ∎

The sequence $x, \mathcal{G}(x), \mathcal{G}^2(x), \ldots$ is called the *orbit* of x. The following theorem concerning orbits is the cornerstone of the perturbation result. It is one of several consequences of the *stable manifold theorem*. A simplified version (to which the reader is referred) is given in the appendix. The following proof assumes that material has been reviewed.

Theorem 12.3   There exists $\varepsilon > 0$ and $\lambda > 0$ such that for all $\mathcal{G} \in \mathcal{B}_\lambda(\mathcal{G}')$ and all j, if the orbit of y (under $\mathcal{G}$) does not leave $\mathcal{B}_\varepsilon(\omega_j)$, then the orbit of y converges.

Proof   Let $T = d\mathcal{G}'_{\omega_j}$, and let $o(x - \omega_j) = \mathcal{G}(x) - \mathcal{G}(\omega_j) - d\mathcal{G}_{\omega_j}(x - \omega_j)$. Next define g by $g(x) = \mathcal{G}(\omega_j) - T\omega_j + (d\mathcal{G}_{\omega_j} - T)(x - \omega_j) + o(x - \omega_j)$.

Note that $\mathcal{G}(\omega_j) - T\omega_j$ is Lipschitz with constant 0 (since it is constant), $d\mathcal{G}_{\omega_j} - T$ is Lipschitz (since it is linear) with constant $\|d\mathcal{G}_{\omega_j} - T\| \to 0$ as $\lambda \to 0$, and $o(x - \omega_j)$ is Lipschitz with constant $o(1)$ for $x \in \mathcal{B}_\varepsilon(\omega_j)$ as $\varepsilon \to 0$ (lemma 12.2). Hence g is Lipschitz with arbitrarily small Lipschitz constant. Moreover,

$$\mathcal{G}(x)$$

$$= \mathcal{G}(\omega_j) + d\mathcal{G}_{\omega_j}(x - \omega_j) + o(x - \omega_j)$$

$$= T(x - \omega_j) + \mathcal{G}(\omega_j) + (d\mathcal{G}_{\omega_j} - T)(x - \omega_j) + o(x - \omega_j)$$

$$= Tx + g(x)$$

Since T is a hyperbolic linear map, let E^+ and E^- be its stable and unstable subspaces (respectively). Let $\| \cdot \|$ be a norm adapted to T and let

$$\alpha = \max\{\|T\big|_{E^+}\|, \|(T\big|_{E^-})^{-1}\|\} < 1$$

Since all norms are equivalent, there exist $\varepsilon_j > 0$ and $\lambda_j > 0$ such that the Lipschitz constant of $g(x)$ is less than $(1 - \alpha)/2$ for $x \in \mathcal{B}_{\varepsilon_j}(\omega_j)$ and $\mathcal{G} \in \mathcal{B}_{\lambda_j}(\mathcal{G}')$. Therefore, the composition of g with the retraction to $\mathcal{B}_{\varepsilon_j}(\omega_j)$ has Lipschitz constant less than $1 - \alpha$, so the stable manifold theorem applies to show that orbits (under $\mathcal{G} = T + g$) which are confined to $\mathcal{B}_{\varepsilon_j}(\omega_j)$ converge (the fixed points of $\mathcal{G}$ belong to $\mathcal{B}_{\varepsilon_j}(\omega_j)$ for sufficiently small λ_j). Now let $\varepsilon = \min \varepsilon_j$ and $\lambda = \min \lambda_j$. ∎

A sequence $x_0, x_1, \ldots, x_k$ is called a ε-chain of length k with respect to $\mathcal{G}$ from x_0 to x_k, provided that $\|x_{i+1} - \mathcal{G}(x_i)\| < \varepsilon$ for $0 \le i < k$. Note that given $\alpha > 0$ there exists $\varepsilon > 0$ such that for all $x \in \Lambda$, for all $\mathcal{G} \in \mathcal{B}_\varepsilon(\mathcal{G}')$, and for all $k > 0$,

$$\mathcal{G}^0(x), \mathcal{G}^1(x), \ldots \mathcal{G}^k(x)$$

is an α-chain with respect to $\mathcal{G}'$ from x to $\mathcal{G}^k(x)$. This follows from the observation that as $\varepsilon \to 0$,

$$\|\mathcal{G}^{i+1}(x) - \mathcal{G}'(\mathcal{G}^i(x))\| \le \sup_{y \in \Lambda} \|\mathcal{G}(y) - \mathcal{G}'(y)\| \to 0$$

Thus statements concerning α-chains with respect to $\mathcal{G}'$ concern orbits of $\mathcal{G}$, provided $\|\mathcal{G} - \mathcal{G}'\|$ is small.

Lemma 12.4 Let $\mathcal{G}'$ be normal. Given $\eta > 0$ there exists $\lambda > 0$ and $\xi > 0$ such that for all length one λ-chains x_0, x_1 with respect to $\mathcal{G}'$,

$$x_0 \in \Lambda \setminus \bigcup \mathcal{B}_\eta(\omega_j) \implies \phi(x_1) > \phi(x_0) + \xi$$

Proof   First, it will be proved by way of contradiction that, for small λ, the function

$$g(\lambda, x) = \inf_{y \in \mathcal{B}_\lambda(\mathcal{G}'(x))} \phi(y) - \phi(x)$$

is positive for $x \in \Lambda \setminus \bigcup \mathcal{B}_\eta(\omega_j)$. Let $\lambda_j \to 0$ and choose corresponding $z_j \in \Lambda \setminus \bigcup \mathcal{B}_\eta(\omega_j)$ such that $g(\lambda_j, z_j) \le 0$. By compactness (and passing to a subsequence if necessary), assume that $z_j \to z \in \Lambda \setminus \bigcup \mathcal{B}_\eta(\omega_j)$. Now by continuity,

$$\phi(\mathcal{G}'(z)) \le \phi(z)$$

which contradicts that ϕ is a Lyapunov function. Hence the continuous function $g(\lambda, x)$ is positive on a compact set of the form

$$[0, \varepsilon] \times \left(\Lambda \setminus \bigcup \mathcal{B}_\eta(\omega_j)\right)$$

Choosing positive ξ less than the minimum of g over this set finishes the proof. ∎

Lemma 12.5 Let $\mathcal{G}'$ be normal. If ε is sufficiently small, then there exists $\eta > 0$ and $\lambda > 0$ such that for all j the following holds: If a λ-chain with respect to $\mathcal{G}'$ enters $\mathcal{B}_\eta(\omega_j)$ and then leaves $\mathcal{B}_\varepsilon(\omega_j)$, say at y, then $\phi(y) > \phi(\omega_j) + 2\eta$.

Proof   Let positive η' and λ' be sufficiently small so that for all j,

$$x \in \mathcal{B}_{\eta'}(\omega_j) \Longrightarrow \mathcal{B}_{\lambda'}(\mathcal{G}'(x)) \in \mathcal{B}_\varepsilon(\omega_j)$$

Apply lemma 12.4 with $\eta = \eta'$ and let the resulting λ be λ''. Using the resulting ξ (from lemma 12.4), choose $\eta < \min\{\eta', \xi/4, \varepsilon\}$ and $\lambda''' < \min\{\lambda', \lambda''\}$ so small that for all j,

$$x \in \mathcal{B}_\eta(\omega_j) \Longrightarrow \phi(\mathcal{B}_{\lambda'''}(\mathcal{G}'(x))) > \phi(\omega_j) - \xi/2$$

Apply lemma 12.4 once more using η as chosen above, letting the resulting λ be λ'''' (the resulting ξ will be used below). Choose $\lambda = \min\{\lambda''', \lambda''''\}$. Finally, let $z \in \mathcal{B}_\varepsilon(\omega_j)$ be the point on the λ-chain just prior to y. Note that $z \notin \mathcal{B}_{\eta'}(\omega_j)$ since $y \notin \mathcal{B}_\varepsilon(\omega_j)$. Hence if ε is sufficiently small, then

$$z \in \Lambda \setminus \bigcup_j \mathcal{B}_{\eta'}(\omega_j)$$

and therefore $\phi(y) > \phi(z) + \xi$. Let w be the last point on the λ-chain prior to z contained in $\mathcal{B}_\eta(\omega_j)$. Then, since ϕ increases along the λ-chain between the point following w and z, it follows from the choice of η that $\phi(z) > \phi(\omega_j) - \xi/2$ and hence it can be concluded that $\phi(y) > \phi(\omega_j) + \xi/2 > \phi(\omega_j) + 2\eta$. ∎

The next step is the definition of sets on which orbits are under control in the sense that lemma 12.5 can be easily applied. Before proceeding, note that a consequence of lemma 12.5 is that if $\phi(\omega_j)$ is maximal (among $\phi(\omega_i)$), then an orbit entering $\mathcal{B}_\eta(\omega_j)$ cannot leave $\mathcal{B}_\varepsilon(\omega_j)$. Otherwise, there would be some y such that $\phi(y) > \phi(\omega_j)$, which is not possible.

Let ψ be the permutation such that $i < j \Longleftrightarrow \phi(\omega_{\psi_i}) < \phi(\omega_{\psi_j})$. Next define, depending on parameters $\gamma_j > 0$,

$$U_j = \{x : \lim_{k \to \infty} (\mathcal{G}')^k(x) = \omega_{\psi_j}\}$$

$$C_j = \bigcup_{i \le j} U_i$$

$$D_j = C_j \setminus \bigcup_{i < j} \mathcal{B}_{\gamma_i}(D_i)$$

Lemma 12.6   The C_j are closed and invariant under $\mathcal{G}'$. Moreover,

$$D_j \subset U_j \subset C_j \subset \bigcup_{i \le j} \mathcal{B}_{\gamma_i}(D_i)$$

Proof   Since the U_j are invariant under $\mathcal{G}'$, the C_j are also. That the C_j are closed follows by reverse induction on j. The base case $j = k$ is trivial, since $C_k = \Lambda$. By the induction hypothesis, assume C_j is closed. Since it is invariant, the dynamical system corresponding to $\mathcal{G}'$ can be restricted to C_j. Note that $\phi(\omega_{\psi_j})$ is maximal over fixed points in C_j. Hence ω_{ψ_j} is an attractor since iterates of $\mathcal{G}'$ converge and ϕ increases along orbits. Therefore the basin of attraction U_j of ω_{ψ_j} is open in C_j, so its complement is closed. The complement is C_{j-1} since the U_i are disjoint. Moreover, C_j is contained in

$$\left(C_j \setminus \bigcup_{i<j} \mathcal{B}_{\gamma_i}(D_i)\right) \cup \bigcup_{i<j} \mathcal{B}_{\gamma_i}(D_i)$$

$$= D_j \cup \bigcup_{i<j} \mathcal{B}_{\gamma_i}(D_i)$$

$$\subset \bigcup_{i \le j} \mathcal{B}_{\gamma_i}(D_i)$$

Therefore D_j is

$$C_j \setminus \bigcup_{i<j} \mathcal{B}_{\gamma_i}(D_i)$$

$$\subset C_j \setminus C_{j-1}$$

$$= U_j$$

$$\subset C_j$$
∎

Lemma 12.7   Let $\eta > 0$. There exists $\varepsilon > 0$ and $\lambda > 0$ such that every λ-chain with respect to $\mathcal{G}'$ beginning at $x \in \mathcal{B}_\varepsilon(D_j)$ enters $\mathcal{B}_\eta(\omega_{\psi_j})$. Moreover, $\varepsilon > 0$ and $\lambda > 0$ are independent of D_i for $i > j$.

Proof   Since D_j is contained in U_j (lemma 12.6), for each $x \in D_j$ there exists k_x such that $\|(\mathcal{G}')^{k_x}(x) - \omega_{\psi_j}\| < \eta$. Since $\mathcal{G}'(x)$ is continuous, there exist ε_x and λ_x such that every λ_x-chain with respect to $\mathcal{G}'$ of length k_x beginning in $\mathcal{B}_{\varepsilon_x}(x)$ enters $\mathcal{B}_\eta(\omega_{\psi_j})$. The sets $\mathcal{B}_{\frac{1}{2}\varepsilon_x}(x)$ are an open cover of D_j. By compactness, let $\mathcal{B}_{\frac{1}{2}\varepsilon_{x_1}}(x_1), \ldots, \mathcal{B}_{\frac{1}{2}\varepsilon_{x_k}}(x_k)$ be a subcover (D_j is closed since it is the intersection of C_j with the complement of an open set). Define $\varepsilon = \min \frac{1}{2}\varepsilon_{x_i}$ and $\lambda = \min \lambda_{x_i}$.

Now if $x \in \mathcal{B}_\varepsilon(D_j)$, then $x \in \mathcal{B}_\varepsilon(y)$ for some $y \in D_j$ and y is contained in some element of the open cover, say $\mathcal{B}_{\frac{1}{2}\varepsilon_{x_i}}(x_i)$. It follows that $x \in \mathcal{B}_{\varepsilon_{x_i}}(x_i)$, since $\|x - x_i\|$ is bounded by $\|x - y\| + \|y - x_i\| < \varepsilon + \frac{1}{2}\varepsilon_{x_i}$. By construction, every λ_x-chain with respect to $\mathcal{G}'$ of length k_x beginning in $\mathcal{B}_{\varepsilon_x}(x)$ enters $\mathcal{B}_\eta(\omega_{\psi_j})$.
∎

Lemma 12.8   Let $\mathcal{G}'$ be normal. Given $\eta > 0$ there exists $\lambda > 0$ such that for all j, every λ-chain beginning at $x \in \mathcal{B}_{\gamma_j}(D_j)$ enters $\mathcal{B}_\eta(\omega_{\psi_j})$. Here the γ_j depend on η and may be taken sufficiently small that

$$\sup_{x \in \mathcal{B}_{\gamma_j}(D_j)} \phi(x) < \phi(\omega_{\psi_j}) + \eta$$

Proof   Choose the parameters γ_j (defining the sets D_j) sequentially ($j = 0, 1, \ldots$) to depend on η as follows. Let γ_j be the ε from lemma 12.7, and let the corresponding λ be λ_j. Now let $\lambda = \min \lambda_j$. This determines the sets D_j up to the parameter η. Since the ε of lemma 12.7 can be arbitrarily small, the γ_j can be arbitrarily small as well.

It will next be shown, by way of contradiction, that the γ_j may be sufficiently small that

$$\sup_{y \in \mathcal{B}_{\gamma_j}(C_j)} \phi(y) < \phi(\omega_{\psi_j}) + \eta$$

This suffices to complete the proof since $D_j \subset C_j$. Let $\gamma_j \to 0$, choose corresponding $y \in \mathcal{B}_{\gamma_j}(C_j)$ such that $\phi(y) > \phi(\omega_{\psi_j}) + \eta/2$, and let $x \in C_j$ be a point minimally distant from y. By compactness (pass to a subsequence if necessary), assume $x_j \to x \in C_j$ as $\gamma_j \to 0$. By continuity of ϕ, it follows that $\phi(x) \geq \phi(\omega_{\psi_j}) + \eta/2$. This contradicts

$$\sup_{x \in C_j} \phi(x)$$

$$= \sup_{i \leq j} \sup_{x \in U_i} \phi(x)$$

$$= \sup_{i \leq j} \phi(\omega_{\psi_i})$$

$$= \phi(\omega_{\psi_j}) \qquad\qquad\qquad \blacksquare$$

Finally, the perturbation result can be proved.

Theorem 12.9   The set of normal heuristics corresponding to the SGA is open (in the space of heuristics corresponding to the SGA).

Proof   Let $\mathcal{G}'$ be normal. The proof is in three parts. The first is to show there exists $\beta > 0$ such that $\mathcal{G}$ is focused for all $\mathcal{G} \in \mathcal{B}_\beta(\mathcal{G}')$.

Choose $\varepsilon' > 0$ so that theorem 12.3 applies, and let the corresponding λ be λ'. Choose $0 < \varepsilon \leq \varepsilon'$ so that lemma 12.5 applies, and let the corresponding λ be λ''. Using the resulting η (from lemma 12.5), apply lemma 12.8, and let the corresponding λ be λ'''. Now let

$\lambda < \min\{\lambda', \lambda'', \lambda'''\}$ and let $\beta > 0$ be so small that if $\mathcal{G} \in \mathcal{B}_\beta(\mathcal{G}')$ then orbits of points under $\mathcal{G}$ are $\frac{\lambda}{2}$-chains with respect to $\mathcal{G}'$.

The proof of the first part proceeds by showing that every λ-chain with respect to $\mathcal{G}'$ will eventually become trapped within some $\mathcal{B}_\varepsilon(\omega_j)$, whereupon it must converge when it corresponds to an orbit under $\mathcal{G}$ (theorem 12.3).

Since $\Lambda = \bigcup U_j \subset \bigcup \mathcal{B}_{\gamma_j}(D_j)$ (lemma 12.6), any $x \in \Lambda$ is contained in some $\mathcal{B}_{\gamma_j}(D_j)$. Hence, by lemma 12.8, every λ-chain beginning at x enters $\mathcal{B}_\eta(\omega_{\psi_j})$. If the λ-chain does not leave $\mathcal{B}_\varepsilon(\omega_{\psi_j})$, then the proof of the first part is complete. Otherwise, lemma 12.5 implies that when it does leave, say at y, then $\phi(y) > \phi(\omega_{\psi_j}) + \eta$. By construction, $x \in \mathcal{B}_{\gamma_j}(D_j) \Longrightarrow \phi(x) < \phi(\omega_{\psi_j}) + \eta$ (lemma 12.8). Therefore, $y \in \mathcal{B}_{\gamma_k}(D_k)$ for some $k > j$.

The previous paragraph may be summarized by: if a λ-chain, upon entering $\mathcal{B}_\eta(\omega_i)$, does not become trapped in $\mathcal{B}_\varepsilon(\omega_i)$, then it enters some $\mathcal{B}_\eta(\omega_k)$ where $\phi(\omega_k) > \phi(\omega_i)$. It follows that the λ-chain must eventually become trapped, since the alternative is an infinite increasing sequence $\phi(\omega_{i_1}) < \phi(\omega_{i_2}) < \phi(\omega_{i_3}), \dots$ which is not possible.

The second part is to show hyperbolicity. Since the spectrum of $d\mathcal{G}_x$ depends continuously on $\mathcal{G}$ and x, it follows that $\mathcal{G} \in \mathcal{B}_\beta(\mathcal{G}')$ is hyperbolic at its fixed points in $\bigcup \mathcal{B}_\varepsilon(\omega_j)$ provided ε and β are sufficiently small. Moreover, lemma 12.4 implies that $\mathcal{G}$ cannot have fixed points in Λ anywhere else.

The final part is to show $\mathcal{G}$ has a complete Lyapunov function. It suffices to show that the existence of an α-chain from x to x with respect to $\mathcal{G}$ for every $\alpha > 0$ implies x is a fixed point (see appendix).

Suppose along some sequence of $\alpha \to 0$ the α-chain from x to x stays within $\mathcal{B}_\varepsilon(\omega_j)$. In this case the shadowing lemma (see appendix) and theorem 12.3 imply the chain must stay within $O(\alpha)$ of the fixed point of $\mathcal{G}$ in $\mathcal{B}_\varepsilon(\omega_j)$. Since α is arbitrarily small, x must be the fixed point.

The alternative leads to a contradiction as follows. Along some sequence of $\alpha \to 0$, choose an element from each α-chain in the complement of $\bigcup \mathcal{B}_\varepsilon(\omega_j)$. By compactness, let y be a limit point in the complement of $\bigcup \mathcal{B}_\varepsilon(\omega_j)$. By construction, there exists an α-chain from y to y for every $\alpha > 0$. But this contradicts the fact that every λ-chain will eventually become trapped within some $\mathcal{B}_\varepsilon(\omega_j)$ (an α-chain with respect to $\mathcal{G}$ is a λ-chain with respect to $\mathcal{G}'$ for small α because orbits with respect to $\mathcal{G}$ are $\frac{\lambda}{2}$-chains). $\blacksquare$

Exercises

1. Establish that $\sup_{x \in \Lambda} \|\mathcal{G}(x) - \mathcal{G}'(x)\| \to 0$ and $\sup_{x \in \Lambda} \|d\mathcal{G}_x - d\mathcal{G}'_x\| \to 0$ provided that $\|\mathcal{G} - \mathcal{G}'\| \to 0$. *Hint:* Functions continuous over a compact domain are uniformly continuous.

2. How do the results in this chapter depend on ϕ being a complete Lyapunov function (as opposed to just a Lyapunov function)?

3. Where in the results of this section (or in their proofs) might it be appropriate for $\mathcal{G}$ to be thought of as being defined on the affine space containing Λ? Would that be a problem? Hint: review chapter 9.

4. Prove that if $\mathcal{M}$ is focused, then there exists $\varepsilon > 0$ such that $\mathcal{G}$ is a contraction mapping for all $\mathcal{F}$ satisfying

$$\sup_{x \in \Lambda} \|d\mathcal{F}_x - I\| < \varepsilon$$

Hint: Review the discussion following theorem 10.7 and the proof of lemma 12.2.

5. Prove that if $\mathcal{G}$ is a contraction mapping, then $\mathcal{G}$ is normal.

6. Generalize theorem 12.9 to a statement concerning arbitrary normal heuristics (which do not necessarily correspond to the SGA).

7. Are any modifications appropriate for the general cardinality case?

12.2   Application

As pointed out in the exercises of the previous section, theorem 12.9 extends beyond the simple genetic algorithm. The methods of this chapter speak to an arbitrary instance of random heuristic search with normal heuristic. To summarize what has been established in the case of the SGA concerning normality, $\mathcal{G}$ is normal in any of the following circumstances:

1. Mixing is cloning (then $\mathcal{G} = \mathcal{F}$ is normal by theorem 10.2 and theorem 10.4).

2. Selection is uniform and mutation is positive (then $\mathcal{G} = \mathcal{M}$ is normal by exercise 5 of section 12.1 and the exercises of section 6.3).

3. Mutation is zero, f is linear, and an arbitrarily small perturbation to f or ϱ is allowed (then $\mathcal{G}$ is normal by theorems 11.6, 11.9, and 12.9).

Theorem 12.9 applies in each of these cases to show nearby heuristics are also normal. In particular, small mutation and crossover rates are allowable in case 1, nearly flat f or ϱ is allowable in case 2, and small mutation rates and nearly linear f suffice for case 3. Moreover, each of these generalized cases may be perturbed to further extend the set of normal heuristics. What the boundaries are to this extension process by way of iterated perturbation is not known. It is conjectured that the set of normal heuristics (corresponding to the SGA) is open and dense in the set of heuristics (corresponding to the SGA) for which mutation satisfies $\mu < 0.5$.

13 Transient Behavior

This chapter is mainly about the relationship between random heuristic search and its heuristic, as population size goes to infinity. A consequence of the results obtained is a view of the SGA's transient behavior in the large population case (a view which speaks also to transient behavior in the small population case, though less forcefully).

The first section concerns the relationship between orbits under τ and orbits under $\mathcal{G}$ and applies it to the influence of transient behavior on asymptotic behavior. The second section, implicitly based on approximating orbits under τ with orbits under $\mathcal{G}$, investigates the rate of convergence of $\mathcal{G}$, and hence addresses the settling time of a transient phase of τ. The final section draws together the results of this chapter to explain the phenomenon of punctuated equilibria.

13.1 Large Populations

Lemma 13.1 Given $\epsilon > 0$ and $\gamma < 1$, there exists N independent of $x \in \Lambda$ such that with probability at least γ,

$$r > N \implies \|\tau(x) - \mathcal{G}(x)\| < \epsilon$$

Proof By theorem 3.4 and exercise 2 of section 3.1, the probability that the discrepancy of $\tau(x)$ with respect to $\mathcal{G}(x)$ is greater than ε is bounded by

$$\sum_{q \in \frac{1}{r} X_n^r} e^{-r\varepsilon + O(\log r)}$$

$$= \binom{n+r-1}{n-1} e^{-r\varepsilon + O(\log r)}$$

$$= O(r^{n-1}) e^{-r\varepsilon + O(\log r)}$$

$$= e^{-r\varepsilon + O(\log r)}$$

Since the right hand goes to zero as $r \to \infty$, the proof is completed by observing that $\tau(x) \to \mathcal{G}(x)$ as the discrepancy goes to zero. ∎

The next theorem shows as $r \to \infty$ that, with probability converging to 1, the transient behavior of a population trajectory converges to the path determined by iterates of $\mathcal{G}$, and the transient phase occupies a time span diverging to infinity.

Theorem 13.2 Given $k > 0$, $\varepsilon > 0$ and $\gamma < 1$, there exists N independent of $x \in \Lambda$ such that with probability at least γ and for all $0 \leq t \leq k$,

$$r > N \implies \|\tau^t(x) - \mathcal{G}^t(x)\| < \varepsilon$$

Proof Induct on k. The base case is lemma 13.1. Since $\mathcal{G}$ is uniformly continuous, choose δ such that

$$\|\tau(x)^{k-1} - \mathcal{G}^{k-1}(x)\| < \delta \Longrightarrow \|\mathcal{G}(\tau(x)^{k-1}) - \mathcal{G}^k(x)\| < \varepsilon/2$$

By the inductive hypothesis, if $n > N_0$ then with probability at least $1 - (1 - \gamma)/2$

$$\|\tau(x)^{k-1} - \mathcal{G}^{k-1}(x)\| < \delta$$

By lemma 13.1, let N_1 be such that with probability at least $1 - (1 - \gamma)/2$

$$n > N_1 \Longrightarrow \|\tau(x)^k - \mathcal{G}(\tau(x)^{k-1})\| < \varepsilon/2$$

It follows that if $n > \max\{N_0, N_1\}$, then with probability at least γ

$$\|\tau(x)^k - \mathcal{G}^k(x)\| \le \|\tau(x)^k - \mathcal{G}(\tau(x)^{k-1})\| + \|\mathcal{G}(\tau(x)^{k-1}) - \mathcal{G}^k(x)\| < \varepsilon \qquad \blacksquare$$

Since $\mathcal{G}$ is related to transient behavior, and since the transient phase occupies a time span diverging to infinity, theorem 13.2 suggests (for large r) that some aspects of steady state (i.e., asymptotic) behavior may be manifestations of transient behavior. Let π be the probability measure corresponding to the steady state distribution of random heuristic search,

$$\pi(A) = \sum_{v \in \frac{1}{r} X_n^k} x_v [v \in A]$$

where x is the steady state distribution (vector) satisfying $x^T = x^T Q$. Thus $\pi(A)$ represents the proportion of time that populations spend in A, averaged over infinitely many generations. Here it is assumed that mutation is positive so that the Markov chain is ergodic. Since π is, for each population size r, a probability measure over the compact set Λ, a theorem of Prokhorov (see appendix) implies that every infinite sequence of π (corresponding to a sequence of r) has an infinite subsequence which *converges weakly* to some probability measure π'. Passing to the subsequence, this means that for every continuous function $h : \Lambda \to [0, 1]$,

$$\int h \, d\pi \longrightarrow \int h \, d\pi'$$

Let $\mathfrak{F}$ be the set of fixed points of $\mathcal{G}$. The next theorem provides a partial answer to how transient behavior influences steady state behavior.

Theorem 13.3 Suppose $\mathcal{G}$ is focused and mutation is positive. If π' is a weak limit point of π as $r \to \infty$, then $\pi'(\mathfrak{F}) = 1$.

Proof   It suffices to show $\pi'(\mathcal{U}) = 1$ for every open set $\mathcal{U}$ containing $\mathfrak{I}$. Since $\mathcal{G}$ is continuous, $\mathfrak{I}$ is compact. Note that $\mathcal{C} = \Lambda \setminus \mathcal{U}$ is also compact, and let ρ be the distance between $\mathcal{C}$ and $\mathfrak{I}$. Let $\mathfrak{I}_{\rho/4}$ be the set of points within a distance of $\rho/4$ from $\mathfrak{I}$. Since $\lim_{t\to\infty} \mathcal{G}^t(x) \in \mathfrak{I}$ for every $x \in \Lambda$, the set $\mathcal{C}$ is the disjoint union of the sets

$$E^j = \{x \in \mathcal{C} : \mathcal{G}^j(x) \notin \mathfrak{I}_{\rho/4} \ \wedge \ t > j \Rightarrow \mathcal{G}^t(x) \in \mathfrak{I}_{\rho/4}\}$$

Therefore,

$$\pi'(\mathcal{U}) = 1 - \pi'(\mathcal{C}) = 1 - \sum \pi'(E^j)$$

The proof is completed by showing $\pi'(E^j) = 0$. Let $h : \Lambda \to [0, 1]$ be a continuous function which is 1 on E^j. Then

$$\pi'(E^j) \le \int h \, d\pi' \le \limsup_{r\to\infty} \int h \, d\pi$$

It therefore remains to show that given $\varepsilon > 0$ there exists N and suitable h such that

$$r > N \Longrightarrow \int h \, d\pi < \varepsilon$$

Let E_δ^j be the set of points less than δ from E^j, and given $y \in E_\delta^j$, let $x \in E^j$ be such that $\|y - x\| < \delta$. Let $\varepsilon > 0$ and let $k > 2j\varepsilon^{-1}$. Since $\mathcal{G}$ is uniformly continuous, choose δ such that for all $0 \le t \le k$

$$\|\mathcal{G}^t(y) - \mathcal{G}^t(x)\| < \rho/4$$

By theorem 13.2, let N be such that with probability at least $1 - \varepsilon/2$ and for all $0 \le t \le k$

$$r > N \Longrightarrow \|\tau^t(y) - \mathcal{G}^t(y)\| < \rho/4$$

Let $d(\cdot, \mathfrak{I})$ be the function measuring distance from $\mathfrak{I}$. Hence if $r > N$ and $j < t \le k$, then with probability at least $1 - \varepsilon/2$, and for all $y \in E_\delta^j$,

$$d(\tau^t(y), \mathfrak{I}) \le \|\tau^t(y) - \mathcal{G}^t(y)\| + \|\mathcal{G}^t(y) - \mathcal{G}^t(x)\| + d(\mathcal{G}^t(x), \mathfrak{I}) < 3\rho/4$$

This means that if the Markov chain was at a state in E_δ^j, then with probability $1 - \varepsilon/2$ it will spend at least the fraction $(k - j)/k > 1 - \varepsilon/2$ of the time outside of E_δ^j provided that $r > N$. Hence choosing h to be zero outside of E_δ^j gives

$$\int h \, d\pi \le \pi(E_\delta^j) < \varepsilon$$

provided that $r > N$.   ∎

Theorem 13.4   Suppose $\mathcal{G}$ is focused and mutation is positive. For every open set U containing $\Im$, $\lim_{r \to \infty} \pi(U) = 1$

Proof   Otherwise, there exists $\varepsilon > 0$ and an infinite sequence of r for which $\pi(U) < 1 - \varepsilon$. By Prokhorov's theorem, a subsequence of the π (i.e., for a suitably chosen divergent sequence of r) converges to some π'. Choosing continuous $h : \Lambda \to [0, 1]$ to be one on $\Im$ and zero in the complement of U,

$$\pi'(\Im)$$

$$\leq \int h \, d\pi'$$

$$= \lim \int h \, d\pi$$

$$\leq \lim \pi(U)$$

$$< 1 - \varepsilon$$

which contradicts theorem 13.3.   ∎

In the large population case, theorem 13.4 indicates where population trajectories predominately spend time; near fixed points of $\mathcal{G}$. Moreover, theorem 13.2 indicates that a trajectory from p moves towards a fixed point of $\mathcal{G}$ by approximately following the path $p, \mathcal{G}(p), \mathcal{G}^2(p), \ldots$ The the next section investigates how quickly this path approaches a fixed point.

Exercises

1. Generalize theorem 13.3 and theorem 13.4 to allow nonzero mutation.

2. Show that theorem 13.3 and theorem 13.4 apply to ergodic RHS with a focused heuristic.

3. Verify theorems 13.2 and 13.4 empirically by way of computer experiments.

4. Show that no modifications are necessary for the general cardinality case.

13.2   Logarithmic Convergence

This section is devoted to the rate of convergence of orbits under a focused heuristic $\mathcal{G}$.

The definition of "logarithmic time to convergence" faces several obstacles. Perhaps the most obvious is the existence of a sequence of initial populations along which the time to convergence diverges to infinity. To circumvent this difficulty, let a probability density ρ be given over Λ and define the probability that the initial population is in A to be

$$\int_A \rho \, d\lambda$$

where λ is surface measure on Λ (i.e., $n - 1$ dimensional Lebesgue measure). The task is then to show that for every ρ and every $\varepsilon > 0$, there exists a set A of probability at least $1 - \varepsilon$ such that if the initial population is in A, then the time to convergence is logarithmic.

The next difficulty is that, typically, a orbit under $\mathcal{G}$ will never reach the limit it is approaching. It is natural, therefore, to let $0 < \delta < 1$ denote how close trajectories are required to get to the limit, and then to require that they do so, within $O(-\log \delta)$ generations.

Logarithmic convergence is defined as follows: for every probability density ρ and every $\varepsilon > 0$, there exists a set A of probability at least $1 - \varepsilon$ such that for all $x \in A$ and $0 < \delta < 1$, the number k of generations required for $\|\mathcal{G}^k(x) - \omega(x)\| < \delta$ is $O(-\log \delta)$, where $\omega(x)$ denotes the limit of $\mathcal{G}^t(x)$ as $t \to \infty$.

The heuristic $\mathcal{G}$ is said to be *regular* if whenever $C \subset \Lambda$ has measure zero, then so does the set $\mathcal{G}^{-1}(C)$. An instance of RHS is regular when its heuristic is.

Theorem 13.5　If $\mathcal{G}$ has an inverse which is continuously differentiable in $\mathcal{G}(\Lambda^o)$, where Λ^o denotes the interior of Λ, then $\mathcal{G}$ is regular.

Proof　Let $\partial \Lambda$ denote $\Lambda \setminus \Lambda^o$, and let C have measure zero. By the change of variable formula,

$$\lambda(\mathcal{G}^{-1}(C))$$

$$= \lambda(\mathcal{G}^{-1}(C \cap \mathcal{G}(\partial \Lambda))) + \lambda(\mathcal{G}^{-1}(C \cap \mathcal{G}(\Lambda^o)))$$

$$\leq \lambda(\partial \Lambda) + \int_{C \cap \mathcal{G}(\Lambda^o)} |\det d\mathcal{G}_x^{-1}| \, d\lambda(x)$$

$$= 0 \qquad\qquad\qquad\qquad\qquad\qquad\qquad\qquad\qquad\qquad\qquad\qquad\qquad\qquad \blacksquare$$

Combining this with theorem 9.3 yields the following.

Theorem 13.6　In the case of the simple genetic algorithm, $\mathcal{G}$ is regular if the crossover rate is less than 1 and the mutation rate is strictly between 0 and 1/2 (provided, in the case of ranking selection, that ϱ is positive).

It is assumed throughout the rest of this section that $\mathcal{G}$ is focused, regular, and has hyperbolic fixed points. Logarithmic convergence is proved only for a suitably chosen norm. The restriction that $0 < \delta < 1$ in the definition of logarithmic convergence is made to streamline the proof given below. Since all norms are equivalent (the dimension of Λ is finite) there is no loss of generality and the norm $\| \cdot \|$ may be chosen so that the diameter of Λ is less than $\alpha < 1$.

The basin of attraction of x is the set

$$\mathcal{B}_x = \{y : \lim_{k \to \infty} \mathcal{G}^k(y) = x\}$$

Let $\mathcal{S}$ be the union of $\mathcal{B}_x$ over stable x, and let $\mathcal{U}$ be the union of $\mathcal{B}_x$ over unstable x. Since $\mathcal{G}$ is assumed to be focused, $\mathcal{S}$ and $\mathcal{U}$ are complements (in Λ).

Lemma 13.7   With respect to any probability density, $\mathcal{U}$ has probability zero.

Proof   Since probabilities are computed by integration with respect to Lebesgue measure, it suffices to show $\lambda(\mathcal{U}) = 0$. Since there are finitely many $\mathcal{B}_x$ (theorem 12.1), and since

$$\mathcal{B}_x = \bigcup_{k \geq 0} \mathcal{G}^{-k}(U)$$

where U is the intersection of a small neighborhood of x with the stable manifold at x, it suffices that $\lambda(U) = 0$. Since x is an unstable fixed point, the stable manifold theorem shows U to be the graph of a function over the stable subspace. Note that there are uncountably many disjoint translates of the graph within a small neighborhood of x (move along any unstable direction). Since λ is translation invariant, it follows that $\lambda(U) = 0$. ∎

Attention will be restricted to $\mathcal{S}$ since lemma 13.7 shows its complement has probability zero. The following theorem shows that the set of typical initial populations may be taken to be compact.

Lemma 13.8   For every probability density ρ and every $\varepsilon > 0$, there exists a compact subset of $\mathcal{S}$ having probability at least $1 - \varepsilon$.

Proof   Let U_x be a small closed neighborhood of the fixed point x and let U be the union of the U_x over stable fixed points x. Define

$$A_k = \bigcup_{0 \leq j \leq k} \mathcal{G}^{-j}(U)$$

and note that the characteristic function of the set A_k (i.e., its indicator function) converges monotonically to the characteristic function of $\mathcal{S}$. Moreover, each A_k is compact. It follows from lemma 13.7 and the monotone convergence theorem that

$$1 = \int_{\mathcal{S}} \rho \, d\lambda = \lim_{k \to \infty} \int_{A_k} \rho \, d\lambda$$

Therefore, a k exists for which the probability of A_k is at least $1 - \varepsilon$. ∎

Given ρ and given $\varepsilon > 0$, let A be a compact subset of $\mathcal{S}$ which exists by lemma 13.8. The next theorem shows it is sufficient to consider local convergence behavior, that is, behavior at a point $x \in A$.

Lemma 13.9   If for every $x \in A$ there exists an integer N_x such that for $0 < \delta < 1$

$$k > -N_x \log \delta \implies \|\mathcal{G}^k(x) - \omega(x)\| < \delta$$

then $\mathcal{G}$ is logarithmically convergent.

Proof   Without loss of generality, the N_x are minimal. Suppose there exists N such that $N_x < N$ for all $x \in A$. In that case the proof would be complete since A has probability at least $1 - \varepsilon$ and for $p \in A$ the number of generations k required for $\|\mathcal{G}^k(p) - \omega(p)\| < \delta$ would be bounded by $-N \log \delta$.

If there were no such N, then let x_j be a sequence for which N_{x_j} diverges. Since A is compact, assume the x_j converge to x. Let U be a small open ball with center $\omega(x)$ such that $y \in U \implies \|\mathcal{G}(y) - \omega(x)\| < \alpha \|y - \omega(x)\|$ for some adapted norm and some $\alpha < 1$. Such a neighborhood exists since the spectral radius of $d\mathcal{G}_{\omega(x)}$ is less than 1. Because the number of fixed points is finite, α may be chosen without regard to which of the stable fixed points $\omega(x)$ is. Let $k > 1$ be such that $\mathcal{G}^k(x) \in U$, and by continuity let V be an open neighborhood of x which is mapped into U by $\mathcal{G}^k$. Hence if $t \geq k$, then

$$\sup_{v \in V} \|\mathcal{G}^t(v) - \omega(x)\| \leq \sup_{u \in U} \|u - \omega(x)\| \alpha^{t-k} < \alpha^{1+t-k}$$

since the norm may be chosen so that the diameter of Λ is less than α. This inequality will be referred to as (∗). Given δ, choose integer t such that $\alpha^{1+t-k} \leq \delta < \alpha^{t-k}$, and let $N = -2k/\log \alpha$. Consider first the case where $t > k$ and note that (in this case)

$$-N \log \delta > (2k/\log \alpha)(t - k) \log \alpha > t$$

Combining this with (∗) yields

$$\sup_{v \in V} \|\mathcal{G}^{\lceil -N \log \delta \rceil}(v) - \omega(x)\| < \sup_{v \in V} \|\mathcal{G}^t(v) - \omega(x)\| < \alpha^{1+t-k} \leq \delta$$

which contradicts that the x_j enter V (since the N_{x_j} are unbounded). The remaining case is $t = k$, in which $\alpha \leq \delta$ holds. Hence

$$\sup_{v \in V} \|\mathcal{G}^{\lceil -N \log \delta \rceil}(v) - \omega(x)\| < \delta$$

is still valid since the diameter of Λ is less than α.   ∎

In the preceding proof, the inequality $y \in U \Longrightarrow \|\mathcal{G}(y) - \omega(x)\| < \alpha\|y - \omega(x)\|$ requires the choice of a suitable norm adapted to $d\mathcal{G}_{\omega(x)}$. Thus the conclusion of theorem 3.4 might appear to be valid only in the basin of attraction of $\omega(x)$. However, there are only finitely many basins (theorem 3.1) and theorem 3.4 is valid in each of them separately. Moreover, if

$$k > -N_x \log \delta \Longrightarrow \|\mathcal{G}^k(x) - \omega(x)\| < \delta$$

for one norm, then the same is true for any other norm by simply adjusting the constant N_x.

Theorem 13.10   If $\mathcal{G}$ is hyperbolic and regular, then $\mathcal{G}$ is logarithmically convergent.

Proof   According to lemma 13.9, all that remains is to show that for every $x \in A$ there exists an integer N_x such that for $0 < \delta < 1$

$$k > -N_x \log \delta \Longrightarrow \|\mathcal{G}^k(x) - \omega(x)\| < \delta$$

It follows from what was shown in the proof of lemma 13.9 that there exists a neighborhood V of x such that if $h > -N \log \delta$ then

$$\sup_{v \in V} \|\mathcal{G}^h(v) - \omega(x)\| < \delta$$

where N depends on x. Since $x \in V$, an acceptable choice is therefore $N_x = \lceil N \rceil$.   ∎

Exercises

1. Give an instance of the SGA and a sequence of initial populations along which the time to convergence diverges to infinity.

2. Two norms are equivalent if each is bounded by a constant multiple of the other. Using the fact that all norms on $\Re^n$ are equivalent, show there is no loss of generality in proving logarithmic convergence for only one norm.

3. Where in this section was the assumption that $\mathcal{G}$ is regular used?

4. Generalize theorem 13.6 to encompass a mutation distribution $\mu \in \Lambda$.

5. Show the definitions and results of this section generalize to the situation where Λ is replaced by the stable manifold $\mathcal{B}$ of a fixed point, A is replaced by $A \cap \mathcal{B}$, and the integral

$$\int_A \rho \, d\lambda$$

is interpreted as a surface integral with respect to surface measure on $\mathcal{B}$.

6. Show that no modifications are necessary for the general cardinality case.

13.3 Summary

Assuming $\mathcal{G}$ is hyperbolic and regular, the view of RHS behavior that emerges is the following. As r increases, and then with probability converging to 1, the initial transient behavior of a population trajectory converges to following the path determined by iterates of $\mathcal{G}$, and the initial transient phase occupies a time span diverging to infinity. Consequently, populations will predominately appear near some fixed point ω of $\mathcal{G}$ since the path $x, \mathcal{G}(x), \mathcal{G}^2(x), \ldots$ approaches a fixed point relatively quickly.

This appears in contrast to the fact that the SGA is an ergodic Markov chain[1]; every state must be visited infinitely often. This is reconciled in *punctuated equilibria*: low probability events may eventually move the system to a population x' contained within the basin of attraction of a different fixed point ω'. Since the behavior of random heuristic search is time independent, the anticipated behavior follows the trajectory $x', \mathcal{G}(x'), \mathcal{G}^2(x'), \ldots$—as if x' were the initial population—to reach a new temporary stasis in the vicinity of ω'.

This cycle of a period of relative stability followed by a sudden change to a new dynamic equilibrium, commonly called *metastability*, is the picture provided by the results of this chapter. It is an open question as to what relationship r must have to n in order that these qualitative aspects of RHS are typically exhibited.

As explained in chapters 3 and 8, metastability is, among other things, a natural consequence of the ergodicity of the Markov Chain, and the interplay between the flow and the lattice available to finite populations for occupation. The relationship of logarithmic convergence to metastability is clarified by reviewing the previous discussion in light of the existence of unstable fixed points and fixed points not within Λ. For focused and hyperbolic RHS, Λ is a finite disjoint union of basins of attraction of fixed points. Although the stable manifolds of unstable fixed points have measure zero, they are interesting because small populations might not be within the basin of attraction of any stable fixed point. Moreover, since the stable manifolds of unstable fixed points have probability zero with respect to every probability density over Λ, it might seem that the logarithmic convergence of RHS does not speak to them.

That is not true, however. Logarithmic convergence is a statement about the underlying flow, and the flow being considered may be taken to be that within the stable manifold $\mathcal{B}$ of an unstable fixed point: the probability density ϱ may be taken over $\mathcal{B}$, the set A may be taken within $\mathcal{B}$, and the integration $\int_A \varrho \, d\lambda$ may be performed with respect to surface measure on $\mathcal{B}$ (see exercise 5 of section 13.2).

Whereas the flow within the stable manifold of an unstable fixed point or of a fixed point not within Λ is relatively unrestricted, finite populations are not; only elements of a finite

---

1. Assuming positive mutation.

lattice are available to them for occupation. Since the lattice has measure zero with respect to every probability density over $\mathcal{B}$, this again suggests that logarithmic convergence does not speak to those regions of Λ most relevant to RHS, the populations themselves.

That suggestion is false however. Consider a small neighborhood U of a lattice point. By continuity of the flow, the transient behavior from the lattice point as given by the flow is nearly the transient behavior from any set $A \subset U$ of positive probability with respect to surface measure on any stable manifold $\mathcal{B}$ of any fixed point. In particular, this continuity together with logarithmic convergence and theorem 13.2 implies that the flow supports an initial transient of RHS which moves towards the unstable fixed point of lowest dimension having stable manifold near the lattice point (simply consider theorem 13.10 on the stable manifold $\mathcal{B}$ of lowest dimension which intersects U in some set A of positive probability with respect to surface measure on $\mathcal{B}$).

This bias of random heuristic search to visit fixed points in order of increasing dimension does not necessarily imply that fixed points of higher dimension (with a larger number of attracting dimensions) are likely to be encountered. As r decreases, fewer points become available for occupation as the lattice becomes increasingly coarse. Search is conducted in lower dimensional faces of Λ, which constrains the system's ability to follow the signal. It is possible that the fixed points of high dimension are not visited, being nowhere close to the low dimensional faces of Λ which can be occupied. Among accessible fixed points, those of higher dimension may be relatively more stable if they have fewer independent unstable directions lying in the low dimensional faces of Λ explored by RHS.

The phenomenon of punctuated equilibria is not confined to the finite population case. The flow is able to support metastability when there are a number of fixed points of various dimensions. This follows from the continuity referred to above, and is illustrated in the following figure.

Metastability near an unstable fixed point, infinite population case.

The bold curves (above) represent a stable manifold flowing into an unstable fixed point of dimension one. The thin curve depicts the flow nearby the stable manifold, and the dots represent an infinite population trajectory. Since the unstable fixed point is a fixed point, the flow must slow in its vicinity (by continuity). Thus populations appear to be stable, for awhile, as the orbit approaches and leaves the fixed point . . . only to approach, perhaps, another unstable fixed point, though of dimension two, whereupon another temporary stasis is experienced, and so on.

Whereas in the infinite population case metastability (if present) eventually terminates with convergence to a fixed point, the finite population case is characterized by a never ending series of transients (assuming ergodicity). As explained above, orbits achieve temporary stasis. That part of an orbit—moving towards and achieving temporary stasis—is referred to as a *transient*. Finite population trajectories are characterized by a series of transients; the first is the *initial* transient. The terms *local dynamics* and *transient behavior* refer to the behavior of the initial transient.

Exercises

1. In a series of computer experiments, explore empirically the connection between r and n and the behavior of RHS as described in this chapter.

2. Since fixed points of high dimension are not visited if nowhere close to the low dimensional faces of Λ which can be occupied, there is a connection between r and the underlying dynamical system (corresponding to $\mathcal{G}$) of the following sort. With increasing population size, an increasing number of fixed points may influence population trajectories; as r increases, the dimension of faces of Λ which can be occupied increases, thereby giving potential access to additional fixed points. Empirically explore this phenomenon.

3. A variant of the previous exercise is that as the population size changes (either by increasing or decreasing), the *location* of lattice points within a particular low diminsional face of Λ can shift, potentially giving or denighing access to fixed points. Empirically explore this phenomenon.

4. As has been explained in the exercises of chapter 8, fixed points can be generalized—as far as metastability is concerned—to regions near lattice points where the flow has stalled. Extend the previous two exercises to this more general phenomenon.

14 Asymptotic Behavior

This chapter builds upon the view of transient behavior summarized, in the large population case, by the previous chapter. There it was seen that random heuristic search with a regular, hyperbolic heuristic exhibits punctuated equilibria; a cycle of periods of relative stability near a fixed point interleaved with sudden change to another dynamic equilibrium near a possibly different fixed point. This suggests that the fixed points can be regarded as "states" and the sudden change can be thought of as a transition between states.

Thus random heuristic search may be modeled by a Markov chain over the fixed points. If the transition probabilities from temporary stasis in the vicinity of one fixed point to temporary stasis near another can be determined, then the punctuated equilibria can in principle be analyzed.

The meta-level view of random heuristic search described above is the subject of this chapter. Only the large population case is analyzed, and attention is focused on asymptotic behavior.

14.1 The Fixed Point Graph

Given an object x with associated numerical quantities, let $|x|$ denote their sum. This provides a flexible and general concept of "cost" or "size" which is notationally convenient. When x is a vector, $|x|$ denotes the sum of its coordinates.

Let $\rho = x_0, \ldots, x_k$ be a sequence of points from Λ, referred to as a *path* of length k from x_0 to x_k. The points $x_1, \ldots, x_{k-1}$ are referred to as *interior points* of ρ. The *cost* of ρ is

$$|\rho| = \alpha_{x_0, x_1} + \cdots + \alpha_{x_{k-1}, x_k}$$

where

$$\alpha_{u,v} = \sum_j v_j \log \frac{v_j}{\mathcal{G}(u)_j}$$

and it is assumed that $\mathcal{G}$ maps Λ into its interior so as to avoid division by zero. Let the stable fixed points of $\mathcal{G}$ in Λ be $\{\omega_0, \ldots, \omega_w\}$. The *fixed point graph* is defined to be the complete directed graph $\mathcal{J}$ on vertices $\{1, \ldots, w\}$ with edge $i \to j$ having weight

$$\rho_{\omega_i, \omega_j} = \inf\{|\rho| : \rho \text{ is a path from } \omega_i \text{ to } \omega_j\}$$

Vertices $i \in \mathcal{J}$ correspond to stable fixed points ω_i of $\mathcal{G}$. A *tributary* of a complete directed graph is a spanning intree (that is, a tree containing every vertex such that all edges point towards the root). Let Tree_k be the set of tributaries rooted at k, and for $t \in \text{Tree}_k$ let its cost $|t|$ be the sum of its edge weights.

A Markov chain is represented by a complete directed graph over $\{1, \ldots, w\}$ when the $i \rightarrow j$ edge for $i \neq j$ is labeled by a weight encoding the i, jth entry of its transition matrix (the $i = j$ entries will be ignored because they can be inferred from the fact that row sums are 1). There is a beautiful connection between a Markov chain's steady state distribution and the tributaries of a graphical representation of this kind:

Theorem 14.1   Let A be a transition matrix for a Markov chain with states $\{0, \ldots, w\}$, and let the corresponding graphical representation have edge $i \rightarrow j$ weighted by $-\log A_{i,j}$ for $i \neq j$. A solution x to the steady state equation $x^T A = x^T$ has components

$$x_k = \sum_{t \in \text{Tree}_k} \exp(-|t|)$$

A *steady state solution* refers to any solution x of the steady state equation. The steady state distribution (vector) of the Markov chain, assuming it exists, is $\pi = x/\mathbf{1}^T x$.

Suppose a graph G is given, similar to that referred to in theorem 14.1 and the discussion in the paragraph preceding it, where $g_{i,j}$ labels its $i \rightarrow j$ edge (for $i \neq j$). Consider the Markov chain $\mathcal{C}_r$, parametrized by r, with $i \rightarrow j$ transition probability $\exp(-rg_{i,j} + o(r))$. It follows from theorem 14.1 that $\mathcal{C}_r$ has steady state solution

$$x = \langle \sum_{t \in \text{Tree}_0} e^{-r(|t|+o(1))}, \ldots, \sum_{t \in \text{Tree}_w} e^{-r(|t|+o(1))} \rangle^T$$

where the Tree_k are computed with respect to G. Suppose further that G has a unique minimum cost tributary rooted at k' and having cost c. In this case, the steady state distribution of $\mathcal{C}_r$ converges as $r \rightarrow \infty$ to point mass at k' since

$$x_k e^{r(c+o(1))}$$

$$= \sum_{t \in \text{Tree}_k} e^{-r(|t|-c+o(1))}$$

$$= o(1)$$

if $k \neq k'$ (because then $|t| > c$), and otherwise

$$x_{k'} e^{r(c+o(1))}$$

$$= 1 + \sum_{t \in \text{Tree}_{k'}} [|t| > c] e^{-r(|t|-c+o(1))}$$

$$= 1 + o(1)$$

By choosing $G = \mathfrak{I}$, a Markov chain $\mathcal{C}_r$ is thereby defined up to $o(r)$ terms as above. The steady state distribution is guaranteed to exist if the Markov chain is ergodic (see appendix); thus $\mathcal{G}$ will be assumed ergodic throughout the rest of this chapter (in the case of the SGA, it suffices that mutation is positive, see theorem 4.7). It is conjectured, though as yet unproven, that an arbitrarily small perturbation of $\mathcal{G}$ (effected in the case of the simple GA by an arbitrarily small perturbation of crossover, mutation or fitness) will guarantee $\mathfrak{I}$ has a unique minimum cost tributary. That such a tributary exists will also be assumed.

A later section will show how $\mathcal{C}_r$ captures the asymptotic behavior of random heuristic search as $r \to \infty$. A consequence will be that, for large populations, RHS will with large probability be asymptotically near that fixed point $\omega_{k'}$ of $\mathcal{G}$ corresponding to the minimum cost tributary of $\mathfrak{I}$.

Exercises

1. Show that theorem 14.1 makes sense even if $A_{i,j} = 0$. *Hint:* $0 = \exp(-\infty) = \exp(\log 0)$.

2. In the Markov chain corresponding to the fixed point graph, the likelihood of a transition from i to j is determined by the minimal cost path from ω_i to ω_j. Interpret this in geometric terms. *Hint:* A path incurs cost to the extent that it is made up of steps which end at a place differing from where $\mathcal{G}$ maps their beginning.

14.2   Approximating Transition Probabilities

This section collects some results which will be needed later.

Theorem 14.2   For any $U \subset \Lambda$,

$$\Pr\{\tau(p) \in U\} = \exp(-r \inf_{q \in U} \alpha_{p,q} + O(\log r))$$

where the constant in the "big O" depends on n.

Proof   By theorem 3.4,

$$\Pr\{\tau(p) \in U\} = \sum_{q \in U} \exp(-r\alpha_{p,q} + O(\log r))$$

A lower bound for the right hand side is

$$\sup_{q \in U} \exp(-r\alpha_{p,q} + O(\log r))$$

An upper bound is

$$\binom{n+r-1}{n-1} \sup_{q \in U} \exp(-r\alpha_{p,q} + O(\log r))$$

$$= O(r^{n-1}) \exp(-r \inf_{q \in U} \alpha_{p,q} + O(\log r)) \qquad \blacksquare$$

Lemma 14.3 If $\mathcal{G}$ maps Λ into its interior, then there exist positive constants α and β depending on $\mathcal{G}$ such that

$$\alpha \|v - \mathcal{G}(u)\|^2 \leq \alpha_{u,v} \leq \beta \|v - \mathcal{G}(u)\|^2$$

In the case of the SGA, it suffices that mutation is positive.

Proof Expanding $\log z$ in powers of $1 - 1/z$ leads to the following asymptotic relation as $u \to v$:

$$v \log \frac{v}{u} = v - u + \frac{(v-u)^2}{v} \left(\frac{1}{2} + o(1)\right)$$

Hence

$$\alpha_{u,v} = \left(\frac{1}{2} + o(1)\right) \sum_i \frac{(v_i - \mathcal{G}(u_i))^2}{v_i}$$

Since continuous $\mathcal{G}$ maps compact Λ into its interior, the denominators in the preceding sum are bounded away from zero as $v \to \mathcal{G}(u)$. This proves the result as $v \to \mathcal{G}(u)$. The restriction (that $v \to \mathcal{G}(u)$) is removed by compactness of Λ and the observation that $\alpha_{u,v} = 0 \iff v = \mathcal{G}(u)$. $\blacksquare$

Combining theorem 14.2 and lemma 14.3 yields

Theorem 14.4 Let d be the standard Euclidean distance from $\mathcal{G}(p)$ to U. If $\mathcal{G}$ maps Λ into its interior, then

$$\Pr\{\tau(p) \in U\} = e^{-rO(d^2) + O(\log r)}$$

where the constant in the "big O" depends on n and $\mathcal{G}$.

The following theorem is a general result of probability theory concerning the characteristic function (see appendix) of a multinomial distribution. Let the current population vector p be fixed, and let $q = \mathcal{G}(p)$. Assuming that $\mathcal{G}$ maps into the interior of Λ, define the random vector ζ by the component equations

$$\zeta_j = \frac{\tau(p)_j - q_j}{\sqrt{q_j/r}}$$

Lemma 14.5 Let $\mathcal{E}$ denote expectation. Then

$$\lim_{r \to \infty} \mathcal{E}(e^{\sqrt{-1}\zeta^T t}) = \exp\left(-\frac{1}{2}\left(\sum t_j^2 - \left(\sum t_j \sqrt{q_j}\right)^2\right)\right)$$

The next result relates to approximating the transition probabilities of RHS by a multi-normal distribution.

Theorem 14.6 Let ξ be random vector of dimension $n - 1$ with density

$$\rho(y) = (2\pi)^{-(n-1)/2} e^{-y^T y/2}$$

and let C be an n by $n - 1$ matrix having orthonormal columns perpendicular to the vector $h = \langle \sqrt{q_0}, \dots, \sqrt{q_{n-1}} \rangle$. Then ζ converges in distribution to $C\xi$ as $r \to \infty$.

Proof   It suffices by the continuity theorem (see appendix) to show

$$\lim_{r \to \infty} \mathcal{E}(e^{\sqrt{-1}\zeta^T t}) = \mathcal{E}(e^{\sqrt{-1}(C\xi)^T t})$$

The right hand side is the characteristic function of a multinormal at $C^T t$,

$$\mathcal{E}(e^{\sqrt{-1}\xi^T(C^T t)}) = \exp\left(-\frac{1}{2} t^T C C^T t\right)$$

By lemma 14.5, the left hand side is

$$\exp\left(-\frac{1}{2} t^T (I - h h^T) t\right)$$

Thus it suffices that $CC^T = I - hh^T$. This follows easily by considering how both sides map the basis consisting of h and the columns of C.   ■

Theorem 14.7   For any open subset U of $\mathbf{1}^\perp$,

$$\Pr\{\tau(p) \in \mathcal{G}(p) + U/\sqrt{r}\} = (2\pi)^{-(n-1)/2} \int_{C^T \text{diag}(h)^{-1}U} e^{-y^T y/2}\, dy + o(1)$$

as $r \to \infty$, provided $\mathcal{G}$ maps into the interior of Λ.

Proof   Using theorem 14.6,

$$\Pr\{\tau(p) \in \mathcal{G}(p) + U/\sqrt{r}\}$$

$$= \Pr\{\sqrt{r}(\tau(p) - q) \in U\}$$

$$= \Pr\{\mathrm{diag}(h)\zeta \in U\}$$

$$= \Pr\{\zeta \in \mathrm{diag}(h)^{-1}U\}$$

$$\rightarrow \Pr\{C\xi \in \mathrm{diag}(h)^{-1}U\}$$

$$\leq \Pr\{\xi \in C^T\mathrm{diag}(h)^{-1}U\}$$

$$\leq \Pr\{C\xi \in (I - hh^T)\mathrm{diag}(h)^{-1}U\}$$

$$= \Pr\{C\xi \in \mathrm{diag}(h)^{-1}U\}$$

The last equality follows from the fact that $I - hh^T$ is the identity on $h^\perp$.   ∎

Exercises

1. What is the dependence on n of the constant in the "big O" of theorem 14.2?

2. Provide complete details for lemma 14.3 and theorem 14.6.

3. Replace the "o(1)" in theorem 14.7 with a more precise error term involving n and r.

14.3   Unstable Fixed Points

The next theorem partially justifies the focus in section 14.1 on stable fixed points. Assuming a normal heuristic (an assumption made throughout the rest of the chapter), the proportion of time random heuristic search spends near unstable fixed points vanishes as $r \rightarrow \infty$. Before proceeding, a completion operator will be defined and a few of its properties will be noted.

Let $\mathcal{S}$ be the basin of attraction for a fixed point of $\mathcal{G}$. Define $\mathcal{S}_0 = \mathcal{S}$ and let $\mathcal{S}_{i+1} = \bigcup \mathcal{S}'$ where the union is over all basins of attraction $\mathcal{S}'$ corresponding to fixed points in the closure of $\mathcal{S}_i$. Since it is assumed that there are finitely many fixed points (theorem 12.1), the sequence $\mathcal{S}_0, \mathcal{S}_1, \ldots$ must become stationary. The *completion* of $\mathcal{S}$ is defined to be the limit of this sequence and is denoted by $\overline{\mathcal{S}}$. For $A \subset \mathcal{S}$, $\overline{A}$ is defined as $\overline{\mathcal{S}}$.

Theorem 14.8

- $\overline{\mathcal{S}}$ is closed.

- If $\mathcal{S}$ corresponds to an unstable fixed point, then $\overline{\mathcal{S}}$ contains no stable fixed point.

- If $x \notin \overline{\mathcal{S}}$ then $\{\mathcal{G}^k(x) : k \geq 0\}$ is a positive distance away from $\overline{\mathcal{S}}$.

Proof   If $\overline{S}$ were not closed, let $\overline{S} = S_i$ and let $x_j \in \overline{S}$ be a sequence converging to $x \notin \overline{S}$. Since $\mathcal{G}$ is focused, x is contained in the basin of attraction of a fixed point ω' in the complement of the closure of S_i (otherwise $x \in S_{i+1} = S_i$). Let U be any open neighborhood of ω', and let V be an open neighborhood of x which is mapped into U by $\mathcal{G}^k$ for some k (the orbit of x converges to ω' and $\mathcal{G}$ is continuous). Since S_i is invariant under $\mathcal{G}$ (it is a union of basins of attraction), it follows that $S_i \cap U \neq \emptyset$ (it contains $\mathcal{G}^k(x_j)$ for some j and k). Hence ω' is in the closure of S_i, a contradiction.

Suppose that ω is a stable fixed point and that S corresponds to an unstable fixed point. If S_i is separated from ω by an open set (true for $i = 0$) then the basin of attraction of ω will not be included in the union defining S_{i+1}. Hence S_i is separated from ω by an open set for all i.

Since $\mathcal{G}$ is focused, the set $\{\mathcal{G}^k(x) : k \geq 0\}$ has the unique limit point ω. It follows that $\{\omega\} \cup \{\mathcal{G}^k(x) : k \geq 0\}$ is a closed set disjoint from $\overline{S}$ (otherwise $x \in \overline{S}$). Hence there is a minimum distance between these disjoint compact sets.   ∎

Theorem 14.9   Let $\mathcal{G}$ be normal, and let $\mathcal{T}$ be the stable manifold of the fixed point ω. There exists an open neighborhood U of ω such that $\mathcal{T} \cap U = \overline{\mathcal{T}} \cap U$.

Proof   If not, let $\mathcal{T}$ correspond to the fixed point ω with basin S, let $\overline{\mathcal{T}} = S_i$, and suppose $x \in (\overline{\mathcal{T}} \cap U) \setminus \mathcal{T}$. Let $y_i = x$ and note that, for some $\varepsilon > 0$,

$$\phi(y_i) < \phi(\lim_{k \to \infty} \mathcal{G}^k(y_i)) - \varepsilon$$

where ϕ is a Lyapunov function for $\mathcal{G}$. Since $\mathcal{G}^\infty(y_i)$ is in the closure of S_{i-1}, there exists $y_{i-1} \in S_{i-1}$ such that

$$\phi(y_i) < \phi(y_{i-1}) - \varepsilon$$

Repeating this construction yields

$$\phi(y_{i-1}) < \cdots < \phi(y_0)$$

It follows that $\phi(y_i) < \phi(\omega) - \varepsilon$, which leads to the contradiction $\phi(\omega) < \phi(\omega)$ as U contracts to ω, provided that ε can be bounded from below. A positive lower bound is provided by lemma 12.4 (since $x \notin \mathcal{T}$, the stable manifold theorem indicates that the orbit of x leaves a fixed neighborhood of ω).   ∎

Theorem 14.10   Suppose $\mathcal{G}$ is ergodic and normal with unstable fixed point ω, and let π be the steady state distribution of random heuristic search. Then there exists a neighborhood U of ω such that $\pi(U) \to 0$ as $r \to \infty$.

Proof   Let $\mathcal{H}_s$ be the subspace corresponding to those eigenvalues of $d\mathcal{G}_\omega$ (abbreviated $d\mathcal{G}$) within the unit disk, let $\mathcal{H}_u$ be the subspace corresponding to those eigenvalues outside the unit disk, and let ρ_s and ρ_u be the corresponding projections. Let the respective unit balls of these spaces be $\mathcal{B}_s$ and $\mathcal{B}_u$. By assumption, $d\mathcal{G}$ has no eigenvalues of modulus 1, and is hence a contraction on $\mathcal{H}_s$ with Lipschitz constant $\alpha < 1$ and an expansion on $\mathcal{H}_u$ with constant $\beta > 1$ with respect to suitable Euclidean norms $\|\cdot\|_s$ and $\|\cdot\|_u$ respectively. Given a vector v, the norm which will be used is $\|v\| = (\|\rho_s v\|_s^2 + \|\rho_u v\|_u^2)^{1/2}$. Note that the distance between the disjoint closed sets $\mathcal{H}_s$ and the boundary of $\mathcal{B}_u$ is 1. Let $\varepsilon > 0$ be sufficiently small that the set $\mathcal{L} + \omega$ where

$$\mathcal{L} = \mathcal{L}_u \times \mathcal{L}_s = \varepsilon \mathcal{B}_u \times \frac{\varepsilon}{1 - \alpha} \mathcal{B}_s$$

is well within the "linear region" where the stable manifold $\mathcal{T}$ at ω is well approximated by $\omega + \mathcal{H}_s$ and $\mathcal{G}(\omega + z)$ is well approximated by $\omega + d\mathcal{G}z$ (for notational convenience and to simplify exposition, they will be treated as equal). Since $\mathcal{G}$ is normal, take the linear region to be so small that $\mathcal{T} = \overline{\mathcal{T}}$ within it (theorem 14.9). Define, for $\varepsilon > 0$,

$$S_\varepsilon = \{x : \|x - \omega\| < \varepsilon\}$$

$$\mathcal{T}_\varepsilon = \{x : \|x - \mathcal{T}\| < \varepsilon\}$$

$$\overline{\mathcal{T}}_\varepsilon = \{x : \|x - \overline{\mathcal{T}}\| < \varepsilon\}$$

The proof is based on the idea that if the Markov chain is at a state $x \in S_\varepsilon$ then it will quickly move to the complement of $\overline{\mathcal{T}}$ whereupon it will spend almost all its time (as $r \to \infty$) at some distance v away from ω. Hence $\pi(S_{\min\{v,\varepsilon\}}) \to 0$ as $r \to \infty$, and so $\pi'(\omega) = 0$ (here π' is as in section 13.1).

The transition from $z + \omega$ to $z' + \omega$ (i.e., $\tau(z + \omega) = z' + \omega$) can be viewed as a Bernoulli trial where "success" means:

1. $\|z' - d\mathcal{G}z\| < \gamma$

2. $z' - d\mathcal{G}z$ has a component in the direction of $\rho_u d\mathcal{G}z$.

Transitions satisfying the first condition are called *semisuccessful*. Note that the probability of a semisuccessful transition is at least $1 - \exp(-\gamma^2 r \theta_1)$ for some $\theta_1 > 0$ (by theorem 14.4).

If $z + \omega \in S_\varepsilon$ and a series of semisuccessful transitions take place, then the resulting state $z^* + \omega$ satisfies $\rho_s z^* \in \mathcal{L}_s$ provided the transitions are within the linear region and $\gamma < \varepsilon$. This is a consequence of the observation that $\rho_s(S_\varepsilon - \omega) \subset \mathcal{L}_s$ and the following transition inequality

$$\| \rho_s z' \|$$

$$\leq \| \rho_s d\mathcal{G} z \| + \gamma$$

$$< \alpha \| \rho_s z \| + \varepsilon$$

$$\leq \frac{\varepsilon}{1 - \alpha}$$

which is valid for any z satisfying $\rho_s z \in \mathcal{L}_s$. The probability of $e^{\gamma r \theta_2}$ consecutive semisuccessful transitions is $1 - o(1)$ as $r \to \infty$ since

$$e^{\gamma r \theta_2} \log(1 - e^{-\gamma^2 r \theta_1})$$

$$\geq \frac{e^{\gamma r (\theta_2 - \gamma \theta_1)}}{e^{-\gamma^2 r \theta_1} - 1}$$

$$= o(1)$$

provided that $\theta_2 < \gamma \theta_1$.

The second condition defining a successful transition says that the asymptotically normally distributed random vector (theorem 14.7) whose addition to $d\mathcal{G} z$ produces z' should lie in a particular half space. Since the normal density is invariant under central inversion, the probability of satisfying the second condition is $1/2 + o(1)$. The probability of a subseries of k consecutive successful transitions out of a series of e^k semisuccessful transitions is therefore at least

$$1 - (1 - (2 + o(1))^{-k})^{e^k/k}$$

$$\geq 1 - \exp\left(-e^k (2 + o(1))^{-k}/k\right)$$

$$= 1 - o(1)$$

provided that $k \to \infty$ as $r \to \infty$. Note that if a series of k successful transitions take place, then the resulting state $z^* + \omega$ satisfies $\| \rho_u z^* \| \geq \beta^k \| \rho_u z \|$ since the second condition defining a successful transition guarantees that the expected motion away from ω (the factor of β provided by $d\mathcal{G}$) takes place at each transition.

Let $V = \{ x : \| \rho_u x \| \leq 1 + \| d\mathcal{G} \| \}$. Using the normal approximation (theorem 14.7) yields

$$\lim_{r \to \infty} \Pr\{ \tau(\xi) \in \mathcal{G}(\xi) + r^{-1} V \} = 0$$

If $\xi \in S_\varepsilon \cap \mathcal{T}_{1/r}$ then, since ω is a fixed point of $\mathcal{G}$, choosing ε sufficiently small guarantees that $\mathcal{G}(\xi)$ is well within the "linear region", and hence, by using the normal approximation once more, $\tau(\xi)$ is well within the linear region with probability $1 - o(1)$ as $r \to \infty$. Thus it is permissible to regard $\mathcal{T}_{1/r} - \omega$ as $(\mathcal{H}_s)_{1/r}$ in the calculation below (the difference between the sets is only relevant outside the linear region and the impact on the probability in question is $o(1)$).

$$\Pr\{\tau(\xi) \in \mathcal{T}_{1/r}\}$$

$$= \Pr\{\tau(\xi) \in \mathcal{G}(\xi) + (\mathcal{T}_{1/r} - \omega) - d\mathcal{G}(\xi - \omega)\}$$

$$\leq \Pr\{\tau(\xi) \in \mathcal{G}(\xi) + \{x : \|\rho_u x\| \leq (1 + \|d\mathcal{G}\|)/r\}\}$$

$$= \Pr\{\tau(\xi) \in \mathcal{G}(\xi) + r^{-1}V\}$$

Hence if $z + \omega \in S_\varepsilon$ then with probability $1 - o(1)$ either $\|\rho_u z\| \geq 1/r$ or $\|\rho_u z'\| \geq 1/r$. Therefore a series of at most $k = \theta_3 \log r$ successful transitions beginning from a point $z + \omega \in S_\varepsilon$ will, with probability $1 - o(1)$ produce a state $z^* + \omega$ satisfying

$$\|\rho_u z^*\|$$

$$\geq \frac{\beta^{\theta_3 \log r}}{r}$$

$$= \exp(\theta_3 \log r \log \beta - \log r)$$

$$> \varepsilon$$

for some $\theta_3 > 0$. In other words, z^* is at least ε away from $\mathcal{H}_s$. Taking $z^* + \omega$ to be the first such state encountered puts the transitions within the linear region and so $\rho_s z^* \in \mathcal{L}_s$. Hence $z^* + \omega \notin \mathcal{T}_\varepsilon$.

To summarize: if $z + \omega \in S_\varepsilon$ then with probability $1 - o(1)$ the next $e^{\gamma r \theta_2}$ transitions are semisuccessful, and a state $z^* + \omega$ in the complement of $\overline{\mathcal{T}}_\varepsilon$ is encountered in fewer than r^{θ_3} transitions (provided θ_2 is sufficiently small and θ_3 is sufficiently large). Next γ will be chosen making it impossible for semisuccessful transitions from $z^* + \omega$ to enter $\overline{\mathcal{T}}_\nu$ (for some $\nu > 0$). This implies that with probability $1 - o(1)$ the proportion of time the Markov chain can spend in $S_{\min\{\nu,\varepsilon\}}$ is $o(1)$.

Since the set of fixed points in the complement of $\overline{\mathcal{T}}$ is closed, let U be a closed neighborhood which separates it from $\overline{\mathcal{T}}$. For $k \geq 0$, define the sets

$$E^k = \{x : k \geq 0 \text{ is minimal such that } j \geq k \Rightarrow \mathcal{G}^j(x) \in U\}$$

It is easily verified that $\mathcal{G}(E^{k+1}) \subset E^k$ and that the sets

$$C^k = \bigcup_{j \leq k} E^j$$

are compact and satisfy $\mathcal{G}(C^{k+1}) \subset C^k$. Define sets F^k inductively as follows. For $x \in C^0$, let O_x^0 be a closed neighborhood separating x from $\overline{\mathcal{T}}$. Since C^0 is compact, let F_0 be the union of a finite subcover of the O_x^0 (their interiors form an open cover of C^0). For $x \in C^j$, let O_x^j be a closed neighborhood separating x from $\overline{\mathcal{T}}$ such that $\mathcal{G}(O_x^j)$ is contained in the interior of some O_y^{j-1} belonging to the finite subcover of C^{j-1}. Since C^j is compact, let F_j be the union of a finite subcover (of the O_x^j). By construction,

- the F^k are closed sets in the complement of $\overline{\mathcal{T}}$
- $\mathcal{G}(F^{k+1})$ is contained in the interior of F^k
- the interiors of the F^k cover the complement of $\overline{\mathcal{T}}$

Because $\mathcal{G}$ is continuous, $\mathcal{G}(F^0)$ is compact and disjoint from $\overline{\mathcal{T}}$ (recall that orbits of points not in $\overline{\mathcal{T}}$ are disjoint from $\overline{\mathcal{T}}$). Therefore let ε be sufficiently small (smaller than chosen before) that $\mathcal{G}(F^0)$ is contained in the complement of $\overline{\mathcal{T}}_{2\varepsilon}$. Since the complement of $\overline{\mathcal{T}}_\varepsilon$ is compact, let the interiors of $F^0, F^1, \ldots, F^K$ be a finite cover. Let ν be the distance from the closure of this cover to $\overline{\mathcal{T}}$. Note that the complement of the interior of F^k is disjoint from $\mathcal{G}(F^{k+1})$, hence let δ_k be the distance between them. Choose positive γ less than the minimum of $\varepsilon, \delta_0, \delta_1, \ldots \delta_{K-1}$. To summarize:

- if x is in the complement of $\overline{\mathcal{T}}_\varepsilon$, then $x \in F^k$ for some $k \le K$
- if $x \in F^k$ for some $k \le K$, then x is in the complement of $\overline{\mathcal{T}}_\nu$
- $\mathcal{G}(F^0)$ is contained in $F^0 \cup \cdots \cup F^K$ at a distance of at least γ from its complement.
- $\mathcal{G}(F^{k+1})$ is contained in F^k at a distance of at least γ from its complement.

It follows that a series of semisuccessful transitions (under τ) from within the cover $F^0, F^1, \ldots, F^K$ cannot escape it, and must therefore remain a distance of ν from $\overline{\mathcal{T}}$. ∎

The following theorem puts the result of theorem 14.10 in a form which will be useful. Recall that the ω_k are the stable fixed points of $\mathcal{G}$.

Lemma 14.11 Under the same hypotheses as theorem 14.10, there exists a function $\varepsilon = o(1)$ such that

$$\pi\left(\bigcup_k \mathcal{B}_\varepsilon(\omega_k)\right) = 1 - o(1)$$

as $r \to \infty$. Moreover, ε may be chosen to converge to 0 (as $r \to \infty$) arbitrarily slowly.

Proof Let $\lambda > 0$. Because the time spent away from stable fixed points vanishes (theorem 14.10 and exercise 2 of section 13.1), there exists n_λ such that if $r \ge n_\lambda$ then

$$\pi\left(\bigcup_k \mathcal{B}_\lambda(\omega_k)\right) > 1 - \lambda$$

Now let λ decrease to 0 and take ε to decrease no faster than would the step function defined by $\varepsilon(n_\lambda) = \lambda$.   ∎

Exercises

1. Compare the completion of a basin of attraction with the sets C_j in lemma 12.6.

2. Show how to use lemma 12.4 to obtain the requisite lower bound needed in theorem 14.9.

3. Verify, as claimed in the proof of theorem 14.10, that $\mathcal{G}(E^{k+1}) \subset E^k$ and that the sets

$$C^k = \bigcup_{j \le k} E^j$$

are compact and satisfy $\mathcal{G}(C^{k+1}) \subset C^k$.

4. In theorem 14.10, the "little o" term in

$$\mathcal{G}(x + \omega) = \omega + d\mathcal{G}_\omega x + o(x)$$

was completely ignored. Show that was justified by giving a more detailed proof including it.

14.4   Asymptotic Approximation

This section presents the main result of the chapter; the approximation, as $r \to \infty$, of normal ergodic RHS by a Markov chain over the fixed points of the heuristic. It is assumed throughout that $\mathcal{G}$ maps Λ into its interior.

The following lemmas will be useful.

Lemma 14.12   Let ρ be a length k path which is constrained to lie a distance of at least $\varepsilon > 0$ away from $\mathfrak{I}$. If $\mathcal{G}$ is focused, then there exist positive constants ν and δ (depending on ε) such that for all $k > 0$

$$|\rho| \ge \left\lfloor \frac{k}{\nu} \right\rfloor \delta$$

Proof   For $\xi \in \Lambda$ let n_ξ be such that $\mathcal{G}^{n_\xi}(\xi)$ is within ε of a fixed point. By continuity, let N_ξ be a neighborhood of ξ such that $\mathcal{G}^{n_\xi}(N_\xi)$ is also within ε of the fixed point. For parameter $\nu > 0$ define the sequence of sets

$$V_0 = \nu(N_\xi - \xi) + \xi$$

$$V_{j+1} = \mathcal{B}_\nu(\mathcal{G}(V_j))$$

Now choose $\nu = \nu_\xi$ sufficiently small such that for all $0 \le i \le n_\xi$

$$V_i \subset \mathcal{G}^i(N_\xi)$$

It follows that if a path ρ of length n_ξ beginning from V_0 does not have a step x_{i-1} to x_i for which $\|x_i - \mathcal{G}(x_{i-1})\| > \nu_\xi$ then ρ cannot stay ε away from $\Im$. On the other hand, if ρ does contain such a step, then $|\rho| > \theta \nu_\xi^2$ for some $\theta > 0$ (lemma 14.3).

The existence of a finite subcover of the V_0 (by compactness of Λ) implies the existence of ν (the maximum of n_ξ) and δ (the minimum of $\theta \nu_\xi^2$) such that every path of length ν maintaining a distance of ε away from $\Im$ has a cost of at least δ. ∎

Lemma 14.13 Let ω and ω' be distinct fixed points of $\mathcal{G}$ (not necessarily stable), and suppose positive ε is $o(1)$ as $r \to \infty$. Then there exists a path ρ' of length K from ω to ω' such that

1. $K \to \infty$ as $r \to \infty$ (ρ' depends on r).
2. The interior points of ρ' come from X_n^r and are at least ε away from $\Im$.
3. $|\rho'| = \rho_{\omega,\omega'} + o(1)$.

Moreover, K may be chosen to diverge arbitrarily slowly.

Proof Let ρ_j be a sequence of paths from ω to ω' such that

$$\lim_{j \to \infty} |\rho_j| = \rho_{\omega,\omega'}$$

Without loss of generality, the length of ρ_j diverges since it can be made longer at an arbitrarily small cost: to increase the length of $\omega, x_1, \ldots, \omega'$ modify it to $\omega, z, x_1, \ldots, \omega'$. The cost of the modified path is

$$\alpha_{\omega,z} + \alpha_{z,x_1} + \alpha_{x_1,x_2} + \cdots \to 0 + \alpha_{\omega,x_1} + \alpha_{x_1,x_2} + \cdots$$

as $z \to \omega$. In particular, it may be assumed that ρ_j has length at least j. Also, by perturbing the interior points of ρ_j as necessary, it may be assumed that no interior point is a fixed point.

As $r \to \infty$, the set X_n^r becomes dense in Λ (theorem 3.1) and the interior points of ρ_j become at least ε away from $\Im$ (since $\varepsilon = o(1)$). Thus if r is sufficiently large, ρ_j can be approximated arbitrarily closely by a path ρ' of the required type such that

$$|\rho'| < |\rho_j| + 1/j$$

Moreover, r may be arbitrarily large with respect to j.   ∎

Theorem 14.14   Suppose $\mathcal{G}$ is ergodic and normal. As $r \to \infty$, the probability measure corresponding to the steady state distribution of random heuristic search converges to point mass at the fixed point corresponding to the minimum cost tributary (provided it exists) of the fixed point graph.

Proof   Consider the auxiliary Markov chain having as "states" the neighborhoods $\mathcal{B}_\varepsilon(\omega_k)$ together with $\mathcal{B}_\varepsilon(\omega_l')$ where the ω_l' are unstable fixed points. Since ε will eventually be chosen according to lemma 14.11, a state is an open ball of radius $o(1)$ as $r \to \infty$. Let S_i be the general name for the ith such state, and to streamline notation, let ω_j denote a general fixed point (possibly unstable). According to lemma 14.11, the time spent away from these states vanishes as $r \to \infty$, and hence the steady state behavior of RHS converges to the steady state behavior of this auxiliary chain, provided that its transition probabilities can be appropriately defined. The auxiliary chain is obtained sequentially in two steps:

1. Aggregate the points (states) of RHS belonging to the sets S_i while leaving all other points alone.

2. Restrict to the subchain over the states S_i.

To streamline notation, the transition probability from state S_i to state S_j is denoted by $A_{i,j}$ and ρ_{ω_i,ω_j} is abbreviated by $\rho_{i,j}$. In accordance with the aggregation and restriction theorems for Markov chains (see appendix), the transition probability $A_{i,j}$ of the auxiliary chain is defined as

$$A_{i,j}$$

$$= \frac{1}{\pi(S_i)} \sum_{x \in S_i} \pi_x \sum_{y \in S_j} Q_{x,y}$$

$$+ \sum_{z_1}^* \frac{1}{\pi(S_i)} \sum_{x \in S_i} \pi_x Q_{x,z_1} \sum_{y \in S_j} Q_{z_1,y}$$

$$+ \sum_{z_1,z_2}^* \frac{1}{\pi(S_i)} \sum_{x \in S_i} \pi_x Q_{x,z_1} Q_{z_1,z_2} \sum_{y \in S_j} Q_{z_2,y}$$

$$+ \ldots$$

where $\sum^*$ denotes summation over the complement of the union of the S_i, and π is the steady state distribution of RHS. By theorem 14.2 the first term is

$$\sum_{y \in S_j} \frac{1}{\pi(S_i)} \sum_{x \in S_i} \pi_x e^{-r(\alpha_{\omega_i,\omega_j}+\alpha_{x,y}-\alpha_{\omega_i,\omega_j}+O(r^{-1}\log r))}$$

$$= \sum_{y \in S_j} e^{-r\alpha_{\omega_i,\omega_j}} \frac{1}{\pi(S_i)} \sum_{x \in S_i} \pi_x e^{-ro(1)}$$

$$= \sum_{y \in S_j} e^{-r(\alpha_{\omega_i,\omega_j}+o(1))}$$

since $S_i \to \{\omega_i\}$ and $S_j \to \{\omega_j\}$ and therefore $\alpha_{x,y} \to \alpha_{\omega_i,\omega_j}$. Similarly, the kth term $(k > 1)$ is

$$\sum_{y \in S_j} t_k \quad \text{where} \quad t_k = \sum_{z_1,\ldots,z_{k-1}}^* e^{-r(\alpha_{\omega_i,z_1}+\cdots+\alpha_{z_{k-1},\omega_j}+o(1))+O(k\log r)}$$

The expression above is also valid for the first term $(k = 1)$ if t_1 is interpreted as $e^{-r(\alpha_{\omega_i,\omega_j}+o(1))}$. Note that each t_k corresponds to a sum over length k paths from ω_i to ω_j. The paths of t_k are constrained to follow along states of RHS—there are r^θ states (here θ is used to represent a positive function of r for which both θ and θ^{-1} are bounded)—and to avoid states of the auxiliary chain (i.e their interior points must be at least ε from $\Im$). According to lemma 14.13, a minimal cost path ρ_K of t_K has cost $\rho_{i,j} + o(1)$ as $K, r \to \infty$. Next define c by

$$\sum_{k>K} t_k = c \sum_{k \leq K} t_k \quad \text{so that} \quad \sum_k t_k = (1+c) \sum_{k \leq K} t_k$$

Since there are at most $r^{k\theta}$ paths of length k, it follows that

$$e^{-r(\rho_{i,j}+o(1))+O(K\log r)}$$

$$\leq \sum_k t_k$$

$$\leq (1+c) \sum_{k \leq K} r^{k\theta} e^{-r(\rho_{i,j}+o(1))+O(k\log r)}$$

$$\leq e^{-r(\rho_{i,j}+o(1))+\log(1+c)+O(K\log r)}$$

Therefore,

$$\sum_k t_k = e^{-r(\rho_{i,j}+o(1))}$$

provided that $\log(1+c) = o(r)$ and $K \to \infty$ at a rate $o(r/\log r)$. This yields

$$A_{i,j}$$

$$= \sum_k \sum_{y \in S_j} t_k$$

$$= \sum_{y \in S_j} e^{-r(\rho_{i,j}+o(1))}$$

$$= e^{-r(\rho_{i,j}+o(1))}$$

since the number of states in RHS is $r^\theta = e^{o(r)}$. Next $\log(1+c) = o(r)$ will be established. Let ρ_k be a minimal cost path of t_k. By choosing $K' > K = O(\log r)$, which is justified since K diverges arbitrarily slowly,

$$c$$

$$= \sum_{k>K} t_k \Big/ \sum_{k \le K} t_k$$

$$\le e^{r(\rho_{i,j}+o(1))} \sum_{k>K} r^{k\theta} e^{-r(|\rho_k|+o(1))+O(k \log r)}$$

$$\le e^{r(\rho_{i,j}+o(1))} \Big(\sum_{k \le K'} e^{-r(\rho_{i,j}+o(1))+O(k \log r)} + \sum_{k>K'} e^{-r(|\rho_k|+o(1))+O(k \log r)} \Big)$$

Estimating the first sum in the second factor as before and applying lemma 14.12 to the second sum produces

$$\le e^{r(\rho_{i,j}+o(1))} \Big(e^{-r(\rho_{i,j}+o(1))+O(K' \log r)} + \sum_{k>K'} e^{-r(k\nu^{-1}-1)\delta+o(r)+O(k \log r)} \Big)$$

$$\le e^{o(r)+O(K' \log r)} + e^{r(\rho_{i,j}+o(1))} \sum_{k>K'} e^{-r(k\nu^{-1}-1)\delta+k\theta \log r}$$

for some θ (perhaps differing from previous use of θ). Choosing $K' = o(r/\log r)$ and bounding the second sum with an integral yields

$$\le e^{o(r)} + e^{r(\rho_{i,j}+\delta+o(1))} \int_{K'}^{\infty} e^{k(\theta \log r - r\nu^{-1}\delta)} \, dk$$

$$\le e^{o(r)} + e^{r(\rho_{i,j}+\delta+o(1))+K'(\theta \log r - r\nu^{-1}\delta)}/(r\nu^{-1}\delta - \theta \log r)$$

provided $r\nu^{-1}\delta > \theta \log r$. Since δ and ν depend on ε, which is varying arbitrarily slowly with respect to r, without loss of generality $r\nu^{-1}\delta > r/\log r$. Thus, for large r, the following bound is obtained

$$c \le e^{o(r)}(1 + e^{r(\rho_{i,j}+\delta-K'/\log r)})$$

Choosing $K' = \sqrt{r}$ gives $c = e^{o(r)}$ as required.

According to the restriction and aggregation theorems for Markov chains (see appendix), the steady state distribution π' of the auxiliary chain satisfies

$$\pi'(S_j) = \frac{\pi(S_j)}{\pi(\bigcup_j S_j)}$$

Applying lemma 14.11 shows $\pi(S_j) = \pi'(S_j) + o(1)$ as $r \to \infty$. Therefore, the auxiliary chain correctly captures the asymptotic behavior of random heuristic search as $r \to \infty$. Moreover, it has been established that the auxiliary chain has transition matrix satisfying

$$A_{i,j} = e^{-r(\rho_{i,j}+o(1))}$$

It follows that the auxiliary chain is identical to the Markov chain $\mathcal{C}_r$, with the exception that it contains states corresponding to unstable fixed points while $\mathcal{C}_r$ does not. The final step in the proof is to show that the steady state distribution of the auxiliary chain converges to the steady state distribution of $\mathcal{C}_r$. This is accomplished via theorem 14.1 by showing that the inclusion of states corresponding to unstable fixed points can not effect where the minimal cost tributary is rooted.

Let t be a minimal cost tributary of the auxiliary chain, and to simplify exposition, nodes (of t) corresponding to stable/unstable fixed points will be referred to as stable/unstable nodes. Also, node S_i will be called "adjacent" to S_j if ω_i is in the closure of the basin of attraction of ω_j.

First consider the case where an unstable interior node x of t does not contain in its subtree every stable node to which it is adjacent. Let the children of x be $y_0, \ldots, y_k$, and let z be a node x is adjacent to which is not in the subtree rooted at x. Modifying t by removing the subtrees rooted at y_i and reattaching them as children of z effects the cost of the tree by at most $o(r)$. Removing x and reattaching it as a child of z has similar cost. The resulting tree has one fewer unstable interior node; x is now a leaf and is adjacent to its parent.

In the case where x contains in its subtree every stable node to which it is adjacent, let z and y_i be as before, except that z is located in the subtree rooted at y_0. Modifying t by removing the subtrees rooted at y_i, for $i > 0$, and reattaching them as children of z effects the cost of the tree by at most $o(r)$. Next remove the subtree rooted at y_0 and reattach it as a child of the parent of x and then remove x and reattach it as a child of z. The resulting tree has one fewer unstable interior node; x is now a leaf and is adjacent to its parent. As before, this is accomplished at a cost of $o(r)$.

The two operations described above may be repeated to transform t into a tree t' which, ignoring $o(r)$ terms, has identical cost. Moreover, t' has all unstable nodes as leaves adjacent to their stable parent nodes. Hence by removing all unstable leaves from t', a tree t'' is obtained which corresponds to $\mathcal{C}_r$ and which, neglecting $o(r)$ terms, has cost identical to t.

Conversely, if t'' is a minimal cost tributary corresponding to $\mathcal{C}_r$, then by adjoining unstable nodes as leaves adjacent to their parents, a tree t corresponding to the auxiliary chain is obtained which, neglecting $o(r)$ terms, has identical cost to t''.

Since, as $r \to \infty$, the $o(r)$ terms have no influence, it follows that the states corresponding to unstable fixed points (i.e., the difference between the auxiliary chain and $\mathcal{C}_r$) can not effect where the minimal cost tributary is rooted.   ■

Exercises

1. Theorem 14.14 was proved by using an auxiliary chain which contains unstable fixed points. Why were they included?

2. The Markov chain $\mathcal{C}_r$ does not include unstable fixed points. Why were they omitted?

3. Theorem 14.14 concerns the approximation, as $r \to \infty$, of the steady state distribution. How, more generally, does C_r approximate normal ergodic RHS in the large population case?

15 Hyperbolicity

As seen in the previous chapters, an important property is hyperbolicity. This chapter is devoted to showing that the set of fitness functions for which $\mathcal{G}$ is hyperbolic forms a dense open subset of the positive orthant when mutation is positive and the selection scheme is proportional. The original proof of hyperbolicity was first obtained jointly with Mary Eberlein. The proof presented in this chapter employs observations which allow a simplified account.

15.1 Polynomials

The key to the hyperbolicity result is being able to express the relevant concepts in the language of polynomials. For convenience, the function $\mathcal{G} = \mathcal{M} \circ \mathcal{F}$ is replaced with $\mathcal{G}' = F\mathcal{M}$, where $F = \mathrm{diag}(f)$. Note that $\mathcal{G}'(x)$ is polynomial in x, and, as the following theorem shows, contains the relevant information (see the exercises of section 16.2 for the correspondence between fixed points of $\mathcal{G}$ and $\mathcal{G}'$).

Throughout this chapter the notation x^{-1} for vector x denotes the vector with ith component $1/x_i$.

Lemma 15.1 Let x be a fixed point of $\mathcal{G}$ and let $y = \mathcal{F}(x)/f^T x$ be the corresponding fixed point of $\mathcal{G}'$. Then

$$\mathrm{spec}(d\mathcal{G}_x) = \mathrm{spec}(d\mathcal{G}'_y(I - y\mathbf{1}^T/\mathbf{1}^T y)) = \mathrm{spec}(d\mathcal{G}'_y) \setminus \{2\} \cup \{0\}$$

Proof Since $\mathcal{G} = F^{-1} \circ \mathcal{G}' \circ \mathcal{F}$, the chain rule yields (see section 7.1 for $d\mathcal{F}$)

$$dG_x$$

$$= F^{-1} d\mathcal{G}'_{\mathcal{F}(x)} \left(\frac{F}{f^T x} - \frac{f \cdot x}{(f^T x)^2} \mathbf{1}^T F \right)$$

$$= F^{-1} d\mathcal{G}'_y \left(F - \frac{f \cdot x}{f^T x} \mathbf{1}^T F \right)$$

$$= F^{-1} d\mathcal{G}'_y \left(I - \frac{y}{\mathbf{1}^T y} \mathbf{1}^T \right) F$$

The second equality above is justified by the linearity of $d\mathcal{G}'_x$ in x (which follows from that of $d\mathcal{M}_x$; see theorem 6.13). Therefore,

$$\mathrm{spec}(d\mathcal{G}_x) = \mathrm{spec}(d\mathcal{G}'_y(I - \frac{y}{\mathbf{1}^T y} \mathbf{1}^T))$$

Let $P = I - y\mathbf{1}^T / \mathbf{1}^T y$. It is easily verified that $Py = 0$ and P^T is the identity on $y^\perp$. Moreover (via theorem 6.16),

$$d\mathcal{G}'_y y$$

$$= F d\mathcal{M}_y y$$

$$= 2F\mathcal{M}(y) = 2\mathcal{G}'(y)$$

$$= 2y$$

Thus 2 is an eigenvalue of $d\mathcal{G}'_y$ with corresponding eigenvector y, and hence $y^\perp$ is invariant under $d\mathcal{G}'_y{}^T$. It follows that

$$P^T d\mathcal{G}'_y{}^T \bigg|_{y^\perp} = d\mathcal{G}'_y{}^T \bigg|_{y^\perp}$$

Applying theorem 6.12,

$$\mathrm{spec}(d\mathcal{G}'_y P)$$

$$= \mathrm{spec}(P^T d\mathcal{G}'_y{}^T \bigg|_{y^\perp}) \cup \{0\}$$

$$= \mathrm{spec}(d\mathcal{G}'_y{}^T \bigg|_{y^\perp}) \cup \{0\}$$

$$= \mathrm{spec}(d\mathcal{G}'_y) \setminus \{2\} \cup \{0\} \qquad\qquad \blacksquare$$

Next consider the rational function q, defined, except at zero, for y in the nonnegative orthant by

$$q(f, y) = \prod_{i,j} (\lambda_i \lambda_j - 1)$$

where the λ's are the eigenvalues of $d\mathcal{G}'_y(I - y\mathbf{1}^T / \mathbf{1}^T y)$ and where f represents the fitness function (recall that a fitness function is identified with a vector through the correspondence $f(i) = f_i$). Since q is symmetric in the roots of the characteristic polynomial, the symmetric function theorem implies that it is a polynomial in the coefficients of that polynomial, i.e., in the entries of $d\mathcal{G}'_y(I - y\mathbf{1}^T / \mathbf{1}^T y)$ which are polynomials in f and $y / \mathbf{1}^T y$.

To make explicit the dependence of $\mathcal{G}'$ on f, it may be written as $\mathcal{G}'_f$ (similarly, $\mathcal{G}$ may be written as $\mathcal{G}_f$). If $y = \mathcal{G}'_f(y)$ corresponds to a nonhyperbolic fixed point x of $\mathcal{G}_f$, then some λ_i in the definition of q has modulus 1 (by theorem 15.1). Thus the i, j factor is zero when λ_j is the conjugate of λ_i. It follows that if $q(f, y)$ is defined and nonzero, and if $\mathcal{G}'_f(y) = y$, then y corresponds to a hyperbolic fixed point x of $\mathcal{G}_f$.

The strategy is to show that the set of fitness vectors

$$U = \{f : \exists y \,.\, \mathcal{G}'_f(y) = y \wedge q(f, y) = 0\}$$

is nowhere dense (in the positive orthant). This would establish the desired result since the complement of the closure of this set is dense and open (in the positive orthant), and for any fitness function f in this complement, $\forall y \,.\, \mathcal{G}'_f(y) = y \Longrightarrow q(f, y) \neq 0$ (i.e., every fixed point x of $\mathcal{G}_f$ is hyperbolic), where the quantification is over y in the domain of q.

The next step is to exploit the dependence on f. Because the selection scheme is proportional, f belongs to the interior of the nonnegative orthant and f^{-1} is therefore well defined. Define φ on the nonnegative orthant, except at zero, by

$$\varphi(x) = \mathrm{diag}(x)/\mathcal{M}(x)$$

Since mutation is assumed positive, $\mathcal{M}$ maps this domain into its interior, and $\varphi(x)$ is continuous. Let the common domain of q and φ (i.e., the nonnegative orthant with zero removed) be referred to as D, and note that on this domain,

$$F\mathcal{M}(x) = x$$

$$\Longleftrightarrow \mathcal{M}(x) = F^{-1}x$$

$$\Longleftrightarrow \mathcal{M}(x) = \mathrm{diag}(x)f^{-1}$$

$$\Longleftrightarrow \mathrm{diag}(x)^{-1}\mathcal{M}(x) = f^{-1}$$

$$\Longleftrightarrow \varphi(x) = f$$

Therefore x is a nontrivial fixed point of $\mathcal{G}'_f$ in the nonnegative orthant if and only if $\varphi(x) = f$. Let $h(y) = q(\varphi(y), y)$. It follows that the defining condition of U is

$$\exists y \,.\, \varphi(y) = f \wedge q(f, y) = 0$$

$$\Longleftrightarrow \exists y \,.\, \varphi(y) = f \wedge h(y) = 0$$

$$\Longleftrightarrow f \in \varphi(h^{-1}(0))$$

Since h is continuous on D, $h^{-1}(0)$ is closed in D. Moreover, the next lemma shows that the closure of $\varphi(h^{-1}(0))$ is contained in $\varphi(h^{-1}(0)) \cup \{0\}$. Therefore, $\varphi(h^{-1}(0))$ is nowhere dense provided it has measure zero. But a rational function preserves zero measure (see exercise 1), so $\varphi(h^{-1}(0))$ is nowhere dense provided $h^{-1}(0)$ has measure zero.

Lemma 15.2   The closure of $\varphi(h^{-1}(0))$ is contained in $\varphi(h^{-1}(0)) \cup \{0\}$.

Proof   Let $x_i \in \varphi(h^{-1}(0))$ be such that the sequence $x_0, x_1, \ldots$ converges to x, and choose $y_i \in h^{-1}(0)$ such that $\varphi(y_i) = x_i$.

Consider first the case where the sequence $y_0, y_i, \ldots$ is unbounded. Note that φ is homogeneous of degree -1 and maps D into itself. Thus its action on the nonnegative orthant is determined by its action on Λ. Since Λ is compact, its image is compact. In particular, the set

$$\varphi(\{y_i/\mathbf{1}^T y_i : i \geq 0\}) = \{\mathbf{1}^T y_i x_i : i \geq 0\}$$

is bounded. It follows, using the unboundedness of the y_i, that $x_i \to 0$.

The remaining case is that the y_i are bounded, and relies on the observation that the y_i are bounded away from 0 (otherwise, a subsequence converges to 0, which, by the homogeneity of φ, implies their images are unbounded, contradicting that $x_0, x_i, \ldots$ converges to x). Let $C \subset h^{-1}(0)$ be a compact subset of D which contains the y_i (recall that $h^{-1}(0)$ is closed in D). Since $\varphi(C)$ is compact, it contains the closure of $\{x_i : i \geq 0\}$. In particular, $x \in \varphi(h^{-1}(0))$.   ■

Theorem 15.3   The set of fitness functions for which $\mathcal{G}$ is hyperbolic forms a dense open subset of the positive orthant when mutation is positive and the selection scheme is proportional.

Proof   By what has already been established, it suffices to show $h^{-1}(0)$ has measure zero. Note that h is a rational function in y; say $h(y) = a(y)/b(y)$. Thus $h^{-1}(0) = a^{-1}(0)$. Since a is polynomial, it is either identically zero or else is zero only on a set of measure zero. The proof is therefore completed by showing that $h(\mathbf{1}) \neq 0$.

Since $\varphi(\mathbf{1}) = \mathbf{1}/n$, it follows from theorem 15.1 that $h(\mathbf{1})$ is

$$\prod_{i,j}(\lambda_i \lambda_j - 1)$$

where the λ are the eigenvalues of $d\mathcal{G}'_{\mathbf{1}} = n^{-1}d\mathcal{M}_{\mathbf{1}}$, except that the eigenvalue 2 is replaced with 0. By theorems 6.7 and 6.13, this spectrum is contained in the unit disk. Therefore,

$$|\lambda_i \lambda_j| = |\lambda_i| \cdot |\lambda_j| < 1$$

for all i, j and $h(\mathbf{1})$ cannot be zero.   ■

Exercises

1. Let $f : U \longrightarrow \mathfrak{R}^n$ be continuously differentiable, where U is an open subset of $\mathfrak{R}^n$. Prove that if $C \subset U$ has Lebesgue measure zero, then so does its image $f(C)$. *Hint:* Since U is a countable union of compact sets, it suffices to consider the case where f is continuously differentiable on an open set O containing the compact closure $\overline{U}$ of U. Use the fact that $\|df_x\|$ is bounded for $x \in \overline{U}$, and thus f can increase the volume of a cover of U by at most some constant factor.

2. This chapter focused attention on fixed points in Λ. What about the proof would not permit the consideration of arbitrary complex fixed points of $\mathcal{G}$?

3. Establish the hyperbolicity result for arbitrary complex fixed points of $\mathcal{G}$.

4. Show the results of this chapter carry over to the general cardinality case.

16 Geometric Invariance

This chapter collects a few invariance results related to the simple genetic algorithm.

The first section presents some simple invariants, briefly touching upon how invariants can relate to the commutativity of diagrams, and foreshadows the role played by schemata with respect to mixing. The second section is devoted to an invariant surface for $\mathcal{G}$ corresponding to the case where proportional selection is used. Although its place in the general scheme of things is unclear, the result is included here because it is interesting and it seems at the present time to fit more naturally in this chapter than in any other.

16.1 Elementary Invariance

Theorem 11.3 is an example of an invariance result: if fitness is linear and mutation is zero, then $\phi(\mathcal{M}(x)) = \phi(x)$ where $\phi(x)$ is average population fitness. The following is a more basic theorem, expressing the fact that crossover cannot create or destroy bits, it only rearranges them.

Theorem 16.1   If mutation is zero, then $\widehat{e_{2^j}}^T \mathcal{M}(x) = \widehat{e_{2^j}}^T x$ for all j.

Proof   Making use of lemma 11.1,

$$\sqrt{n} e_{2^j}^T W \mathcal{M}(x)$$

$$= \sum_i (-1)^{i^T 2^j} \sum_{u,v} x_u x_v M_{i \oplus u, i \oplus v}$$

$$= \sum_{u,v} x_u x_v (-1)^{u^T 2^j} [u^T 2^j = v^T 2^j]$$

$$= \frac{1}{2} \sum_{u,v} x_u x_v (-1)^{u^T 2^j} (1 + (-1)^{v^T 2^j + u^T 2^j})$$

$$= \frac{1}{2} \sum_{u,v} x_u x_v (-1)^{u^T 2^j} + \frac{1}{2} \sum_{u,v} x_u x_v (-1)^{v^T 2^j}$$

$$= \sqrt{n} e_{2^j}^T W x \qquad\blacksquare$$

The interpretation given in the preceding paragraph (that crossover cannot create or destroy bits, it only rearranges them) may be understood as follows. The proportion of population x having a 1 in the kth bit position is

$$\sum_i i^T 2^k x_i$$

$$= \frac{1}{2} \sum_i (1 - (-1)^{i^T 2^k}) x_i$$

$$= \frac{1}{2} (1 - \sum_i (-1)^{i^T 2^k} x_i)$$

$$= \frac{1}{2} (1 - \sqrt{n}(e_{2^k}^T W)x)$$

$$= \frac{1}{2} (1 - \sqrt{n}\widehat{e_{2^k}}^T x)$$

By theorem 16.1, x may be replaced with $\mathcal{M}(x)$ in the last expression. Therefore the proportion of 1s in each bit position is preserved by $\mathcal{M}$.

The next theorem does not require zero mutation, it applies in particular to mutation alone (by choosing zero crossover). Both theorems 16.1 and 16.2 can be viewed as statements concerning the Walsh basis.

Theorem 16.2   For all k, both $\mathcal{L}\{\widehat{e_j} : j \in \Omega_k\}$ and $\mathcal{L}\{\widehat{e_j} : j \notin \Omega_k\}$ are invariant under $\mathcal{M}$.

Proof   Consider the second space first. Let $x = \sum \alpha_i \widehat{e_i}$ be an element of $\mathcal{L}\{\widehat{e_j} : j \notin \Omega_k\}$; thus $u \in \Omega_k \Longrightarrow \alpha_u = 0$. By theorem 6.16 and theorem 6.15,

$$\widehat{e_j}^T \mathcal{M}(x)$$

$$= \frac{1}{2} \widehat{e_j}^T d\mathcal{M}_x x$$

$$= \sqrt{n} \sum_{u,v} \alpha_u \alpha_v \hat{M}_{u,v} \widehat{e_j}^T \widehat{e_{u \oplus v}}$$

$$= \sqrt{n} \sum_u \alpha_u \alpha_{u \oplus j} \hat{M}_{u,u \oplus j}$$

It follows from theorem 6.5 that $\hat{M}_{u,u \oplus j} = 0$ unless $u \in \Omega_j$. If $j \in \Omega_k$, then $\Omega_j \subset \Omega_k$ and the coefficients α_u in the sum are zero.

Next let $x = \sum \alpha_i \widehat{e_i}$ be an element of $\mathcal{L}\{\widehat{e_j} : j \in \Omega_k\}$. As before, for $j \notin \Omega_k$,

$$\widehat{e_j}^T \mathcal{M}(x) = \sqrt{n} \sum_u \alpha_u \alpha_{u \oplus j} \hat{M}_{u,u \oplus j}$$

where nonzero terms are subscripted by elements of Ω_j. Since $u \notin \Omega_k \Longrightarrow \alpha_u = 0$, every term will be zero provided that

$$u \in \Omega_j \Longrightarrow u \notin \Omega_k \vee u \oplus j \notin \Omega_k$$

This implication follows from the fact that $u \oplus (u \oplus j) = j \notin \Omega_k$.   ∎

Invariants can speak to the commutativity of diagrams. For example, consider the following.

$$
\begin{array}{ccc}
x & \longrightarrow & \mathcal{M}(x) \\
\Xi \downarrow & & \downarrow \Xi \\
\Xi x & \xrightarrow{\tilde{\mathcal{M}}} & \Xi \mathcal{M}(x)
\end{array}
$$

Here Ξ is a linear map, and $\tilde{\mathcal{M}}$ is defined by commutativity (of the diagram). The mixing scheme $\mathcal{M}$ is polynomial, and is homogeneous of degree 2. One could wonder if $\tilde{\mathcal{M}}$ might have similar properties. For instance, could $\tilde{\mathcal{M}}$ also be homogeneous of degree 2?

Suppose this were the case. In particular, $\tilde{\mathcal{M}}(0) = 0$. If x existed such that $\Xi x = 0$ and $\Xi \mathcal{M}(x) \neq 0$, then a contradiction is obtained:

$$\tilde{\mathcal{M}}(\Xi x) = \tilde{\mathcal{M}}(0) = 0 \neq \Xi \mathcal{M}(x) = \tilde{\mathcal{M}}(\Xi x)$$

Therefore $\Xi x = 0$ implies $\Xi \mathcal{M}(x) = 0$, which makes the kernel of Ξ an invariant of $\mathcal{M}$.

According to theorem 16.2, the subspace $\mathcal{L}\{\widehat{e_j} : j \notin \Omega_k\}$ is an invariant of $\mathcal{M}$. This suggests that a collection $\{\Xi_k\}_{k \in \Omega}$ of maps, such that the kernel of Ξ_k is $\mathcal{L}\{\widehat{e_j} : j \notin \Omega_k\}$, might be compatible with the assumptions above. The following chapters will show this is indeed the case, and will identify each Ξ_k with a family of schemata.

The counterpart of theorem 16.1 for selection is the explicit condition on arbitrary selection schemes:

$$x_j = 0 \Longrightarrow \mathcal{F}(x)_j = 0$$

In particular, $\mathcal{H}\{e_j : j \in A\}$ is invariant under $\mathcal{F}$ for any $A \subset \Omega$ and an arbitrary selection scheme. This section closes with a similar property for $\mathcal{G}$ in the zero mutation case. Theorem 16.4 is another statement of the fact that neither crossover nor selection can create bits. The following theorem prepares the way. Let C be the $\ell \times 2^\ell$ matrix defined by $C_{i,j} = j^T 2^i$.

Lemma 16.3   For all k, $x \in \mathcal{L}\{e_j : j \in \Omega_k\} \Longleftrightarrow k^T C x = \mathbf{1}^T C x$.

Proof   Note that $(k^T C)_j = k^T j$. If $x \in \mathcal{L}\{e_j : j \in \Omega_k\}$ then $x_j > 0 \Rightarrow j \in \Omega_k$. Thus

$$k^T C x$$

$$= \sum_{j \in \Omega_k} k^T j x_j$$

$$= \sum_{j \in \Omega_k} \mathbf{1}^T j x_j$$

$$= \mathbf{1}^T C x$$

Conversely, if $x \notin \mathcal{L}\{e_j : j \in \Omega_k\}$ then $x_{j'} > 0$ for some $j' \notin \Omega_k$, and $k^T j' < \mathbf{1}^T j'$. Note that $k^T j \leq \mathbf{1}^T j$ for all j. Therefore

$$k^T C x$$

$$= \sum k^T j x_j$$

$$< \sum \mathbf{1}^T j x_j$$

$$= \mathbf{1}^T C x \qquad \blacksquare$$

Theorem 16.4   If mutation is zero, then $\mathcal{H}\{e_j : j \in \Omega_k\}$ is invariant under $\mathcal{G}$ for all k.

Proof   The invariance of $\mathcal{H}\{e_j : j \in \Omega_k\}$ under $\mathcal{F}$ has already been noted (above). For $x \in \mathcal{H}\{e_j : j \in \Omega_k\}$, it follows from theorem 16.1 that for all $0 \leq i < \ell$

$$(e_0 - e_{2^i})^T W x = (e_0 - e_{2^i})^T W \mathcal{M}(x)$$

But $2^{\ell/2-1}(e_0 - e_{2^i})^T W e_j = j^T 2^i$, hence $C x = C \mathcal{M}(x)$. The proof is completed by appealing to lemma 16.3,

$$k^T C \mathcal{M}(x)$$

$$= k^T C x$$

$$= \mathbf{1}^T C x$$

$$= \mathbf{1}^T C \mathcal{M}(x) \qquad \blacksquare$$

The next theorem gives a sufficient condition for invariance of the interior of Λ.

Theorem 16.5   If selection is positive and $\mu_0 > 0$, then $x_j > 0 \implies \mathcal{G}(x)_j > 0$ for all j.

Proof   If $x_j > 0$ then $s_j = \mathcal{F}(x)_j > 0$ since selection is positive. Therefore

$\mathcal{M}(s)_j$

$\geq s_j^2 M_{0,0}$

$= s_j^2 \sum_{i,j,k} \mu_i \mu_j \dfrac{\chi_k + \chi_{\bar{k}}}{2}[i \otimes k \oplus \bar{k} \otimes j = 0]$

$\geq s_j^2 \mu_0^2$

> 0 ∎

Exercises

1. To what extent can theorem 16.2 hold for selection?

2. Is there a positive mutation analogue of theorem 16.4?

3. Show theorem 16.1 carries over to the general cardinality case, provided 2 is replaced by c. *Hint:* Use exercises 7 and 6 of section 6.4

4. The *interpretation* of (the binary version of) theorem 16.1 extends, in the general cardinality case, to

$$\sum [i_k = a]x_i = \sum [i_k = a]\mathcal{M}(x)_i$$

Show this equality holds in the general cardinality case. *Hint:* Do not attempt to obtain it via the general cardinality version of theorem 16.1.

5. Show theorem 16.2 carries over to the general cardinality case. *Hint:* Consider answering the question, of how Ω_k should be defined, by maintaining the proof technique.

6. Show theorem 16.4 carries over to the general cardinality case. Does the definition of Ω_k need to be as restrictive as required by the previous exercise?

7. Show theorem 16.5 carries over to the general cardinality case.

16.2   Proportional Selection and the GA Surface

This section assumes proportional selection. The definition of $\mathcal{G}$ is slightly inconvenient because of the occurrence of division: $\mathcal{G}(x) = \mathcal{M}(f \cdot x / f^T x)$. This may be remedied (as in chapter 15) by defining $\mathcal{G}'(x) = F\mathcal{M}(x)$ where $F = \operatorname{diag}(f)$. Since

$$\mathcal{G} = F^{-1} \circ \mathcal{G}' \circ \mathcal{F} \sim F^{-1} \circ \mathcal{G}' \circ F$$

it follows that $\mathcal{G}' \sim F \circ \mathcal{G} \circ F^{-1}$ so that properties of either are easily transferred to the other.

The function $\mathcal{G}$ has the pleasant property that it maps Λ into itself. However, there is a corresponding surface, the *GA surface*, which is the analogue of Λ and is invariant under $\mathcal{G}'$.

The intuition behind the existence of this surface is simple. Since $\mathcal{G}'(\alpha x) = \alpha^2 \mathcal{G}'(x)$, points far from the origin—large α—should map even farther away because of the α^2 factor. Similarly, points near the origin—small α—should map even closer. Thus iterating $\mathcal{G}'$ beginning from x converges to ∞ for large x and to 0 for small x. One would expect the boundary between these two cases to be a surface which $\mathcal{G}'$ maps into itself.

Let $|\cdot|$ be a continuous function satisfying all of the properties of a norm with the possible exception of the triangle inequality, and let $\mathcal{B}$ be its unit ball in the nonnegative orthant

$$\mathcal{B} = \{\frac{x}{|x|} : x \in \Lambda\}$$

Let $\varphi_{t+1} = |\mathcal{G}'(s^t)|$ and let $s^{t+1} = \varphi_{t+1}^{-1}\mathcal{G}'(s^t)$. If $|\cdot|$ is $\|\cdot\|_1$, then $\mathcal{B}$ is Λ and this inductive definition of s^t coincides with previous usage so that s^t is the selection vector for generation t if the next population is taken to be the expected next generation. When alternate choices for $|\cdot|$ are made, the length but not the direction of s^t may change. The *GA surface* corresponding to the simple genetic algorithm with proportional selection is the set

$$\mathcal{S} = \{s^0 \prod_{i=1}^{\infty} \varphi_i^{-2^{-i}} : s^0 \in \mathcal{B}\}$$

Theorem 16.6   The GA surface $\mathcal{S}$ is independent of the choice of $|\cdot|$, and is mapped by $\mathcal{G}'$ into itself. If $\mathcal{G}$ is focused, then $\mathcal{S}$ is the graph of a differentiable function.

Proof   First suppose that $|\cdot|$ is $\|\cdot\|_1$. A typical point of $\mathcal{S}$ is

$$s^0 \exp\{-\sum_{i=1}^{\infty} 2^{-i} \log \varphi_i\}$$

Since $\mathcal{G}'$ has quadratic components and s^t is nonnegative, $\varphi_{t+1} = \|\mathcal{G}'(s^t)\|_1$ is differentiable whenever s^t is. Moreover, φ_{t+1} is both uniformly bounded from above and away from 0 from below because F is invertible and

$$\|\mathcal{G}'(s^t)\|_1 \in \|F\mathcal{M}(\Lambda)\|_1 \subset \|F\Lambda\|_1$$

Thus $s^{t+1} = \varphi_{t+1}^{-1}\mathcal{G}'(s^t)$ is differentiable if s^t is. Hence, by induction on t, s^t and therefore φ_{t+1} are differentiable. The uniform bounds on φ_{t+1} imply

$$d \sum_{i=1}^{\infty} 2^{-i} \log \varphi_i = \sum_{i=1}^{\infty} 2^{-i} \varphi_i^{-1} d\varphi_i$$

since the sum may be differentiated term by term, provided the sum of differentials converges. Differentiating the relations defining s^i and φ_i leads to

$$d\varphi_{i+1} = \mathbf{1}^T F d\mathcal{M}_{s^i} \prod_{j=0}^{i-1} \varphi_{j+1}^{-1} (I - \varphi_{j+1}^{-1} \mathcal{G}'(s^j) \mathbf{1}^T) F d\mathcal{M}_{s^j}$$

Let $\lim_{j \to \infty} s^j = s^*$ and let s be the fixed point on $\mathcal{S}$ corresponding to s^* (i.e., $s \sim s^*$). Since $\mathcal{G}'(\alpha x) = \alpha^2 \mathcal{G}'(x)$,

$$\lim_{j \to \infty} \varphi_j = \mathbf{1}^T \mathcal{G}'(s/\mathbf{1}^T s) = 1/\mathbf{1}^T s.$$

Therefore

$$\lim_{j \to \infty} \|\varphi_{j+1}^{-1} (I - \varphi_{j+1}^{-1} \mathcal{G}'(s^j) \mathbf{1}^T) F d\mathcal{M}_{s^j}\|_1 = \|(I - s\mathbf{1}^T/\mathbf{1}^T s) F d\mathcal{M}_s\|_1$$

Using the same techniques which were employed in the proof of lemma 15.1, the spectral radius of $(I - s\mathbf{1}^T/\mathbf{1}^T s) F d\mathcal{M}_s$ is less than 2. It follows that

$$d\varphi_i = \mathbf{1}^T A(i)$$

where the matrix $A(i)$ satisfies $\|A(i)\| = O(\alpha^i)$ and $\alpha < 2$ with suitable choice of norm. Hence the series

$$\sum_{i=1}^{\infty} 2^{-i} \varphi_i^{-1} d\varphi_i = \mathbf{1}^T \sum_{i=1}^{\infty} 2^{-i} \varphi_i^{-1} A(i)$$

converges since the ith term has norm $O((\alpha/2)^i)$. Now drop the assumption that $|\cdot|$ is $\|\cdot\|_1$. Note that

$$\mathcal{G}'(s^0 \prod_{i=1}^{\infty} \varphi_i^{-2^{-i}})$$

$$= \mathcal{G}'(s^0) \prod_{i=1}^{\infty} \varphi_i^{-2^{1-i}}$$

$$= s^1 \varphi_1 \prod_{i=1}^{\infty} \varphi_i^{-2^{1-i}}$$

$$= s^1 \prod_{i=1}^{\infty} \varphi_{i+1}^{-2^{-i}}$$

Since the last expression is the point on $\mathcal{S}$ corresponding to $s^1 \epsilon \mathcal{B}$, it has been established that $\mathcal{G}'(\mathcal{S}) \subset \mathcal{S}$. The proof is finished by noting that $\mathcal{S}$ does not depend on $|\cdot|$ since $\mathcal{S}$ is an invariant surface of $\mathcal{G}'$ in the nonnegative orthant, and $\mathcal{G}'$ does not depend on $|\cdot|$. ∎

Choosing $|\cdot|$ to be $\|\cdot\|_1$, any probability vector $s \in \Lambda$ may be regarded as a point of $\mathcal{S}$ through the correspondence

$$s \longleftrightarrow s^0 \prod_{i=1}^{\infty} \varphi_i^{-2^{-i}} \quad \text{(where } s = s^0)$$

Since this correspondence is continuous, the GA surface is compact. A sequence $x_1, x_2, x_3,$ ... in $\mathcal{S}$ moves *downhill* if

$$|x_i| > |x_{i+1}|$$

except when $x_i = x_{i+1}$. Note that the concept of downhill depends on the choice of $|\cdot|$. A particularly natural sequence to consider is the trajectory followed by the selection vectors

$$s, \mathcal{G}'(s), \mathcal{G}'^2(s), \ldots$$

for arbitrary initial vector $s \in \mathcal{S}$.

Theorem 16.7   Let $r_j = \varphi_j/\varphi_{j+1}$. A necessary and sufficient condition for the sequence of selection vectors with initial vector s^0 to move downhill on $\mathcal{S}$ is that, for all j,

$$1 > \sqrt{r_j \sqrt{r_{j+1} \sqrt{r_{j+2} \sqrt{\cdots}}}}$$

except when s^0 is a fixed point of $\mathcal{G}'$.

Proof

$$\frac{|\mathcal{G}'^j(s^0)|}{|\mathcal{G}'^{j-1}(s^0)|}$$

$$= \frac{|s^j \prod_{i=1}^{\infty} \varphi_{i+j}^{-2^{-i}}|}{|s^{j-1} \prod_{i=1}^{\infty} \varphi_{i+j-1}^{-2^{-i}}|}$$

$$= \prod_{i=1}^{\infty} (\frac{\varphi_{i+j-1}}{\varphi_{i+j}})^{2^{-i}}$$

$$= \sqrt{r_j \sqrt{r_{j+1} \sqrt{r_{j+2} \sqrt{\cdots}}}} \qquad \blacksquare$$

It is of some interest to consider theorem 16.7 when $|\cdot|$ is $\|\cdot\|_1$. For this choice,

$$\varphi_t = \|F\mathcal{M}(s^{t-1})\|_1 = \mathbf{1}^T F p^t$$

Hence φ_t is the average population fitness of population p^t. Appealing to theorem 11.6 yields the following.

Theorem 16.8   By choosing $|\cdot| = \|\cdot\|_1$, the sequence $s, \mathcal{G}'(s), \mathcal{G}'^2(s), \ldots$ of selection vectors moves downhill on the GA surface provided mutation is zero and fitness is linear.

Exercises

1. Show that if $\mathcal{G}(x) = x$, then $\mathcal{G}'(y) = y$ where $y = (\mathbf{1}^T Fx)^{-2} Fx$ is the corresponding fixed point of $\mathcal{G}'$.

2. Show that if $\mathcal{G}'(x) = x$, then $\mathcal{G}(y) = y$ where $y = (\mathbf{1}^T F^{-1}x)^{-1} F^{-1}x$ is the corresponding fixed point of $\mathcal{G}$.

3. Show that if x is a fixed point of $\mathcal{G}'$ then $(\mathbf{1}^T x)^2 = \mathbf{1}^T F^{-1}x$. *Hint:* do the previous exercise.

4. Complete the sketch of theorem 16.6.

5. Show, by counter example, that theorem 16.8 does not hold for general fitness functions.

6. Compute the GA surface and visualize its height using $|\cdot| = \|\cdot\|_1$ for the nonlinear fitness functions listed in section 9.3. In these examples, to what extent does downhill motion on the GA surface accurately predict evolutionary trajectories?

7. Show the results of this section carry over to the general cardinality case.

8. Generalize the GA surface to other heuristics—which have no connection to the SGA. *Hint:* Think about $\mathcal{G}'(\alpha x) = \alpha^2 \mathcal{G}'(x)$.

17 Quotients

This chapter considers interpreting random heuristic search as taking place on equivalence classes. One might imagine that there is nothing to do, because the search space Ω can simply be taken to be the collection of equivalence classes. While trivial (and to some extent missing the point), this observation is nevertheless important: preconceived notions of "microscopic" vs "macroscopic" or "genotype" vs "phenotype" are irrelevant to the scope, power, and application of the paradigm; choosing Ω to be a space of "phenotypes"— which is nothing more than a set of equivalence classes—brings the full force of the theory of RHS to bear at what one might call the "macroscopic" level.

If, however, an instance of random heuristic search is already defined, the interesting question is whether that instance is compatible with a given equivalence relation. Put another way: given a microscopic definition of random heuristic search, is a macroscopic model compatible with it?

The first section is a general discussion of equivalence. Its focus is the compatibility issue and its main results are conditions under which a given instance of random heuristic search, defined over some fixed Ω, can be naturally viewed as taking place on equivalence classes. The second section presents simple conditions under which the standard genetic operators are compatible with equivalence relations. This leads, in the case of crossover, to schemata (a later chapter explores schemata in greater depth).

17.1 Equivalence

In this chapter, $\equiv$ will be used to denote an equivalence relation on Ω. Because Ω can naturally be regarded as a subset of Λ through the correspondence

$$i \in \Omega \longleftrightarrow e_i \in \Lambda$$

the equivalence relation $\equiv$ may be regarded as applying to the unit basis vectors, i.e.,

$$e_i \equiv e_j \Longleftrightarrow i \equiv j$$

This relation on the vertices of Λ is extended to all of Λ by

$$x \equiv y \Longleftrightarrow \forall t \, . \, \sum [i \equiv t] x_i = \sum [i \equiv t] y_i$$

The fact that this coincides with the previous definition in the case where x and y are unit basis vectors is a simple exercise. The practice of using $\equiv$ for both an equivalence relation on Ω and on Λ will be continued, since context makes the meaning clear. Moreover, $\equiv$ can without modification be regarded as an equivalence relation on all of $\Re^n$ as the definition given above makes sense for any $x, y \in \Re^n$. Explicit mention will be made when this general case ($\equiv$ an equivalence relation on $\Re^n$) is intended.

Let $\Lambda/\!\equiv$ denote the set of equivalence classes of $\equiv$ in Λ, and let $\Omega/\!\equiv$ denote the set of equivalence classes of $\equiv$ in Ω. The notation $[a]$ will be used to denote the equivalence class of a ($[a] \in \Omega/\!\equiv$ when $a \in \Omega$, and $[a] \in \Lambda/\!\equiv$ when $a \in \Lambda$). Later in this section, the notation $[h]$ will be used to denote a function. Previous usage of $[expr]$ to denote an indicator function will also be maintained; the type of the argument to $[\cdot]$ will disambiguate between these possible meanings.

An element $v \in \Re^n$ is said to be *dominated by* $\equiv$, denoted $v \prec \equiv$, provided that

$$i \equiv j \Longrightarrow v_i = v_j$$

The next theorem records some elementary properties of equivalence.

Theorem 17.1   Let $x \equiv y$ and $u \equiv v$ (here, $\equiv$ is regarded as an equivalence relation on all of n-space). Then $x \pm u \equiv y \pm v$ and $\alpha x \equiv \alpha y$ for all $\alpha \in \Re$. If $v \prec \equiv$, then $v^T x = v^T y$ and $v \cdot x \equiv v \cdot y$.

Proof   Note that

$$\sum [i \equiv t](x \pm u)_i$$

$$= \sum [i \equiv t]x_i \pm \sum [i \equiv t]u_i$$

$$= \sum [i \equiv t]y_i \pm \sum [i \equiv t]v_i$$

and

$$\sum [i \equiv t](\alpha x)_i$$

$$= \alpha \sum [i \equiv t]x_i$$

$$= \alpha \sum [i \equiv t]y_i$$

Also, $v^T x$ is

$$\sum_{[t] \in \Omega/\equiv} \sum [i \equiv t]v_i x_i$$

$$= \sum_{[t] \in \Omega/\equiv} v_t \sum [i \equiv t]x_i$$

$$= \sum_{[t] \in \Omega/\equiv} v_t \sum [i \equiv t]y_i$$

and

$$\sum [i \equiv t] v_i x_i$$

$$= v_t \sum [i \equiv t] x_i$$

$$= v_t \sum [i \equiv t] y_i \qquad \blacksquare$$

Theorem 17.2 Elements of $\Lambda/\equiv$ (i.e., equivalence classes) are convex, compact sets.

Proof Suppose $a \equiv b$. By theorem 17.1,

$$\alpha a + (1 - \alpha) b \equiv \alpha a + (1 - \alpha) a = a$$

Therefore, $a \equiv b \Longrightarrow \alpha a + (1 - \alpha) b \equiv a \equiv b$ which proves convexity. As for compactness, suppose $x^j \in \Lambda$ are all equivalent and $x^j \to x$. In particular,

$$\sum [i \equiv t] x_i^0 = \sum [i \equiv t] x_i^j \longrightarrow \sum [i \equiv t] x_i$$

by continuity. Hence x is in the same equivalence class as the x^j. $\qquad \blacksquare$

The following theorem establishes a correspondence between equivalence classes in Ω and equivalence classes in Λ.

Theorem 17.3 Let $\mathcal{C}$ be an equivalence class in $\Omega/\equiv$, and let Let $\mathcal{K}$ be an equivalence class in $\Lambda/\equiv$. Then

- $\mathcal{H}(\{e_k : k \in \mathcal{C}\}) \in \Lambda/\equiv$
- $\{k : e_k \in \mathcal{K}\} \in \{\emptyset\} \cup \Omega/\equiv$
- $\mathcal{H}(\{e_k : e_k \in \mathcal{K}\}) \in \{\emptyset, \mathcal{K}\}$

Proof Since the convex hull is, by theorem 17.2, already known to be contained in some element of $\Lambda/\equiv$, the key to establishing the first assertion is to show, given $k' \in \mathcal{C}$ that

$$x \equiv e_{k'} \Longrightarrow x \in \mathcal{H}(\{e_k : k \in \mathcal{C}\})$$

Therefore assume

$$\sum_i [i \equiv t] x_i = \sum_i [i \equiv t] (e_{k'})_i = [k' \equiv t]$$

If $t \in \mathcal{C}$ it follows that $\sum_i [i \equiv t] x_i = 1$, and because $x \in \Lambda$, all other components must be zero, i.e., $i \notin \mathcal{C} \implies x_i = 0$. This, however, implies that $x \in \mathcal{H}(\{e_k : k \in \mathcal{C}\})$.

Analogously, if $e_i, e_j \in \mathcal{K}$ then $e_i \equiv e_j$ hence $i \equiv j$. Thus the second assertion is established by showing, given $e'_k \in \mathcal{K}$ that

$$i \equiv k' \implies e_i \in \mathcal{K}$$

But $i \equiv k'$ implies $e_i \equiv e'_k$ hence $e_i \in \mathcal{K}$ because $\mathcal{K}$ is an equivalence class.

Finally, the previous two assertions establish that if the convex hull is nonempty, then it is an equivalence class. But $\mathcal{H}(\{e_k : e_k \in \mathcal{K}\})$ is nonempty when it intersects $\mathcal{K}$, in which case it must be $\mathcal{K}$ since equivalence classes are either identical or disjoint. ∎

Let T be a collection of equivalence class representatives. That is, T is minimal with respect to containment such that

$$\Lambda \subset \bigcup_{t \in T} [t]$$

Given a stochastic function h on Λ (i.e., $h(x)$ is, for every $x \in \Lambda$, a random vector taking values in Λ), define stochastic $[h] : T \longrightarrow T$ by

$$[h](t) = t' \iff h(t) \in [t']$$

In particular, $\Pr\{[h](t) = t'\} = \Pr\{h(t) \in [t']\} = \Pr\{h(t) \equiv t'\}$. The function $[h]$ is called the *quotient* of h with respect to T. If h is deterministic, it may nevertheless be regarded as stochastic by $\Pr\{h(x) = y\} = [y = h(x)]$ and in that case the definition of $[h]$ reduces to

$$[h](t) = t' \in T \text{ such that } h(t) \in [t']$$

The function h is said to be *compatible with* $\equiv$ if

$$x \equiv y \implies \forall t \in T . \ \Pr\{h(x) \in [t]\} = \Pr\{h(y) \in [t]\}$$

In that case, $[h]$ is referred to as the quotient of h. When h is deterministic, this reduces to $x \equiv y \implies h(x) \equiv h(y)$. Stochastic functions h and g are said to be *independent* provided that, for all w, x, y, z,

$$\Pr\{g(w) = x \wedge h(y) = z\} = \Pr\{g(w) = x\} \Pr\{h(y) = z\}$$

It is an easy exercise that any two deterministic functions are independent. Given functions h and g, to say "as stochastic functions, $h = g$" is to indicate that for all x and y

$$\Pr\{h(x) = y\} = \Pr\{g(x) = y\}$$

The stochastic functions dealt with in this book take values in a finite set. It follows from the finiteness assumption that the independence of stochastic functions h and g is equivalent to the independence, for all w and y, of the random vectors $g(w)$ and $h(y)$. The statement that $h = g$ as stochastic functions is equivalent to the assertion that $h(x)$ and $g(x)$ are identically distributed for all x.

Theorem 17.4   If stochastic functions g and h are independent and compatible with $\equiv$, then $[g]$ and $[h]$ are independent, $g \circ h$ is compatible with $\equiv$, and, as stochastic functions, $[g \circ h] = [g] \circ [h]$.

Proof   Suppose that $x \equiv y$. Note that

$\Pr\{g \circ h(x) \in [t]\}$

$= \displaystyle\sum_{t' \in T} \sum_{z \in [t']} \Pr\{g(z) \in [t]\} \Pr\{h(x) = z\}$

$= \displaystyle\sum_{t' \in T} \Pr\{g(t') \in [t]\} \sum_{z \in [t']} \Pr\{h(x) = z\}$

$= \displaystyle\sum_{t' \in T} \Pr\{g(t') \in [t]\} \Pr\{h(x) \in [t']\}$

But the last expression is invariant under replacing x with y (h is compatible), which establishes the compatibility of $g \circ h$. To see that $[g \circ h] = [g] \circ [h]$, suppose $x \in [t'']$ and note that the first expression above is $\Pr\{[g \circ h](t'') = t\}$. Assuming the independence of $[g]$ and $[h]$, the last expression above is

$\displaystyle\sum_{t' \in T} \Pr\{[g](t') = t\} \Pr\{[h](t'') = t'\} = \Pr\{[g] \circ [h](t'') = t\}$

It therefore remains to establish the independence of $[g]$ and $[h]$. Note that

$\Pr\{[g](t) = t'\} \Pr\{[h](t'') = t'''\}$

$= \Pr\{g(t) \in [t']\} \Pr\{h(t'') \in [t''']\}$

$= \displaystyle\sum_{u \in [t']} \sum_{v \in [t''']} \Pr\{g(t) = u\} \Pr\{h(t'') = v\}$

$= \displaystyle\sum_{u \in [t']} \sum_{v \in [t''']} \Pr\{g(t) = u \wedge h(t'') = v\}$

$$= \Pr\{g(t) \in [t'] \wedge h(t'') \in [t''']\}$$

$$= \Pr\{[g](t) = t' \wedge [h](t'') = t'''\} \qquad \blacksquare$$

Equivalence can be expressed in terms of the linear operator Ξ defined by

$$\Xi_{[i],j} = [i \equiv j]$$

where the rows are indexed by elements of $\Omega/\equiv$ and the columns are indexed by Ω. Note that $\Xi x = \Xi y$ if and only if for all i

$$\sum_j [i \equiv j] x_j = \sum_j [i \equiv j] y_j$$

Therefore elements $x, y \in \Lambda$ are equivalent precisely when $\Xi x = \Xi y$. Since equivalence corresponds to having the same image under Ξ, the equivalence classes must be preimages under Ξ, that is

$$\Lambda/\equiv \ = \Lambda \cap \{\Xi^{-1}x : x \in \Xi\Lambda\}$$

Thus, given any collection T of equivalence class representatives, the map

$$\Xi : T \longrightarrow \Xi\Lambda$$

is an isomorphism. Hence $\Lambda/\equiv$, which is represented by T, may be identified with $\Xi\Lambda$. Note further that

$$(\mathbf{1}^T \Xi)_j = \sum_{[i] \in \Omega/\equiv} [i \equiv j] = 1$$

Hence the image of Λ under Ξ consists of nonnegative vectors of dimension $|\Omega/\equiv|$ which sum to 1. Therefore $\Xi\Lambda$, which has been identified with $\Lambda/\equiv$, represents the state space for random heuristic search over the search space $\Omega/\equiv$. The set $\Xi\Lambda$ is called the *quotient representation space*, Ξ is the *quotient map*, and $\Omega/\equiv$ is the *quotient search space*.

Given $h : \Lambda \to \Lambda$ and a collection T of equivalence class representatives, the map $[h] : T \to T$ induces a function $\tilde{h}$ on the quotient space ($\tilde{h}$ is also called the quotient of h) by commutativity of the following diagram.

$$
\begin{array}{ccc}
t & \longrightarrow & [h](t) \\
\Xi \downarrow & & \downarrow \Xi \\
\Xi t & \xrightarrow{\ \tilde{h}\ } & \Xi h(t)
\end{array}
$$

The distribution of $\tilde{h}(\Xi t)$ could depend on the choice of T, however.

Theorem 17.5   In order, for every $t \in T$, that the distribution of $\tilde{h}(\Xi t)$ be independent of the collection T of equivalence class representatives, it is necessary and sufficient that h is compatible with $\equiv$. When h is deterministic and compatible with Ξ, $\tilde{h}$ is completely determined by the following commutative diagram.

$$
\begin{array}{ccc}
x & \xrightarrow{\hspace{2cm}} & h(x) \\[2pt]
\Xi \Big\downarrow & & \Big\downarrow \Xi \\[2pt]
\Xi x & \xrightarrow{\ \ \tilde{h}\ \ } & \Xi h(x)
\end{array}
$$

Proof   If h were not compatible, then $\Pr\{h(x) \equiv t\} \neq \Pr\{h(y) \equiv t\}$ for some t and some x, y such that $\Xi x = \Xi y$. It follows that the event $\Xi h(x) = \Xi t$ has probability different from that of the event $\Xi h(y) = \Xi t$. Thus the distribution of $\tilde{h}(\Xi x)$ depends upon which of x or y is chosen to represent $[x]$.

On the other hand, compatibility of h with $\equiv$ implies that the events $\Xi h(x) = \Xi t$ and $\Xi h(y) = \Xi t$ have equal probability for every t. Thus either definition, $\tilde{h}(\Xi x) = \Xi h(x)$ or $\tilde{h}(\Xi y) = \Xi h(y)$, produce results which, as stochastic functions, are equal.   ∎

Given h compatible with $\equiv$, the function $\tilde{h}$ is referred to as the *quotient* of h (with respect to $\equiv$). To simplify exposition, $\Omega/\equiv$ will be denoted by $\tilde{\Omega}$, and the image of $x \in \Lambda$ under the quotient map will be denoted by $\tilde{x}$.

Lemma 17.6   If $t \in X_n^k$, then

$$
\sum_{v \in X_n^k} [v \equiv t] \prod_{j \in \Omega} \frac{x_j^{v_j}}{v_j!} = \prod_{j \in \tilde{\Omega}} \frac{\tilde{x}_j^{\tilde{t}_j}}{\tilde{t}_j!}
$$

In particular, if $x \equiv y$ then the expression above is invariant under replacing x with y.

Proof   Induct on the cardinality of $\Omega/\equiv$. The base case is that all elements of Ω are equivalent. By theorem 17.2, the convex hull of the basis vectors (i.e., Λ) is contained within a single equivalence class. Hence by theorem 17.1, all of X_n^k is also contained within a single equivalence class. Therefore, the expression above reduces to the multinomial theorem (lemma 3.2).

For the inductive step, assume $\Omega/\equiv = \{[w_0], \ldots [w_h]\}$ where, without loss of generality, the search space Ω is $\{0, \ldots n-1\}$ and $[w_h] = \{u, u+1, \ldots, n-1\}$ (reindex if necessary). Let $\pi : \Re^n \longrightarrow \Re^u$ be projection to the first u components, and let $\pi' : \Re^n \longrightarrow \Re^{n-u}$ be projection to the last $n - u$ components. Note that

$$\sum_{v \in X_n^k} [v \equiv t] \prod_{j < n} \frac{x_j^{v_j}}{v_j!}$$

$$= \sum_{v \in X_n^k} \prod_{j \le h} [\sum_{i \equiv w_j} v_i = \sum_{i \equiv w_j} t_i] \prod_{j < n} \frac{x_j^{v_j}}{v_j!}$$

$$= \sum_{v \in X_n^k} [\sum_{i \equiv w_h} v_i = \sum_{i \equiv w_h} t_i] \prod_{j \equiv w_h} \frac{x_j^{v_j}}{v_j!} \prod_{j < h} [\sum_{i \equiv w_j} v_i = \sum_{i \equiv w_j} t_i] \prod_{j < u} \frac{x_j^{v_j}}{v_j!}$$

$$= \sum_{l \le k} \sum_{v' \in X_{n-u}^l} \sum_{v \in X_u^{k-l}} [\mathbf{1}^T v' = \mathbf{1}^T \pi'(t)] \prod_{j < n-u} \frac{x_{j+u}^{v'_j}}{v'_j!} [v \equiv \pi(t)] \prod_{j < u} \frac{x_j^{v_j}}{v_j!}$$

$$= \sum_{l \le k} (\sum_{v' \in X_{n-u}^l} [l = \mathbf{1}^T \pi'(t)] \prod_{j < n-u} \frac{x_{j+u}^{v'_j}}{v'_j!}) (\sum_{v \in X_u^{k-l}} [v \equiv \pi(t)] \prod_{j < u} \frac{x_j^{v_j}}{v_j!})$$

The first parenthesized expression is nonzero only when $l = \mathbf{1}^T \pi'(t)$ and then is an instance of the base case of the induction (in dimension $n - u$). The induction hypothesis (in dimension u) applies to the second parenthesized expression. Making the respective substitutions leads to

$$\frac{\tilde{x}_{w_h}^{\tilde{t}_{w_h}}}{\tilde{t}_{w_h}} \prod_{j \in \tilde{\Omega} \setminus \{[w_h]\}} \frac{\tilde{x}_j^{\tilde{t}_j}}{\tilde{t}_j!} \qquad\qquad\qquad ∎$$

The preceding theorem provides a bridge between $\mathcal{G}$ and τ, implying that compatibility of the former means compatibility of the latter.

Theorem 17.7 If $\mathcal{G}$ is compatible with $\equiv$, then τ is compatible with $\equiv$.

Proof Suppose $x \equiv y$. By theorem 3.4 the probability of transition into $[t]$ from x is

$$r! \sum_{v \in X_n^r} [v/r \equiv t] \prod \frac{\mathcal{G}(x)_j^{v_j}}{v_j!}$$

Since $\mathcal{G}$ is compatible with $\equiv$, it follows that $\mathcal{G}(x) \equiv \mathcal{G}(y)$ and hence, by theorem 17.1 and lemma17.6, the expression above is invariant under replacing x with y.   ∎

The basic framework is now in place for interpreting random heuristic search as operating on equivalence classes, given that $\mathcal{G}$ is compatible with $\equiv$. The following theorem, whose proof is an exercise, integrates the preceding results.

Theorem 17.8   Let $p, q \in \Lambda$ and suppose $\mathcal{G}$ is compatible with $\equiv$. Then, for all $k > 0$,

$$\mathcal{G}^k(p) \equiv q \Longleftrightarrow \tilde{\mathcal{G}}^k(\tilde{p}) = \tilde{q}$$

and

$$\Pr\{\tau^k(p) \equiv q\} = \Pr\{\tilde{\tau}^k(\tilde{p}) = \tilde{q}\}$$

Moreover, for $p, q \in \frac{1}{r} X_n^r$,

$$\Pr\{\tilde{\tau}(\tilde{p}) = \tilde{q}\} = r! \prod_{j \in \tilde{\Omega}} \frac{\tilde{\mathcal{G}}(\tilde{p})_j^{r\tilde{q}_j}}{(r\tilde{q}_j)!}$$

Exercises

1. Verify that $e_i \equiv e_j \Longleftrightarrow i \equiv j$ is a special case of

$$x \equiv y \Longleftrightarrow \forall t \, . \, \sum [i \equiv t] x_i = \sum [i \equiv t] y_i$$

2. Verify that $x \equiv y$ if and only if $x - y$ is contained in the kernel of Ξ.

3. Use the previous exercise to give alternate proofs of theorems 17.1 and 17.2.

4. Show that the number of equivalence classes in $\Lambda/\equiv$ is either one or else is infinite.

5. Show any two deterministic functions are independent.

6. The assumption was made that all stochastic functions dealt with in this book take values in a finite set. What difficulties arise if uncountably many values are taken on?

7. Prove theorem 17.8.

8. Show that if $\mathcal{G}$ is not compatible with $\equiv$, then no matter how $\tilde{\tau}$ is defined as an instance of RHS,

$$\Pr\{\tau(p) \equiv q\} = \Pr\{\tilde{\tau}(\tilde{p}) \equiv \tilde{q}\}$$

cannot hold in general.

17.2   Operators

The next series of results establishes a condition under which some common selection schemes are compatible with $\equiv$.

Theorem 17.9   If the fitness f is dominated by $\equiv$, then the proportional selection scheme is compatible with $\equiv$.

Proof   Let $x \equiv y$. Since $f \prec \equiv$, theorem 17.1 gives

$$\mathcal{F}(x) = (f \cdot x)/f^T x \equiv (f \cdot y)/f^T y \qquad \blacksquare$$

Theorem 17.10   If the fitness f is dominated by $\equiv$, then the ranking selection scheme is compatible with $\equiv$.

Proof   Assume $x \equiv y$. It suffices to show that

$$\sum [i \equiv k] \int_{\sum [f_j < f_i] x_j}^{\sum [f_j \le f_i] x_j} \varrho(z)\, dz$$

is unchanged by replacing x with y. This in turn follows from the observation that the limits of integration are invariant under replacing x with y. This will be demonstrated for the lower limit (the upper limit is similar). Using the fact that $f \prec \equiv$,

$$\sum [f_j < f_i] x_j$$

$$= \sum_{[t] \in \Omega/\equiv} \sum_{j \in [t]} [f_j < f_i] x_j$$

$$= \sum_{[t] \in \Omega/\equiv} \sum_{j \in [t]} [f_t < f_i] x_j$$

$$= \sum_{[t] \in \Omega/\equiv} [f_t < f_i] \sum_{j \in [t]} x_j$$

$$= \sum_{[t] \in \Omega/\equiv} [f_t < f_i] \sum [j \equiv t] x_j$$

The last expression is invariant under replacing x with y since $x \equiv y$. $\blacksquare$

Theorem 17.11   If the fitness f is dominated by $\equiv$, then the tournament selection scheme is compatible with $\equiv$.

Proof   Assume $x \equiv y$. It suffices to show that

$$\sum_i [i \equiv t] \sum_{v \in X_n^k} \mathcal{F}'(v/k)_i \prod_{j<n} \frac{x_j^{v_j}}{v_j!}$$

is unchanged by replacing x with y. By theorem 17.10, this can be written in the form

$$\sum_i [i \equiv t] \sum_{[t] \in \Lambda/\equiv} \sum_{v \in k[t] \cap X_n^k} \mathcal{F}'(v/k)_i \prod_{j<n} \frac{x_j^{v_j}}{v_j!}$$

$$= \sum_i [i \equiv t] \sum_{[t] \in \Lambda/\equiv} \sum_{v \in k[t] \cap X_n^k} \mathcal{F}'(t)_i \prod_{j<n} \frac{x_j^{v_j}}{v_j!}$$

$$= \sum_i [i \equiv t] \sum_{[t] \in \Lambda/\equiv} \mathcal{F}'(t)_i \sum_{v \in k[t] \cap X_n^k} \prod_{j<n} \frac{x_j^{v_j}}{v_j!}$$

The inner sum is invariant under replacing x with y by lemma 17.6.   ∎

An equivalence relation $\equiv$ is called *uniform with respect to translation* provided that for all $i, j, h, k \in \Omega$,

$$i \equiv j \implies |(i \oplus [h]) \cap [k]| = |(j \oplus [h]) \cap [k]|$$

That is, the cardinality of the intersection of the equivalence class of k with the translate by j of the equivalence class of h depends on the class of j rather than the particular value of j.

The next theorem is a sufficient, though not necessary, condition for the mutation scheme to be compatible with $\equiv$.

Theorem 17.12   If the mutation distribution μ is dominated by $\equiv$, and if $\equiv$ is uniform with respect to translation, then the mutation scheme is compatible with $\equiv$.

Proof   Assume $x \equiv y$. By exercise 10 of section 6.1 it suffices to show that

$$\sum_h [h \equiv t] \sum_j x_j \mu_{j \oplus h}$$

is unchanged by replacing x with y. This expression may be written as

$$\sum_h [h \equiv t] \sum_j x_j \mu_{j \oplus h} \sum_{[i] \in \Omega/\equiv} [j \oplus h \equiv i]$$

$$= \sum_h [h \equiv t] \sum_{[i] \in \Omega/\equiv} \sum_j [j \oplus h \equiv i] \mu_{j \oplus h} \sum_{[k] \in \Omega/\equiv} [j \equiv k] x_j$$

Since $\mu \prec \equiv$, the summation maybe rearranged to yield

$$\sum_{[k] \in \Omega/\equiv} \sum_j [j \equiv k] x_j \sum_{[i] \in \Omega/\equiv} \mu_i \sum_h [h \equiv t][j \oplus h \equiv i]$$

Note that the condition $[h \equiv t][j \oplus h \equiv i]$ is equivalent to $h \in [t] \wedge h \in j \oplus [i]$. Hence the inner sum is just the cardinality of $(j \oplus [i]) \cap [t]$. Using the uniformity of $\equiv$ with respect to translation, the expression above is

$$\sum_{[k] \in \Omega/\equiv} \sum_j [j \equiv k] x_j \sum_{[i] \in \Omega/\equiv} \mu_i |(k \oplus [i]) \cap [t]|$$

$$= \sum_{[k] \in \Omega/\equiv} \sum_{[i] \in \Omega/\equiv} \mu_i |(k \oplus [i]) \cap [t]| \sum_j [j \equiv k] x_j$$

Since $x \equiv y$, the inner sum is unchanged by replacing x with y. ∎

As has by now become apparent to those familiar with classical "GA theory", schemata have been left behind, playing no part in the theoretical development so far. This is not to suggest that they can have no role, but their natural place in the general landscape had not, until now, been come upon.

For those not already familiar with the concept, a *schema* is a subset S of Ω maximal with respect to the condition that, for some given $U \subset \{0, \ldots, \ell - 1\}$,

$$\forall u \in U . \forall s, s' \in S . s \otimes 2^u = s' \otimes 2^u$$

Theorem 17.13   If crossover is separating and the crossover scheme is compatible with $\equiv$, then the elements of $\tilde{\Omega}$ must be schemata.

Proof   Assume that the crossover scheme is compatible with $\equiv$, let $\mathcal{C} \in \Omega/\equiv$, and let $\mathcal{K} = \mathcal{H}(\{e_k : k \in \mathcal{C}\})$. Note that

$$\left(\mathcal{M} \Big|_{\mu = e_0} \right)(e_k) = e_k$$

It follows, using the compatibility of crossover and theorem 17.3, that

$$(\mathcal{M}\Big|_{\mu=e_0})(\mathcal{K}) \subset \mathcal{K}$$

Therefore, by theorems 10.7 and 17.2,

$$x \in \mathcal{K} \implies \lim_{j \to \infty} (\mathcal{M}\Big|_{\mu=e_0})^j(x) \in \mathcal{K}$$

Choosing $x \sim \sum_{k \in \mathcal{C}} e_k$, and applying theorem 10.14 yields an element y (the limit above) satisfying

$$\langle \prod_{i=0}^{\ell-1} \sum_{k \in \mathcal{C}} [k \otimes 2^i = 0 \otimes 2^i], \ldots, \prod_{i=0}^{\ell-1} \sum_{k \in \mathcal{C}} [k \otimes 2^i = \mathbf{1} \otimes 2^i] \rangle \sim y \in \mathcal{K}$$

Let $U = \{u : \forall s, s' \in \mathcal{C} \,.\, s \otimes 2^u = s' \otimes 2^u\}$. The proof is completed by showing, given $s' \in \mathcal{C}$, that

$$(\forall u \in U \,.\, s \otimes 2^u = s' \otimes 2^u) \implies s \in \mathcal{C}$$

Suppose to the contrary that $s \notin \mathcal{C}$, then $e_s^T y = 0$ since $y \in \mathcal{K} = \mathcal{H}(\{e_k : k \in \mathcal{C}\})$. That is,

$$\exists i \,.\, \sum_{k \in \mathcal{C}} [k \otimes 2^i = s \otimes 2^i] = 0$$

Thus every term of the sum is zero (i.e., $k \in \mathcal{C} \implies k \otimes 2^i \neq s \otimes 2^i$), and in particular $s' \otimes 2^i \neq s \otimes 2^i$. Therefore $i \notin U$, since by assumption $\forall u \in U \,.\, s \otimes 2^u = s' \otimes 2^u$. But $i \notin U$ means, by the definition of U, that $s'' \otimes 2^i \neq s' \otimes 2^i$ for some $s'' \in \mathcal{C}$. Thus it may now be concluded that $s'' \otimes 2^i = s \otimes 2^i$, contracting $k \in \mathcal{C} \implies k \otimes 2^i \neq s \otimes 2^i$. ∎

Exercises

1. Use the result of exercise 2 in section 17.1 to give an alternate proof of theorem 17.9.

2. A function f expressible in the form $f(x) = h(\mathbf{1}^T x)$ for some function h is called a *function of unitation*. Define $\equiv$ in a nontrivial way so that, for any fitness function of unitation, proportional, ranking, and tournament selection are compatible with $\equiv$.

3. Show that the condition $f \prec \equiv$ in theorem 17.9 is necessary as well as sufficient, provided that $|\Omega/\!\equiv| > 1$.

4. Show that for ranking and tournament selection, the condition $f \prec \equiv$ in theorem 17.9 is not necessary, even when $|\Omega/\!\equiv| > 1$.

5. Obtain a necessary and sufficient condition on f for the ranking and tournament selection schemes to be compatible with $\equiv$. *Hint:* Consider sorting Ω by fitness, and requiring that equivalent elements sort together.

6. Define $\equiv$ in a nontrivial way so that any mutation distribution which is a function of unitation is dominated by $\equiv$.

7. For the choice of $\equiv$ in the previous exercise, is the mutation scheme compatible with $\equiv$ when mutation corresponds to a rate? *Hint:* Does exercise 6 of section 4.1 speak to whether $\equiv$ is uniform with respect to translation?

8. What is the general cardinality analogue of theorem 17.12?

9. Show that any equivalence relation corresponding to schemata is uniform with respect to translation.

10. Appropriately generalize the concept of schemata and repeat the previous exercise for the general cardinality case.

11. Show theorem 17.13 carries over to the general cardinality case.

18 Models

In situations where $\mathcal{G}$ is compatible with a nontrivial equivalence relation, one may construct a course-grained model $\tilde{\tau}$ of τ over a simplified search space $\tilde{\Lambda}$ of reduced complexity, with complete assurance that the macroscopic model accurately reflects the dynamics of τ over Λ.

In the case of the simple genetic algorithm, however, there are hardly any interesting quotients to consider (the next chapter will explain this in some detail). When $\mathcal{G}$ is not compatible with the equivalence relation (and, by theorem 17.8, neither is τ), the dauntless may nevertheless choose to proceed at the peril of sacrificing any expectation that the equivalence class of a future generation has any relationship—besides serendipitous—to that predicted by $\tilde{\tau}$.

Depending upon one's goals, that is entirely appropriate: one may choose to sacrifice absolute truth in the pursuit of a more manageable model (in rough analogy to forsaking actual data for a linear regression). Moreover, $\tilde{\mathcal{G}}$ is perfectly well defined with respect to any choice T of equivalence class representatives, whether or not it happens to be compatible with the underlying equivalence relation. And, given any definition of $\tilde{\mathcal{G}}$ on the quotient space, one may consider the instance of random heuristic search over $\tilde{\Omega}$ having $\tilde{\mathcal{G}}$ as its heuristic.

Whereas the freedom allowed by the approach described in the previous paragraph— define $\tilde{\mathcal{G}}$ based on a choice for T, then take $\tilde{\tau}$ corresponding to $\tilde{\mathcal{G}}$—provides flexibility and hope of obtaining a reasonable fit by judicious choice of representatives, one may well wind up in the situation of having a simple model about which nothing has been proved *except internally;* the resulting model is an instance of RHS, so the general theory of random heuristic search may be brought to bear *on the model* . . . but the degree to which the model represents τ is another matter altogether!

When proof is an irrelevant concept, the outcome described above is of no consequence. Moreover, estimating $\tilde{\mathcal{G}}$—rather than defining it with respect to T—may provide further simplification. If confidence in the model is desired, one may resort to empirical means, assuming the model's complexity is not a computational barrier.

The first section of this chapter considers choosing equivalence class representatives and how, when they are suitably chosen, the quotient map takes a particularly simple form. The second section touches upon invariance considerations in choosing equivalence class representatives and considers an extended example in the exercises. The final section touches upon the special case where the heuristic is compatible and is projectively (i.e., ignoring magnitude) a linear transformation.

18.1   Natural Representatives

Theorem 17.2 suggests one method of choosing equivalence class representatives; the elements of $\Lambda/\!\equiv$ are convex compact sets, thus the average of $[t]$ is a natural candidate to represent $[t]$. Alternatively, one might pick a maximal element of $[t]$, with respect to entropy for instance, as a representative (models employing some sort of maximum entropy assumption are not uncommon). Or perhaps representatives could be chosen in some natural way with respect to the underlying equivalence relation on Ω.

The latter possibility is considered first; suppose T is chosen such that $t \in T \Longrightarrow t \prec \equiv$. Note that in this case $t_i = |[i]|^{-1} \sum [j \equiv i]\, t_j$.

Lemma 18.1   If $\Xi x = \Xi y$ and $x \prec \equiv$, then the entropy of x is greater than or equal to that of y.

Proof: Let T be a set of equivalence class representatives. The entropy of x is

$$-\sum x_i \log x_i$$

$$= -\sum_{t \in T} \sum_i [i \equiv t]\, x_i \log x_i$$

$$= -\sum_{t \in T} \log x_t \sum_i [i \equiv t]\, x_i$$

$$= -\sum_{t \in T} \log \frac{\sum_j [j \equiv t]\, x_j}{|[t]|} \sum_i [i \equiv t]\, x_i$$

$$= -\sum_{t \in T} \log \frac{\sum_j [j \equiv t]\, y_j}{|[t]|} \sum_i [i \equiv t]\, y_i$$

Subtracting the entropy of y from this gives

$$\sum_{t \in T} \sum_i [i \equiv t](y_i \log y_i \ - \ y_i \log \frac{\sum_j [j \equiv t]\, y_j}{|[t]|})$$

$$= \sum_{t \in T} \sum_i [i \equiv t]\, y_i \log \frac{y_i |[t]|}{\sum_j [j \equiv t]\, y_j}$$

Using $\log x \geq 1 - 1/x$ in the expression above leads to a lower bound of 0.   ∎

A consequence of lemma 18.1 is that choosing representatives to be dominated by $\equiv$ implies that representatives have maximum entropy.

Next consider choosing representatives by averaging, that is

$$T = \{\frac{1}{\lambda([x])} \int_{[x]} y \, d\lambda : x \in \Lambda\}$$

where λ represents surface measure on $[x] \subset \Lambda$.

Lemma 18.2   Let T be the set of equivalence class representatives given by averaging. The representative $t \in T$ of $[x]$ has ith component

$$t_i = \frac{(\Xi x)_{[i]}}{|[i]|}$$

In particular, $t \prec \equiv$.

Proof   Since the equivalence class $[x] = \Lambda \cap \Xi^{-1}(\Xi x)$ is a product of simplices, the integral factors, giving the product of their barycenters. Thus the representative $t \in T$ of $[x]$ has ith component

$$t_i = \frac{(\Xi x)_{[i]}}{|[i]|}$$

and hence $t_i = t_j$ whenever $i \equiv j$. In particular, $t \prec \equiv$.   ∎

Lemmas 18.2 and 18.1 taken together establish the equivalence of all three proposed methods of choosing equivalence class representatives.

Theorem 18.3   The following methods of choosing a set T of equivalence class representatives are equivalent.

- Choose T such that $t \in T \Longrightarrow t \prec \equiv$.
- Choose T such that $t \in T \Longrightarrow t$ has maximum entropy among $[t]$.
- Choose T by averaging (as in lemma 18.2).

This choice for T (as in theorem 18.3) is particularly convenient because it allows the following simple characterization of $\tilde{\mathcal{G}}$.

Theorem 18.4   If equivalence class representatives are chosen as in theorem 18.3, then

$$\tilde{\mathcal{G}} = \Xi \circ \mathcal{G} \circ D\Xi^T$$

where D is the diagonal matrix having iith entry $|[i]|^{-1}$. The representative t of x is given by $t = D\Xi^T \Xi x$. Moreover, $\Xi D\Xi^T = I$, and $\mathbf{1}^T \Xi = \mathbf{1}^T$.

Proof   The ith component of $D\Xi^T\Xi x$ is

$$D_{i,i} \sum_{u,v} \Xi_{u,i}\Xi_{u,v}x_v$$

$$= \frac{1}{|[i]|} \sum_{u,v}[i \in u][v \in u]x_v$$

$$= \frac{1}{|[i]|} \sum_{v}[i \equiv v]x_v$$

$$= \frac{(\Xi x)_{[i]}}{|[i]|}$$

which, by lemma 18.2, is the ith component of the representative of x. The i, jth entry of $\Xi D\Xi^T$ is

$$\sum_{u,v} \Xi_{i,u}\frac{[u = v]}{|[u]|}\Xi_{j,v}$$

$$= \sum_{u}[u \in i]\frac{1}{|[u]|}[u \in j]$$

$$= \frac{[i = j]}{|[i]|}\sum_{u}[u \in i]$$

$$= [i = j]$$

The jth component of $\mathbf{1}^T\Xi$ is

$$\sum_{i}[j \in i] = 1$$

By what has already been established, to show $\tilde{\mathcal{G}}$ is $\Xi \circ \mathcal{G} \circ D\Xi^T$ it suffices that

$$\tilde{\mathcal{G}}(\Xi t) = \Xi\mathcal{G}(t)$$

This, however, is the definition of $\tilde{\mathcal{G}}(\Xi t)$ for $t \in T$.   ∎

18.2   Invariant Representatives

A possible consideration in choosing equivalence class representatives is invariance. Suppose there exists a set T of representatives such that $\mathcal{G} : T \to T$. If T is chosen as in theorem 18.3, invariance is equivalent to the condition $t \prec \, \equiv \, \Longrightarrow \mathcal{G}(t) \prec \, \equiv$. Because the hierarchical relationship

$$[\mathcal{G}(t)] = \tilde{\mathcal{G}}([t])$$

holds for $t \in T$, invariance of T under $\mathcal{G}$ has the following consequence.

Theorem 18.5   If T is invariant under $\mathcal{G}$, then $[\mathcal{G}^k(t)] = \tilde{\mathcal{G}}^k([t])$ for all k, provided $t \in T$. Moreover, the local dynamics of τ as viewed in the quotient space $(\Xi\,\tau(t),\ \Xi\,\tau^2(t),\ \ldots)$ is attracted to the local dynamics of $\tilde{\mathcal{G}}$ as population size increases, for population trajectories beginning in T.

Proof   By theorem 13.2, the local dynamics of τ is attracted to the local dynamics of $\mathcal{G}$ as $r \to \infty$. Thus, given $h > 0$, $\varepsilon > 0$ and $\gamma < 1$, there exists N such that with probability at least γ and for all $0 \le k \le h$

$$r > N \quad \Longrightarrow \quad \| \Xi\tau^k(t) - \Xi\mathcal{G}^k(t) \| \, < \varepsilon$$

The proof is completed by showing $\Xi\mathcal{G}^k(t) = \tilde{\mathcal{G}}^k(\Xi t)$ via induction on k. The base case ($k = 1$) is trivial. For the inductive step, note that

$$\Xi\mathcal{G}^{k-1}(\mathcal{G}(t))$$

$$= \tilde{\mathcal{G}}^{k-1}(\Xi\mathcal{G}(t))$$

$$= \tilde{\mathcal{G}}^{k-1}(\tilde{\mathcal{G}}(\Xi t)) \qquad\qquad\qquad\qquad \blacksquare$$

Theorem 18.5 is important because it establishes links between $\mathcal{G}$, τ, $\tilde{\mathcal{G}}$, and $\tilde{\tau}$ in situations where compatibility with the underlying equivalence relation is lacking.

The next theorem gives sufficient conditions for invariance in the context of the simple genetic algorithm.

Recall that the probability i is used as a crossover mask is χ_i, and the probability that i is used as a mutation mask is μ_i. Crossover and mutation are called *symmetric* if for all permutations σ of bit positions

$$\chi_k = \chi_{\sigma(k)}$$

$$\mu_k = \mu_{\sigma(k)}$$

Theorem 18.6 If mutation and crossover are symmetric, then for all i and j, and all permutations σ of bit positions

$$M_{i,j} = M_{\sigma(i),\sigma(j)}$$

where M is the mixing matrix. In this case the set T of equivalence class representatives as in theorem 18.3 is invariant under $\mathcal{G}$ (assuming proportional, ranking, or tournament selection), provided:

- fitness is dominated by $\equiv$,
- each equivalence class is invariant under every permutation σ,
- given equivalent elements i and j (of Ω) there exists a permutation σ such that $\sigma(i) = j$.

Proof

$M_{x,y}$

$$= \sum_{i,j,k} \mu_i \mu_j \frac{\chi_k + \chi_{\overline{k}}}{2} [(x \oplus i) \otimes k \oplus (y \oplus j) \otimes \overline{k} = 0]$$

$$= \sum_{i,j,k} \mu_i \mu_j \frac{\chi_k + \chi_{\overline{k}}}{2} [\sigma((x \oplus i) \otimes k \oplus (y \oplus j) \otimes \overline{k}) = 0]$$

$$= \sum_{i,j,k} \mu_i \mu_j \frac{\chi_k + \chi_{\overline{k}}}{2} [(\sigma(x) \oplus \sigma(i)) \otimes \sigma(k) \oplus (\sigma(y) \oplus \sigma(j)) \otimes \sigma(\overline{k}) = 0]$$

$$= \sum_{i,j,k} \mu_{\sigma^{-1}(i)} \mu_{\sigma^{-1}(j)} \frac{\chi_{\sigma^{-1}(k)} + \chi_{\sigma^{-1}(\overline{k})}}{2} [(\sigma(x) \oplus i) \otimes k \oplus (\sigma(y) \oplus j) \otimes \overline{k} = 0]$$

Since mutation and crossover are symmetric,

$$\mu_{\sigma^{-1}(i)} \mu_{\sigma^{-1}(j)} \frac{\chi_{\sigma^{-1}(k)} + \chi_{\sigma^{-1}(\overline{k})}}{2}$$

$$= \mu_i \mu_j \frac{\chi_k + \chi_{\overline{k}}}{2}$$

and therefore $M_{i,j} = M_{\sigma(i),\sigma(j)}$. By theorems 17.9, 17.10, and 17.11, T is invariant under $\mathcal{F}$. It therefore remains to show that T is invariant under the mixing scheme $\mathcal{M}$. Let $i \equiv j$ and let $\sigma(i) = j$. Appealing to lemma 18.2,

$$\mathcal{M}(x)_j$$

$$= \sum_{u,v} x_u x_v M_{u\oplus j, v\oplus j}$$

$$= \sum_{s,t\in T} \sum_{u,v} [u \equiv s][v \equiv t] x_u x_v M_{u\oplus j, v\oplus j}$$

$$= \sum_{s,t\in T} \frac{\tilde{x}_{[s]}\tilde{x}_{[t]}}{|[s]|\,|[t]|} \sum_{u,v} [u \equiv s][v \equiv t] M_{u\oplus j, v\oplus j}$$

It therefore suffices that the inner sum is invariant under replacing j with i. Note that the sum in question may be written as

$$\sum_{u,v} [\sigma(u) \equiv s][\sigma(v) \equiv t] M_{\sigma(u)\oplus\sigma(i),\sigma(v)\oplus\sigma(i)}$$

$$= \sum_{u,v} [u \equiv \sigma^{-1}(s)][v \equiv \sigma^{-1}(t)] M_{\sigma(u\oplus i),\sigma(v\oplus i)}$$

$$= \sum_{u,v} [u \equiv s][v \equiv t] M_{u\oplus i, v\oplus i} \qquad\blacksquare$$

Assuming compatibility and invariance are not considerations, the choice of equivalence might depend upon the main points of interest. For example, it may be natural, in the context of function optimization, to equivalence class based on function value; i.e., let elements of Ω be equivalent when they have the same fitness.

David Goldberg coined the term "function of unitation" to refer to a function (defined on a set of binary strings) whose value at x depends only on $\mathbf{1}^T x$. The following exercises illustrate the application of preceding theory to functions of unitation. In the context of GAs applied to functions of unitation, the principle of invariance and some of its implications were first explored by Rabinovich and Wigderson.

Exercises

1. Define equivalence classes based on

$$i \equiv j \iff \mathbf{1}^T i = \mathbf{1}^T j$$

Show that functions of unitation are dominated by $\equiv$.

2. A function f of unitation is called *injective* provided $f(i) = f(j) \Longrightarrow \mathbf{1}^T i = \mathbf{1}^T j$. Show that if f is an injective function of unitation, then the definition of equivalence (exercise 1) coincides with equivalence based on fitness (i.e., $f(i) = f(j) \Longleftrightarrow i \equiv j$).

3. Show that if $\mathcal{F}$ is the proportional, ranking, or tournament selection scheme, and if f is a function of unitation, then $p \prec \equiv \Longrightarrow \mathcal{F}(p) \prec \equiv$.

4. Show that when mutation is given by a rate, it is compatible with $\equiv$.

5. Show that crossover is not necessarily compatible with $\equiv$.

6. Let T be the set of equivalence class representatives as given in theorem 18.3 ($\equiv$ is defined in exercise 1). Assuming f is a function of unitation, show that T is invariant under $\mathcal{F}$, but it is not necessarily invariant under $\mathcal{G} = \mathcal{M} \circ \mathcal{F}$.

7. Show that for functions of unitation, T (as in the previous exercise) is invariant under $\mathcal{G}$ if mutation is given by a rate and crossover is uniform. *Hint:* Apply theorem 18.6.

8. Prove the following:

Theorem 18.7   Let mutation and crossover be symmetric, let f be a function of unitation, and let the selection scheme be proportional, ranking, or tournament. Suppose the set T of equivalence class representatives is given as in theorem 18.3, where $\equiv$ is defined by unitation ($\mathbf{1}^T i = \mathbf{1}^T j \Longleftrightarrow i \equiv j$). Then $[\mathcal{G}^k(t)] = \tilde{\mathcal{G}}^k([t])$ for all k, provided $t \in T$. Moreover, the local dynamics of τ as viewed in the quotient space (i.e., $\Xi \tau(t)$, $\Xi \tau^2(t)$, ...) is attracted to the local dynamics of $\tilde{\mathcal{G}}$ as population size increases, for population trajectories beginning in T.

9. Assuming the hypotheses of theorem 18.7, let $\mathcal{G}'$ and τ' denote $\mathcal{G}$ and τ, respectively, subject to the restriction that crossover is zero. Justify the following argument and conclusions: $\tilde{\mathcal{G}}'$ is well defined independent of T, and the hierarchical relationships

$$[\mathcal{G}'^k(x)] = \tilde{\mathcal{G}}'^k([x])$$

$$\Pr\{\tau'^k(p) \equiv q\} = \Pr\{\tilde{\tau}'^k(\tilde{p}) = \tilde{q}\}$$

hold for all k and every initial population. For small crossover, the local dynamics of $\tilde{\mathcal{G}}$ is nearly that of $\tilde{\mathcal{G}}'$, which is the image under Ξ of the local dynamics of $\mathcal{G}'$, which is nearly the image under Ξ of the local dynamics of $\mathcal{G}$, which coincides with that of τ as viewed in the quotient space as population size increases. Therefore,

• As the crossover rate decreases, the local dynamics of τ as viewed in the quotient space converges to that of $\tilde{\tau}$.

• As the population size increases and the crossover rate decreases, the local dynamics of τ as viewed in the quotient space converges to that of $\tilde{\mathcal{G}}$.

10. Assuming zero crossover, show that $\mathcal{M}$ is given by matrix multiplication with the matrix U having entries $U_{i,j} = \mu_{i \oplus j}$.

11. Using the notation of the previous exercises, show that if the fitness scheme is proportional, then

$$\mathcal{G}'(x) = \frac{Ax}{\mathbf{1}^T Ax}$$

where $A = U \operatorname{diag}(f)$, and

$$\tilde{\mathcal{G}}'(\tilde{t}) = \frac{B\tilde{t}}{\mathbf{1}^T B\tilde{t}}$$

where $B = \Xi A D \Xi^T$. Given zero mutation, show this simplifies to

$$\tilde{\mathcal{F}}(\tilde{x}) = \frac{\operatorname{diag}(\langle f_{2^0-1}, \ldots, f_{2^\ell-1} \rangle) \tilde{x}}{\langle f_{2^0-1}, \ldots, f_{2^\ell-1} \rangle^T \tilde{x}}$$

18.3   Linear Heuristics

A heuristic $\mathcal{G}$ is called *linear* if it is projectively (i.e., ignoring magnitude) a linear transformation, i.e.,

$$\mathcal{G} = \frac{Ax}{\mathbf{1}^T Ax}$$

In this case, A is called the matrix of the heuristic.

Theorem 18.8   Suppose $\mathcal{G}$ is a linear heuristic with matrix A which is compatible with an equivalence relation $\equiv$. Then $\tilde{\mathcal{G}}$ is a linear heuristic with matrix $B = \Xi A D \Xi^T$ (the matrices D and Ξ are as in theorem 18.4). Moreover, if $\mathbf{1}^T$ is a left eigenvector of A, then

$$Ax = \lambda x \implies B\Xi x = \lambda \Xi x$$

Proof   Since $\mathcal{G}$ is compatible with $\equiv$, equivalence class representatives can be chosen arbitrarily (theorem 17.5). Hence theorem 18.4 applies, which establishes the first part of the proof. If $\mathbf{1}^T A = \alpha \mathbf{1}^T$, then for any $x \in \Lambda$,

$$\mathbf{1}^T B \Xi x$$

$$= \mathbf{1}^T \Xi A D \Xi^T \Xi x$$

$$= \mathbf{1}^T A D \Xi^T \Xi x$$

$$= \alpha \mathbf{1}^T D \Xi^T \Xi x$$

$$= \alpha \mathbf{1}^T x$$

$$= \mathbf{1}^T A x$$

Hence if x is an eigenvector of A with eigenvalue λ, the following diagram commutes

$$
\begin{array}{ccc}
x & \xrightarrow{} & Ax = \lambda x \\
\Xi \downarrow & & \downarrow \Xi \\
\Xi x & \xrightarrow{B} & \Xi Ax = \lambda \Xi x
\end{array}
$$

To see this, first note that when omitting "$= \lambda x$" and "$= \lambda \Xi x$" from the diagram, commutativity holds for an open set of x—which are not eigenvalues of U—and so it holds for all x; next restore the assumption that x is an eigenvalue. ∎

The function $\mathcal{G}'$ considered in the exercises of the preceding section (see exercise 11) coincides with the linear heuristic $\mathcal{F}_\mu$ corresponding to mutating the result of proportional selection (see section 4.3 of chapter 4),

$$\mathcal{F}_\mu(x) = \frac{Ax}{\mathbf{1}^T A x}$$

where $A = U \operatorname{diag}(f)$ and $U_{i,j} = \mu_{i \oplus j}$. Let $\equiv$ be an equivalence relation with which $\mathcal{F}_\mu(x)$ is not necessarily compatible, and consider the "model"

$$\tilde{\mathcal{F}}_\mu(\tilde{t}) = \frac{B\tilde{t}}{\mathbf{1}^T B\tilde{t}}$$

where $B = \Xi A D \Xi^T$. The heuristic $\mathcal{F}_\mu$ is called *simple* if the matrix B of the model $\tilde{\mathcal{F}}_\mu$ is diagonalizable (simplicity implicitly involves the equivalence relation $\equiv$).

Theorem 18.9   For any mutation distribution μ and any equivalence relation $\equiv$, the set

$$S = \{ f : \mathcal{F}_\mu \text{ is simple (given fitness vector } f) \}$$

is open and dense.

Proof   By choosing $f_i = 1/D_{i,i}$, the matrix B of the heuristic of the model becomes the real symmetric matrix $\Xi U \Xi^T$. In this case, B has real eigenvalues and eigenvectors, and $Z^{-1} B Z$ is diagonal where Z is the matrix whose columns are normalized eigenvectors of B. Diagonalizability of B persists as f is perturbed since the eigenvalues and eigenvectors depend continuously on f and the nonvanishing of the Gramian $\det(Z^T Z)$ characterizes diagonalizability. Thus S is open. S is nowhere dense because the vanishing of the Gramian on an open set would imply it vanishes identically. ∎

Assuming simple $\mathcal{F}_\mu$, let $\mathrm{diag}(h) = Z^{-1}BZ$ where Z is the matrix whose columns are the normalized eigenvectors of B and h contains the eigenvalues of B. Assume further that B is invertible. Regarding $\tilde{\mathcal{F}}_\mu$ as acting on the sphere, call it $\mathcal{F}_\mu^*$ in that context, it follows that

$$\mathcal{F}_\mu^*(x)$$

$$= \frac{Bx}{\|Bx\|}$$

$$= \frac{Z\,\mathrm{diag}(h)Z^{-1}x}{\|Z\,\mathrm{diag}(h)Z^{-1}x\|}$$

$$= Z^*\mathcal{F}(Z^{-1}x)$$

where $\mathcal{F}$ is the proportional selection scheme corresponding to the fitness vector h (ignoring the fact that the entries of h might not be positive) and where Z^* is the linear operator Z regarded as acting on the sphere, that is, $Z^*x = Zx/\|Zx\|$. Regarding $\mathcal{F}$ as acting on the sphere, call it $\mathcal{F}^*$ in that context, it follows that

$$\mathcal{F}_\mu^*(Z^*x) = Z^*\mathcal{F}^*(x)$$

where Z^* is invertible and continuously differentiable, and the following diagram commutes

$$
\begin{array}{ccc}
x & \longrightarrow & \mathcal{F}^*x \\
\Big\downarrow{\scriptstyle Z^*} & & \Big\downarrow{\scriptstyle Z^*} \\
Z^*x & \longrightarrow & \mathcal{F}_\mu^*(Z^*x)
\end{array}
$$

Hence the dynamics of $\mathcal{F}_\mu^*$ is the image under Z^* of pure selection dynamics $\mathcal{F}^*$ Of course, this may be over complex space because there is no guarantee that the eigenvalues of B are real. This "equivalence" (via Z^*) between mutation and selection was noted by Jonathan Rowe.

Exercises

1. Provide details for the proof of theorem 18.9. *Hint:* If $f = \mathbf{1}$, then B is diagonalized by unitary Z. Modify the columns of Z as f changes (subtract out directions spanned by

rows of $B - \lambda I$ where the λ are eigenvalues of B) to obtain a new matrix Z containing "eigenvectors"—some of which which may in fact be zero. The Gramian in question (of Z, indicating nondefective B by a nonzero value) will be a polynomial in f and the eigenvalues of B; the square of its norm is (by the symmetric function theorem) a polynomial in f.

2. Generalize the concept of simplicity from $\mathcal{F}_\mu$ to an arbitrary linear heuristic, and prove a corresponding generalized version of theorem 18.9.

3. Analyze (as in the exercises of the preceding section) degenerate Royal Road functions, which have the following form. Let $\mathbf{1} = a_1 \oplus \cdots \oplus a_k$ where $a_i \otimes a_j = a_i \delta_{i,j}$. The fitness of x is given by $\sum g_i (x \otimes a_i)$ where g is some positive real vector. Equivalence class based on fitness, and choose representatives as in theorem 18.3. *Hint:* Royal Road functions support compatibility to a lesser degree than do functions of unatation.

19 Schemata

This chapter is almost an afterthought, devoted to schemata. Whereas schemata have historically been appealed to as a means of explaining the behavior of genetic search, much has been claimed and little of relevance has been proved. The most mystical part of classical "GA theory" is the role played by schemata.

Rather than attempting to bring rigor to a muddled subject (though to some extent that might inadvertently be accomplished) this final chapter is devoted to a less ambitious goal; shedding light on interrelationships between schemata, $\mathcal{M}$, $\mathcal{F}$, and the Walsh transform, within the context of equivalence relations.

The first section reinterprets schemata in terms of the theoretical framework presented in previous chapters. The second section considers their interrelationship with $\mathcal{M}$. The final section brings $\mathcal{F}$ into the picture, concluding with a result about the shape selection must have, given natural assumptions, for the GA's heuristic to be compatible with equivalence relations. The Walsh transform is woven throughout.

19.1   Definition

Schemata are reinterpreted as members of some *schemata family*. Any $\xi \in \Omega$ represents a schemata family, and the matrix Ξ defined by

$$\Xi_{i,j} = [j \otimes \xi = i]$$

is called the operator associated with the family. Here Ξ has $2^{1^T \xi}$ rows and n columns. Integers in the interval $[0, 2^{1^T \xi})$ and elements of Ω_ξ are regarded as being the same through the injection corresponding to ξ (see section 4.1 for definition and example of this injection). Hence the rows of Ξ are indexed by Ω_ξ and the columns are indexed by Ω.

The elements of the schemata family represented by ξ are subsets which partition Ω. Thus a schema is an equivalence class and the schemata family can be thought of as an equivalence relation (the equivalence of elements x and y will be denoted by $x \equiv y$). Each equivalence class contains exactly one element from Ω_ξ, referred to as its *canonical representative*. Thus the schemata family represented by ξ may be identified with Ω_ξ. In general, element j is related to canonical representative i if and only if $\Xi_{i,j} = 1$ (regarding rows as indexed by Ω_ξ and columns as indexed by Ω).

For example, let $\Omega = \{0, 1, 2, 3, 4, 5, 6, 7, 8\}$ and $\xi = 5$. Then $\Omega_\xi = \{0, 1, 4, 5\}$ and

$$\Xi = \begin{pmatrix} 1 & 0 & 1 & 0 & 0 & 0 & 0 & 0 \\ 0 & 1 & 0 & 1 & 0 & 0 & 0 & 0 \\ 0 & 0 & 0 & 0 & 1 & 0 & 1 & 0 \\ 0 & 0 & 0 & 0 & 0 & 1 & 0 & 1 \end{pmatrix}$$

The schemata, identified with their canonical representatives, are

$$
\begin{aligned}
0 &\longleftrightarrow \{0, 2\} \\
1 &\longleftrightarrow \{1, 3\} \\
4 &\longleftrightarrow \{4, 6\} \\
5 &\longleftrightarrow \{5, 7\}
\end{aligned}
$$

The image of a vector x under Ξ is

$$
\Xi x = \begin{pmatrix} x_0 + x_2 \\ x_1 + x_3 \\ x_4 + x_6 \\ x_5 + x_7 \end{pmatrix}
$$

In other words, the ith component of Ξx is the summation of x_j over all j belonging to schema i; schema i refers to that schema containing canonical representative i. Considering this using summation notation yields

$$
(\Xi x)_i
$$

$$
= \sum_j [j \otimes \xi = i] x_j
$$

$$
= \sum_{j \in \Omega_\xi} \sum_{j' \in \Omega_{\overline{\xi}}} [(j \oplus j') \otimes \xi = i] x_{j \oplus j'}
$$

$$
= \sum_{j' \in \Omega_{\overline{\xi}}} \sum_{j \in \Omega_\xi} [j = i] x_{j \oplus j'}
$$

$$
= \sum_{j' \in \Omega_{\overline{\xi}}} x_{i \oplus j'}
$$

The indices in the last sum show the members of the schemata family represented by ξ are the cosets of the subgroup $\Omega_{\overline{\xi}}$. Hence every column of Ξ contains exactly one 1 (in the row indicating the coset to which the column index belongs) and the first nonzero entry in row i (regarding rows as indexed by elements of Ω_ξ through the injection corresponding to ξ) is in column i (regarding columns as indexed by elements of Ω). Therefore Ξ is in row echelon form and has full row rank. The kernel of Ξ is easily determined via the Walsh transform.

Theorem 19.1   The kernel of Ξ is $\mathcal{L}\{\widehat{e_k} : k \notin \Omega_\xi\}$

Proof   Neglecting nonzero factors, the ith component of $\Xi \widehat{e_k}$ is

$$\sum_{j \in \Omega_{\overline{\xi}}} (-1)^{(\xi \otimes k \oplus \overline{\xi} \otimes k)^T j} = \sum_{j \in \Omega_{\overline{\xi}}} (-1)^{j^T \overline{\xi} \otimes k}$$

The latter sum is zero because $\overline{\xi} \otimes k \neq 0$ (since $k \notin \Omega_\xi$). The dimension of the kernel is $n - 2^{1^T \xi}$ since Ξ has full row rank, and there are exactly $n - 2^{1^T \xi}$ independent vectors in $\{\widehat{e_k} : k \notin \Omega_\xi\}$.   ∎

Note that $\Xi e_x = e_{\xi \otimes x}$ (where $\xi \otimes x \in \Omega_\xi$ is regarded as an integer in the interval $[0, 2^{1^T \xi})$ via the injection corresponding to ξ). In particular, the image of every basis vector is nonnegative. Since Ξ is nonnegative, it follows that its kernel, with the exception of zero, is disjoint from the nonnegative orthant. The following results shed further light on what multiplication by Ξ means.

Let ρ_ξ be projection to Ω_ξ,

$$\rho_\xi e_j = [j \in \Omega_\xi] e_j$$

Note that $\{e_j : j \in \Omega_\xi\}$ is a basis for the range of ρ_ξ. Hence the matrix of ρ_ξ is similar to that for Ξ. It has $2^{1^T \xi}$ rows which are indexed by elements of Ω_ξ and n columns which are indexed by elements of Ω. Recall (section 6.1) that the Walsh transform of ρ_ξ is $\widehat{\rho_\xi} = W \rho_\xi W$ (of course, the dimension of W on the left is $2^{1^T \xi}$ by $2^{1^T \xi}$ and the dimension of W on the right is n by n). It is an easy exercise to verify the following.

Theorem 19.2

$$\widehat{\rho_\xi} = 2^{-1^T \overline{\xi}} \Xi$$

As an application of this equality, note that

$$\Xi e_x = \Xi e_y$$

$$\Longleftrightarrow \widehat{\rho_\xi} e_x = \widehat{\rho_\xi} e_y$$

$$\Longleftrightarrow \rho_\xi \widehat{e_x} = \rho_\xi \widehat{e_y}$$

$$\Longleftrightarrow k \in \Omega_\xi \Longrightarrow \frac{(-1)^{x^T k}}{\sqrt{n}} = \frac{(-1)^{y^T k}}{\sqrt{n}}$$

$$\Longleftrightarrow k \in \Omega_\xi \Longrightarrow k^T x = k^T y$$

$$\Longleftrightarrow \xi \otimes x = \xi \otimes y$$

$$\Longleftrightarrow x \equiv y$$

This chain of equivalences establishes the following.

Theorem 19.3   The following are equivalent:

- $\Xi e_x = \Xi e_y$
- $\rho_\xi \widehat{e}_x = \rho_\xi \widehat{e}_y$
- $k \in \Omega_\xi \Longrightarrow k^T x = k^T y$
- $\xi \otimes x = \xi \otimes y$
- $x \equiv y$

Exercises

1. To how many schemata families does a schema belong?

2. What is the cardinality of schema i (for $i \in \Omega_\xi$)?

3. Considering all schemata families, how many distinct schema are there?

4. Given population vector x, show the ith component of Ξx is the proportion of population x belonging to schema i.

5. Show $\Xi e_x = e_{\xi \otimes x}$, where $\xi \otimes x \in \Omega_\xi$ is regarded as an integer in the interval $[0, 2^{1^T \xi})$ via the injection corresponding to ξ.

6. Show that $\Omega_{\overline{\xi}}$ is a subgroup of Ω.

7. Show that the members of a schemata family represented by ξ are the cosets of $\Omega_{\overline{\xi}}$.

8. Show Ξ is in row echelon form and has full row rank.

9. Show $\Xi \sigma_k = \Xi$ for all $k \in \Omega_{\overline{\xi}}$.

10. What can be said concerning $\mathcal{L}\{e_k : k \in \Omega_\xi\}$ $\mathcal{L}\{\widehat{e}_k : k \notin \Omega_\xi\}$?

11. The operator Ξ is not invertible unless $\xi = \mathbf{1}$. Excluding this case, give necessary and sufficient conditions on $\xi_1, \ldots, \xi_k$ so that x may be recovered from $\Xi_1 x, \ldots, \Xi_k x$.

12. Prove theorem 19.2.

13. Show the equivalence of $\Xi(x * y) = (\Xi x) * (\Xi y)$ and $\rho_\xi(x \cdot y) = (\rho_\xi x) \cdot (\rho_\xi y)$. *Hint:* See exercises 6 and 8 of section 6.1.

14. Extend this section to the general cardinality case. *Hint:* Base equivalence on the relationship $\Xi x = \Xi y \Longleftrightarrow x \otimes \xi = y \otimes \xi$, where ξ are constrained to be binary.

19.2 Mixing

Because the objects coincide, the operator associated with a schemata family was given the same name as the quotient map of the previous chapter. The preceding section has identified the quotient search space with Ω_ξ. The operator Ξ associated with a schemata family is precisely the quotient map corresponding to $\equiv$.

Section 16.1 raised the question of whether $\tilde{\mathcal{M}}$ in the commutative diagram

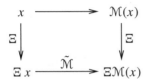

might be homogeneous of degree two. This section shows that to be the case by constructing $\tilde{\mathcal{M}}$ explicitly. Given $\xi \in \Lambda$, let $n_\xi = 2^{\mathbf{1}^T \xi}$ and define the set Λ_ξ by

$$\Lambda_\xi = \{ \langle x_0, \ldots, x_{n_\xi - 1} \rangle : \mathbf{1}^T x = 1, x_j \geq 0 \}$$

In other words, Λ_ξ is defined as Λ for the choice of $n = n_\xi$. As in the previous section, the indices of $x \in \Lambda_\xi$ can regarded as elements of Ω_ξ (and so also as schemata!) through the injection corresponding to ξ.

Let $\mathcal{M}_\xi : \Lambda_\xi \longrightarrow \Lambda_\xi$ be defined as $\mathcal{M}$ for the choice of $n = n_\xi$ with the exception that the mutation distribution is $\Xi \mu$, and the crossover distribution is $\Xi \chi$. Let the corresponding mixing matrix be denoted by M_ξ.

Theorem 19.4 If mutation is independent, then

$$\Xi \mathcal{M}(x) = \mathcal{M}_\xi(\Xi x)$$

Proof The kth component of $\Xi \mathcal{M}(x)$ is

$$\sum_{k' \in \Omega_{\bar{\xi}}} \mathcal{M}(x)_{k \oplus k'}$$

$$= \sum_{u,v \in \Omega_\xi} \sum_{u',v' \in \Omega_{\bar{\xi}}} x_{u \oplus u'} x_{v \oplus v'} \sum_{k' \in \Omega_{\bar{\xi}}} M_{u \oplus u' \oplus k \oplus k', v \oplus v' \oplus k \oplus k'}$$

$$= \sum_{u,v \in \Omega_\xi} \sum_{u' \in \Omega_{\bar{\xi}}} x_{u \oplus k \oplus u'} \sum_{v' \in \Omega_{\bar{\xi}}} x_{v \oplus k \oplus v'} \sum_{k' \in \Omega_{\bar{\xi}}} M_{u \oplus k', v \oplus u' \oplus v' \oplus k'}$$

Since mutation is independent, it can be performed after crossover. Appealing to Theorem 4.3, the innermost sum above is

$$\sum_{k'\in\Omega_{\bar{\xi}}} \sum_{i,j\in\Omega_\xi} \sum_{i',j'\in\Omega_{\bar{\xi}}} \mu_{i\oplus i'} \frac{\chi_{j\oplus j'} + \chi_{\overline{j\oplus j'}}}{2}$$

$$[(u\oplus k')\otimes(j\oplus j')\oplus(\overline{j\oplus j'})\otimes(v\oplus u'\oplus v'\oplus k') = i\oplus i']$$

Note that the indicator function is equivalent to

$$[k'\otimes j'\oplus(\bar{\xi}\oplus j')\otimes(u'\oplus v'\oplus k') = i'][u\otimes j\oplus(\xi\oplus j)\otimes v = i]$$

The first factor of this is equivalent to $[k' = i'\oplus(\bar{\xi}\oplus j')\otimes(u'\oplus v')]$ which determines k'. It follows that the sum above is

$$\sum_{i,j\in\Omega_\xi}[u\otimes j\oplus(\xi\oplus j)\otimes v = i]\sum_{i'\in\Omega_{\bar{\xi}}}\mu_{i\oplus i'}\sum_{j'\in\Omega_{\bar{\xi}}}\frac{\chi_{j\oplus j'}+\chi_{\overline{j\oplus j'}}}{2} = (M_\xi)_{u,v}$$

Therefore, the The kth component of $\Xi\mathcal{M}(x)$ is

$$\sum_{u,v\in\Omega_\xi}(M_\xi)_{u,v}\sum_{u'\in\Omega_{\bar{\xi}}}x_{u\oplus k\oplus u'}\sum_{v'\in\Omega_{\bar{\xi}}}x_{v\oplus k\oplus v'}$$

$$= \sum_{u,v\in\Omega_\xi}(M_\xi)_{u,v}(\Xi x)_{u\oplus k}(\Xi x)_{v\oplus k}$$

$$= \mathcal{M}_\xi(\Xi x)_k \qquad\qquad\qquad\qquad\qquad\qquad\qquad\qquad \blacksquare$$

The hypothesis of independent mutation was used in the proof of theorem 19.4 only to interchange the order of crossover and mutation. Hence the result holds for arbitrary mutation, provided crossover is performed first. Theorem 19.4 has the consequence that

$$\Xi x = \Xi y \implies \Xi\mathcal{M}(x) = \mathcal{M}_\xi(\Xi x) = \mathcal{M}_\xi(\Xi y) = \Xi\mathcal{M}(y)$$

Thus $\mathcal{M}$ is compatible with $\equiv$, and $\mathcal{M}_\xi$ coincides with the quotient $\tilde{\mathcal{M}}$ of $\mathcal{M}$ referred to in theorem 17.5.

Exercises

1. If x is a fixed point of $\mathcal{M}$, what is the corresponding fixed point of $\tilde{\mathcal{M}}$?

2. Explain how theorem 19.4 shows that the conditions of theorem 17.12 are not necessary.

3. Show that mutation is independent if and only if $\mu = (K\mu)\cdot(\overline{K}\mu)$ for all k, where K and $\overline{K}$ are the operators associated with the schemata families represented by k and $\overline{k}$, respectively.

4. Is the result of the previous exercise valid in the general cardinality case?

5. The commutative diagram in this section is valid for any choice of schema family corresponding to any $\xi \in \Omega$. Moreover, it is valid *simultaneously*, for *every* $\xi \in \Omega$, in *parallel*. This situation might be called *"implicit parallelism"*. Interpret implicit parallelism as the fact that a vector may be projected to many subspaces.

6. Show theorem 19.4 carries over to the general cardinality case.

19.3   Selection

If selection could satisfy $\Xi\mathcal{F}(x) = \mathcal{F}_\xi(\Xi x)$, then $\mathcal{G}$ would also be well defined on schemata:

$$\Xi\mathcal{G}(x) = \Xi\mathcal{M}(\mathcal{F}(x)) = \mathcal{M}_\xi(\Xi\mathcal{F}(x)) = \mathcal{M}_\xi(\mathcal{F}_\xi(\Xi x)) = \mathcal{G}_\xi(\Xi x)$$

There is little hope however, even if $\mathcal{F}_\xi(\Xi x)$ is defined to be $\Xi\mathcal{F}(x)$ and $\mathcal{G}_\xi$ is defined to be $\mathcal{M}_\xi \circ \mathcal{F}_\xi$. The problem is with the definition of $\mathcal{F}_\xi$. For example, suppose x and y are such that $\rho_\xi \hat{x} = \rho_\xi \hat{y}$. This is equivalent to $\Xi x = \Xi y$ via theorem 19.3. By definition of $\mathcal{F}_\xi$,

$$\Xi\mathcal{F}(x) = \mathcal{F}_\xi(\Xi x) = \mathcal{F}_\xi(\Xi y) = \Xi\mathcal{F}(y)$$

It follows that $\rho_\xi W\mathcal{F}(x) = \rho_\xi W\mathcal{F}(y)$ (via theorem 19.3). This is summarized by the following theorem, whose statement emphasizes the geometry of the situation. The proof is left as an exercise.

Theorem 19.5   The equation $\mathcal{F}_\xi(\Xi x) = \Xi\mathcal{F}(x)$ can be used to define $\mathcal{F}_\xi$ if and only if

$$(x - y) \in \widehat{e_k}^\perp \implies (\mathcal{F}(x) - \mathcal{F}(y)) \in \widehat{e_k}^\perp$$

for all $x, y \in \Lambda$ and $k \in \Omega_\xi$. Moreover, in that case $\Xi\mathcal{G}(x) = \mathcal{G}_\xi(\Xi x)$ where $\mathcal{G}_\xi = \mathcal{M}_\xi \circ \mathcal{F}_\xi$.

This will be pursued further for the case of proportional selection. Let $0 < \xi < 1$ so that both Ω_ξ and $\Omega_{\overline{\xi}}$ contain more than one element. When $\xi = 1$, the schemata are singleton sets and correspond to elements of Ω. When $\xi = 0$, there is only the single schema Ω. The condition $0 < \xi < 1$ simply rules out these two degenerate schemata families. Let $a \equiv b$ be two distinct elements of schema $i \in \Omega_\xi$ and define

$$y = (x_b - x_a)(e_a - e_b) + x$$

Since $\Xi e_a = \Xi e_b$ (via theorem 19.3), it follows that $\Xi y = \Xi x$. Defining $\mathcal{F}_\xi$ by the equation $\mathcal{F}_\xi(\Xi x) = \Xi \mathcal{F}(x)$ yields $\Xi \mathcal{F}(x) = \Xi \mathcal{F}(y)$. Now Choose x such that $x_a \neq x_b$ and note that

$$\Xi(\mathcal{F}(x) - \mathcal{F}(y))$$

$$= \Xi \left(\frac{f \cdot x}{f^T x} - \frac{f \cdot (x_b - x_a)(e_a - e_b) + f \cdot x}{f^T (x_b - x_a)(e_a - e_b) + f^T x} \right)$$

$$\sim \Xi \left((f \cdot x)(x_b - x_a)(f_a - f_b) - (f^T x)(x_b - x_a)(f_a e_a - f_b e_b) \right)$$

$$\sim \Xi (f \cdot x)(f_a - f_b) - (f^T x)(f_a e_{\xi \otimes a} - f_b e_{\xi \otimes b})$$

where subscripts $\xi \otimes a$ and $\xi \otimes b$ are regarded as integers in the interval $[0, 2^{\mathbf{1}^T \xi})$ via the injection corresponding to ξ. Let $j \in \Omega_\xi$ be distinct from i and observe the jth component of e_i is zero. Since $i = \xi \otimes a = \xi \otimes b$, it follows that the jth component of $\Xi(\mathcal{F}(x) - \mathcal{F}(y))$ is a nonzero multiple of $\Xi(f \cdot x)$. Because f is a positive vector and x may be chosen positive, $\Xi(f \cdot x) > 0$ which contradicts $\Xi \mathcal{F}(x) = \Xi \mathcal{F}(y)$.

What has been shown is that, in general, it is not possible to make proportional selection well defined on a nontrivial schemata family. It seems unlikely that any reasonable selection scheme would be.

Exercises

1. Prove theorem 19.5. *Hint:* Use theorem 19.1 to interpret what $\Xi x = 0$ means.

2. Show ranking selection is not well defined on any nontrivial schemata family. *Hint:* Use a similar approach as in the proportional selection case.

3. Repeat the previous exercise for tournament selection.

4. Show, for any given schemata family, that $x \equiv y \implies \mathcal{F}(x) \equiv \mathcal{F}(y)$ does hold for particular functions.

5. Is the result of the previous exercise interesting?

6. What can be said in the general cardinality case?

20 Appendix

A basic understanding of the rudiments of algebra, calculus, probability, and topology is assumed. The sections of this appendix review selected background material from these areas, summarizing from the following technical references:

E. Akin (1993), *The General Topology of Dynamical Systems*. American Mathematical Society.

F. R. Ghantmacher (1977), *Matrix Theory*. Chelsea.

R. Engelking (1989), *General Topology*, Heldermann Verlag Berlin.

S. Lang (1971), *Algebra*, Addison-Wesley.

L. H. Loomis & S. Sternberg (1968), *Advanced Calculus*, Addison-Wesley.

A. Renyi (1970), *Probability Theory*, North-Holland.

H. L. Royden (1968), *Real Analysis*, Macmillan.

20.1 Analysis

The collection $\mathcal{A}$ of subsets of X is a *σ-field* if

1. $\emptyset \in \mathcal{A}$
2. $A \in \mathcal{A} \Longrightarrow X \setminus A \in \mathcal{A}$
3. $A_n \in \mathcal{A}, n = 1, 2, \ldots \Longrightarrow \bigcup A_n \in \mathcal{A}$

An ordered pair $(X, \mathcal{A})$, where $\mathcal{A}$ is a σ-field over X, is a *measurable space*. Elements of $\mathcal{A}$ are called *measurable sets*. A *measure* is an extended real-value function λ (i.e., λ takes values in $\Re \cup \{-\infty, +\infty\}$) defined on the σ-field $\mathcal{A}$ of a measurable space $(X, \mathcal{A})$ such that

1. $\lambda(\emptyset) = 0$
2. $E \in \mathcal{A} \Longrightarrow \lambda(E) \geq 0$
3. If $A_n \in \mathcal{A}, n = 1, 2, \ldots$ are disjoint, then $\lambda(\bigcup A_n) = \sum \lambda(A_n)$

Let $x, y \in \Re^n$. The *Euclidean distance* between x and y is $\|x - y\|_2$ where

$$\|z\|_2 = (z^T z)^{1/2}$$

To streamline notation, $\| \cdot \|_2$ is usually abbreviated by $\| \cdot \|$. A set $U \subset \Re^n$ is *open* if for every $u \in U$ there exists $\varepsilon > 0$ such that the sphere

$$\mathcal{B}_\varepsilon(u) = \{z : \|z - u\| < \varepsilon\}$$

is contained in U. The interior of a set is the union of all open sets it contains. A *neighborhood* of x is a set containing $\mathcal{B}_\varepsilon(x)$ for some $\varepsilon > 0$. In the case $X = \mathfrak{R}^n$, the smallest σ-field $\mathcal{A}$ containing the open sets is called the *Borels*. *Lebesgue measure* is the unique measure λ on the Borels for which $\lambda(E)$ is, for every parallelepiped E, the volume of E. That is,

$$\lambda([a_1, b_1] \times \cdots \times [a_n, b_n]) = (b_1 - a_1) \cdots (b_n - a_n)$$

A *simple function* has the form

$$\varphi(x) = \sum_{i=1}^{k} c_i[x \in A_i]$$

where the c_i are real and the A_i are measurable sets. If $E \subset \mathcal{A}$, then the integral of φ over E with respect to λ is

$$\int_E \varphi \, d\lambda = \sum_{i=1}^{k} c_i \lambda(E \cap A_i)$$

A *measurable function* is a real-valued function h on X such that for each t,

$$\{x : h(x) < t\} \in \mathcal{A}$$

The corresponding integral of a nonnegative measurable function h is

$$\sup_{0 \le \varphi \le h} \int_E \varphi \, d\lambda$$

where the supremum is taken with respect to simple functions φ (assuming the supremum is finite—otherwise, h is not integrable). When h is not nonnegative, the integral is defined by

$$\int_E h \, d\lambda = \int_E h^+ \, d\lambda - \int_E h^- \, d\lambda$$

The integral is extended to functions taking values in $\mathfrak{R}^n$ by

$$e_i^T \int_E \varphi \, d\lambda = \int_E e_i^T \varphi \, d\lambda$$

and is extended to complex space by simply integrating real and imaginary parts.

A collection $\mathcal{U}$ of open sets is an *open cover* of $X \subset \mathfrak{R}^n$ if each element of X is contained in some element of $\mathcal{U}$. A subset X of $\mathfrak{R}^n$ is *bounded* if there exists a number d which is larger than the (Euclidean) distance of every element $x \in X$ to the origin. The set X is *closed* if its complement is open. A point x is a *limit point* of the set X if every neighborhood of x intersects $X \setminus \{x\}$. A set is closed if it contains its limit points. The closure of a set is the intersection of all closed sets containing it. A set is *nowhere dense* provided its closure contains no nonempty open set. The following are equivalent:

- X is closed and bounded.
- Every sequence of elements of X has a convergent subsequence.
- Every open cover of X has a finite subcover.

A set X satisfying the above properties is called *compact*.

A function h is *continuous* if the inverse image of every open set is open. If X is compact and $h : X \to \mathfrak{R}^n$ is continuous, then

- $h(X)$ is compact (in particular, h is bounded).
- $\forall \varepsilon > 0 \,.\, \exists \delta > 0 \,.\, \|x - y\| < \delta \Longrightarrow \|h(x) - h(y)\| < \varepsilon$

A function h possessing the latter property is called *uniformly continuous*. Continuous functions are measurable. A sequence h_n of functions is said to converge *almost everywhere* provided the set of x for which $h_n(x)$ does not converge has measure zero. The set of measurable functions is closed with respect to limits (if h_n are measurable and $h_n \to h$, then h is measurable), and if h is measurable and g differs from h on a set of measure zero, then g is measurable.

Let X be a compact subset of $\mathfrak{R}^n$. Let S be the set of continuous real-valued functions on X. If λ and $\{\lambda_i\}$ are measures, then λ_i *converges weakly* to λ on X means that

$$\int_X h \, d\lambda_i \longrightarrow \int_X h \, d\lambda \quad \text{for every } h \in S \text{ as } i \to \infty$$

Suppose $h : U \to \mathfrak{R}^n$ where $U \subset \mathfrak{R}^m$ is open. The *differential* of h at x is the linear transformation dh_x satisfying

$$h(x + y) = h(x) + dh_x y + o(y)$$

The matrix of the differential (when it exists) has i, jth entry $\partial e_i^T h / \partial x_j$. A point $x \in \mathfrak{R}^m$ is a *critical point* of h if dh_x has rank less than n. The function h is *continuously differentiable* if dh_x depends continuously on x (which is the case when the partials $\partial e_i^T h / \partial x_j$ are continuous).

Sard's theorem   If h is continuously differentiable, then the image (under h) of the set of critical points (of h) has Lebesgue measure zero.

Mean Value Theorem   If h is continuous and λ is Lebesgue measure, then there exists $\xi \in [a, b]$ such that

$$\int_{[a,b]} h \, d\lambda = (b - a)h(\xi)$$

Inverse Function Theorem   If h is continuously differentiable and if dh_x is invertible, then h, restricted to some open neighborhood of x, has a continuously differentiable inverse.

Change of Variable   If $h : E \subset \Re^n \to \Re^n$ is injective, continuously differentiable and has no critical points in the open set E, if $g : h(E) \to \Re^n$ is integrable, and if λ is Lebesgue measure, then

$$\int_{h(E)} g \, d\lambda = \int_E g \circ h(x) \, |\det(dh_x)| \, d\lambda(x)$$

It follows that if $h : \Re^n \to \Re^n$ is continuously differentiable, and A is a set of Lebesgue measure zero, then $h(A)$ has Lebesgue measure zero.

Monotone Convergence Theorem   If h_n is a monotone increasing sequence of nonnegative measurable functions which converges to h then

$$\int h \, d\lambda = \lim \int h_n \, d\lambda$$

assuming the right hand side exists (otherwise, h is not integrable).

Dominated Convergence Theorem   If h_n is a sequence of integrable functions converging almost everywhere to h, and if there exists integrable g such that $|h_n| < g$, then h is integrable and

$$\int h \, d\lambda = \lim \int h_n \, d\lambda$$

Fundamental Theorem of Calculus If h is continuous and g is an anti-derivative of h, then

$$\int_{[a,b]} h \, d\lambda = g(b) - g(a)$$

20.2 Algebra

A commutative diagram consists of objects connected by arrows, which represent functions between objects, such that the composition of functions along any path depends only on the beginning and ending objects of the path.

A *group* is a set, say G, closed under an associative binary operation, say $\cdot$, for which there exists an identity element and inverses (in G). An *Abelian* group satisfies the additional condition that $\cdot$ is commutative. In that case, the binary operation of the group is usually written as $+$. A subset S (of G) is a *subgroup* if it is a group with respect to the same operation ($\cdot$). A *coset* of S is a set of the form

$$a \cdot S = \{a \cdot s : s \in S\}$$

Each coset has the same cardinality, and they partition G. For example, a subspace of $\mathfrak{R}^n$ is a subgroup (with respect to $+$), and each of its cosets (i.e., translates) is an *affine space*. An example of a nonabelian group is the set of invertible matrices (over $\mathfrak{R}^n$) under multiplication.

A *ring* is an Abelian group, say G, with respect to an operation, say $+$, closed under an additional associative binary operation, say $\cdot$, which has an identity element (in G) and distributes over $+$. A ring is commutative if $\cdot$ is commutative. A commutative ring for which there exists inverses (in G) with respect to $\cdot$ is a *field*.

A polynomial $h(t_1, \ldots, t_k)$ is *symmetric* if it is invariant under every permutation of its variables. Let A be a commutative ring and let R be the commutative ring of polynomials having variables $t_1, \ldots, t_k$ and coefficients in A. Consider the polynomial $g(x)$ with coefficients in R defined by

$$g(x)$$
$$= (x - t_1) \cdots (x - t_k)$$
$$= x^k - s_1 x^{k-1} + \cdots + (-1)^k s_k$$

The polynomials $s_1, \ldots, s_k$ are called *elementary symmetric polynomials*.

Symmetric Function Theorem   If f is a symmetric polynomial having coefficients in a commutative ring A, then f is expressible as a polynomial (with coefficients in A) in the elementary symmetric polynomials.

The zero set of a finite collection of polynomials over a field k is called an *affine variety*. If k is the real or complex field, then an affine variety is either closed and nowhere dense or else is all of space.

The *eigenvalues* of a matrix A (with real or complex entries) are the solutions to

$$\det(xI - A) = 0$$

The polynomial (in x) on the left hand side of this equation is called the *characteristic polynomial*. When A is symmetric, the eigenvalues of A are real.

A (right) *eigenvector* of A is a vector v such that $Av = \alpha v$ for some eigenvalue α. A left eigenvector of A is a vector v such that $v^T A = \alpha v^T$ for some eigenvalue α. If A has distinct eigenvalues, then to each eigenvalue corresponds a unique eigenvector (up to magnitude) and the eigenvectors span all of space.

The determinant $\det(A^T A)$ is the *Gramian* of the columns of A, and is nonzero if and only if they are independent. Since the eigenvalues of $A^T A$ depend continuously on the entries of A, and since the determinant is their product (with multiplicity), a nonzero Gramian remains so after a small perturbation of A. Thus the set of matrices with full column rank is open. The same is true concerning row rank.

A *norm* is a nonnegative function υ on vectors satisfying

1. $x \neq 0 \implies \upsilon(x) \neq 0$
2. $\upsilon(\alpha x) = |\alpha| \upsilon(x)$
3. $\upsilon(x + y) \leq \upsilon(x) + \upsilon(y)$

The domain of υ is extend to matrices as follows

$$\upsilon(A) = \sup_{\upsilon(x) \leq 1} \upsilon(Ax)$$

The three properties above are preserved, and the following additional properties hold

$$\upsilon(Ax) \leq \upsilon(A)\upsilon(x)$$

$$\upsilon(AB) \leq \upsilon(A)\upsilon(B)$$

An example of a norm is given by $\upsilon_1(x) = \|x\|_1$. Let $|A|$ denote the matrix with i, jth entry $|A_{i,j}|$, and let $A \leq B$ indicate that $\forall i, j \,.\, A_{i,j} \leq B_{i,j}$. The following properties are easily verified

$$|AB| \leq |A|\,|B|$$

$$\upsilon_1(A) \leq \upsilon_1(|A|)$$

$$|A| \leq |B| \implies \upsilon_1(|A|\,|C|) \leq \upsilon_1(|B|\,|C|)$$

A *semigroup* is a set closed under an associative binary operation. If $\mathcal{S}$ is a semigroup of matrices (under matrix multiplication) then

$$\upsilon_{\mathcal{S}}(x) = \sup_{S \in \mathcal{S}} \upsilon(Sx)$$

defines the norm $\upsilon_{\mathcal{S}}$ provided the supremum exists. An immediate consequence of the definition is that

$$S \in \mathcal{S} \implies \upsilon_{\mathcal{S}}(S) \leq 1$$

An *inner product* is a bilinear map (i.e., linear in each coordinate), usually denoted by $(\cdot, \cdot)$ which is conjugate symmetric ((x, y) is the complex conjugate of (y, x)) and positive ($x \neq 0 \implies (x, x) > 0$). A norm $\| \cdot \|$ is a *Euclidean norm* if there exists an inner product for which

$$\|x\|^2 = (x, x)$$

The *spectrum* of the linear transformation A is its set of eigenvalues, the *spectral radius*, denoted by $\varsigma(A)$, is the maximum modulus of its eigenvalues. Given $\varepsilon > 0$, a norm can always be found such that the norm of A is within ε of the spectral radius of A. Moreover,

$$\varsigma(A) = \inf \|A\|$$

where the infimum is taken over all Euclidean norms. The standard inner product on $\mathfrak{R}^n$ is defined by $(x, y) = x^T y$. Given vector x and inner product $(\cdot, \cdot)$, the space of vectors *orthogonal* (perpendicular) to x is $x^\perp = \{y : (x, y) = 0\}$. By a suitable choice of basis, this is equivalent to $x^\perp = \{y : y^T x = 0\}$. All norms on $\mathfrak{R}^n$ are equivalent, in the sense that given norms $\| \cdot \|$ and $\| \cdot \|'$, there exist positive constants α, β such that for all x, $\alpha \|x\| < \|x\|' < \beta \|x\|$.

Spectral Mapping Theorem   If h is a function analytic (i.e., differentiable as a function of a complex variable—a function which is everywhere analytic is called *entire*) on some neighborhood of $\mathrm{spec}(A)$, then $h(\mathrm{spec}(A)) = \mathrm{spec}((h(A)))$.

A linear map $A : \mathfrak{R}^n \to \mathfrak{R}^n$ is *contractive* if $\|A\| < 1$ for some norm, A is *expansive* if A^{-1} is contractive, and A is *hyperbolic* when it satisfies either of the following equivalent conditions

• A has no eigenvalue of modulus 1.

• $\mathfrak{R}^n$ is the direct sum of invariant (under A) subspaces E^+ and E^- such that A restricted to E^+ is contractive and A restricted to E^- is expansive.

When A is hyperbolic, there exists an inner product for which the corresponding Euclidean norm is such that $\|A^+\| < \alpha < 1$ and $\|(A^-)^{-1}\| < \beta < 1$ where A^+ is the restriction of A to E^+ and A^- is the restriction of A to E^-. Moreover, the inner product may be chosen such that E^+ and E^- are orthogonal ($x \in E^+$, $y \in E^- \implies (x, y) = 0$), α is arbitrarily close to $\varsigma(A^+)$, and β is arbitrarily close to $1/\varsigma(A^-)$. Such a norm is said to be *adapted* to A.

The $k \times k$ identity matrix is denoted by I_k. The *simple Jordan submatrix* $J_k(a)$ is the matrix identical to aI_k except that its subdiagonal is 1. For example,

$$J_4(a) = \begin{pmatrix} a & 0 & 0 & 0 \\ 1 & a & 0 & 0 \\ 0 & 1 & a & 0 \\ 0 & 0 & 1 & a \end{pmatrix}$$

Given any $n \times n$ matrix A there exists a similarity transformation S such that $J = S^{-1}AS$ consists of simple Jordan submatrices along the diagonal and zeros elsewhere. This matrix J is called the *Jordan canonical form* of A.

The number of independent eigenvectors of A is given by the number of Jordan submatrices. Hence a matrix need not have a basis of eigenvectors; such matrices are called *defective*. The columns of S however coincide with the eigenvectors of A when A is not defective. In the defective case, the columns of S are still a convenient basis. Suppose J has Jordan submatrix $J_{k+1}(\lambda)$ in columns j through $j + k$. The columns of S corresponding to $J_{k+1}(\lambda)$ are $S_j, \ldots S_{j+k}$ and satisfy the relations

$$AS_{j+i} = \lambda S_{j+i} + S_{j+i+1}$$

where S_{j+i} is interpreted as 0 if $i > k$. This follows from equating columns j through $j + k$ in the identity $AS = SJ$. Note that in particular the span of those columns of S corresponding to a simple Jordan submatrix is invariant under A.

If the Jordan canonical form of A consists of the single simple Jordan submatrix $J_n(\lambda)$ then it is easily proved by induction on l that

$$A^l \sum_{j=0}^{n-1} c_j S_j = \sum_{j=0}^{n-1} S_j \sum_{k=0}^{l} \binom{l}{k} \lambda^{l-k} c_{j-k}$$

where c_j is interpreted as 0 if $j < 0$. Since the span of columns of S corresponding to a simple Jordan submatrix is invariant under A, it follows that for the general case $J = \text{diag}(J_{n_1}(\lambda_{n_1}), \ldots, J_{n_m}(\lambda_{n_m}))$ the result is

$$A^l \sum_{j=0}^{n-1} c_j S_j = \sum_{i=1}^{m} \sum_{v_i \le j < v_{i+1}} S_j \sum_{\substack{k=0 \\ j-k \ge v_i}}^{l} \binom{l}{k} \lambda_{n_i}^{l-k} c_{j-k}$$

where $v_i = \sum_{j<i} n_j$.

If every entry of A is positive, then A is called a *positive matrix*. In this case, a theorem of Perron states that A has a positive simple eigenvalue λ (i.e., λ is a root of multiplicity one of the equation $\det(\alpha I - A) = 0$) which exceeds the modulus of all other eigenvalues. Corresponding to λ is a positive eigenvector x. Moreover, the only positive eigenvector of A is x. Taking $J_1(\lambda)$ as the first simple Jordan submatrix in J and using the formula above yields

$$A^l \sum_{j=0}^{n-1} c_j S_j$$

$$= \lambda^l c_0 x + \sum_{i=2}^{m} \sum_{v_i \leq j < v_{i+1}} S_j \sum_{k=0}^{n_i-1} O(l^k) \lambda_{n_i}^{l-k}$$

$$= \lambda^l c_0 x + \sum_{i=2}^{m} \sum_{v_i \leq j < v_{i+1}} S_j \lambda^l O(l^n |\lambda_{n_i}/\lambda|^l)$$

$$= \lambda^l (c_0 x + o(1) \sum_{j=1}^{n-1} S_j)$$

A consequence is that if $\lambda = 1$, then $\lim_{l \to \infty} A^l$ exists and is projection to the space spanned by x. The same conclusion holds if A is nonnegative and A^k is positive (the spectral mapping theorem shows A has maximal eigenvalue 1 when A^k does). The formula above implies that for arbitrary A, if the spectral radius of A is less than 1 then $\sup_k \upsilon(A^k) < \infty$ for any norm υ, since $\lim_{l \to \infty} A^l x = 0$ for every x in the closed (compact) unit ball.

A symmetric matrix A is called *positive definite* if every eigenvalue is positive. This is equivalent to

$$x^T A x \leq 0 \Longrightarrow x = 0$$

where superscript T is interpreted as conjugate transpose.

20.3   Probability

A Kolmogorov probability space is a triple $(X, \mathcal{A}, \lambda)$ where $(X, \mathcal{A})$ is a measurable space and λ is a measure (not necessarily Lebesgue measure) satisfying $\lambda(X) = 1$. The measure λ is called a *probability measure* and elements A of $\mathcal{A}$ and are called *events*. The probability of an event A, denoted $\Pr\{A\}$, is given by $\lambda(A)$. A *random variable* is a measurable function h on X. A *random vector* h has random variables (on the same probability space) as components. The *distribution function* of a random vector h is the function

$$D(x_0, \ldots, x_k) = \Pr\{h_0 < x_0 \wedge \ldots \wedge h_k < x_k\} = \lambda(\{h \in X : h_0 < x_0 \wedge \ldots \wedge h_k < x_k\})$$

If the function d defined by

$$d(x_0, \ldots, x_k) = \frac{\partial^k D(x_0, \ldots, x_k)}{\partial x_0 \ldots \partial x_k}$$

exists, it is called the *density function* (of h) and

$$\Pr\{h \in A\} = \int [x \in A]\, dD(x_0, \ldots, x_k) = \int [x \in A]d(x_0, \ldots, x_k)\, dx_0, \ldots, dx_k$$

The *expectation* (or *mean*) of a random vector h is

$$\mathcal{E}(h) = \int h\, d\lambda = \int x\, dD(x_0, \ldots, x_k)$$

and its *variance* is

$$\mathcal{E}(\|h - \mathcal{E}(h)\|^2)$$

The *characteristic function* $\varphi(t)$ of h is the expectation of $\exp\{\sqrt{-1}\, t^T h\}$.

A sequence D_n of distribution functions is said to *converge completely* to a distribution function D if $D_n(t) \to D(t)$ at all continuity points t of D. In this case, if h_n and h are the corresponding random vectors, then the sequence h_n is said to converge to h *in distribution*.

Continuity Theorem   Let D_n be a sequence of distribution functions, and let φ_n be the corresponding sequence of characteristic functions. Then D_n converges completely to a distribution function D if and only if φ_n converges to a function φ which is continuous at the origin. In that case, φ is the characteristic function of a random vector with distribution D.

Let X be compact. A theorem of Prokhorov implies that every infinite sequence of probability measures on $(X, \mathcal{A})$ has an infinite subsequence which converges weakly to a probability measure on $(X, \mathcal{A})$.

Consider a system which at each time step $0, 1, 2, \ldots$ is in exactly one state of the set of states $S = \{S_1, \ldots S_n\}$. Suppose that $Q_{i,j}$ is the *transition probability* of the system being in state S_j at time $t + 1$ given that it was in state S_i at time t. Assume further that the matrix Q is independent of t and of the initial state of the system. These circumstances define a *homogeneous Markov chain* with a finite number of states.

Note that **1** is an eigenvector of Q with eigenvalue 1. Let $p_{i,j}^k$ be the probability of the system being in state S_j at time t given that it began in state S_i at time $t - k$. It follows by induction (on k) that

$$p_{i,j}^k = (Q^k)_{i,j}$$

If for some k the entries of the matrix Q^k are positive, then the Markov chain is called *ergodic* and the limit

$$\lim_{k \to \infty} Q^k = Q^\infty$$

exists. Let v_j^t be the probability of the system being in state S_j at time t. Assuming the chain is ergodic, consider the following chain of equalities

$$\pi_j$$

$$= \lim_{t \to \infty} v_j^t$$

$$= \lim_{t \to \infty} \sum_i v_i^0 p_{i,j}^t$$

$$= (v^0)^T Q_j^\infty$$

$$= (v^0)^T Q^\infty Q_j$$

Hence π (as defined above) is a left eigenvector of Q corresponding to the eigenvalue 1. Since Q is independent of v^0, so to is π. The vector π represents the *steady state distribution*, and π_j represents the proportion of time (asymptotically, as $t \to \infty$) that the system spends in state S_j.

An application of this theory is to random heuristic search; states are population vectors, which are elements of the compact set Λ. Let $\mathcal{A}$ be the Borels of Λ. The steady state distribution can be thought of as a probability measure according to

$$\pi(A) = \sum_i \pi_i [S_i \in A]$$

thus making $(\Lambda, \mathcal{A}, \pi)$ a Kolmogorov probability space. Identifying steady state distributions of Markov chains corresponding to ergodic RHS with measures on Λ in this way, a consequence of Prokhorov's theorem is:

Weak Limits Every infinite collection of steady state distributions has a weakly convergent subsequence.

Let the nonempty sets $P_1, \ldots, P_l$ partition S. Let π be the steady state distribution corresponding to Q. Consider a Markov chain having as states the sets P_j, transition matrix Q', and steady state distribution π'.

Aggregation   If the transition matrices Q and Q' are related by

$$Q'_{i,j} = \frac{1}{\pi(P_i)} \sum_{x \in P_i} \pi_x \sum_{y \in P_j} Q_{x,y}$$

then $\pi'_j = \pi(P_j)$.

Consider a Markov chain having as states the elements of some nonempty subset S' of S, transition matrix Q', and steady state distribution π'.

Restriction   If the transition matrices Q and Q' are related by

$$Q'_{i,j}$$

$$= Q_{i,j}$$

$$+ \sum_{z_1}^{*} Q_{i,z_1} Q_{z_1,j}$$

$$+ \sum_{z_1,z_2}^{*} Q_{i,z_1} Q_{z_1,z_2} Q_{z_2,j}$$

$$+ \ldots$$

where $\sum^{*}$ denotes summation over the complement of S', then $\pi'_j = \pi_j / \pi(S')$.

20.4   Dynamical Systems

A discrete dynamical system is a function $g : X \to X$, and what is of interest is aspects of the behavior of orbits

$$x, g(x), g^2(x), \ldots$$

A superficial introduction to parts of the subject is provided by the text of the preceding chapters. This section of the appendix is mainly concerned with a group of results that, collectively, are referred to as the *stable manifold theorem*. The account presented here is less general than possible, being specialized to the case $X = \Re^n$.

Let $A : \mathfrak{R}^n \to \mathfrak{R}^n$ be a hyperbolic linear map. The corresponding spaces E^+ and E^-, mentioned in the previous section, are unique and are referred to as the *stable space* and *unstable space* respectively.

A map $q : \mathfrak{R}^n \to \mathfrak{R}^n$ is *Lipschitz* if there exists a constant α such that

$$\|q(x) - q(y)\| \le \alpha \|x - y\|$$

The smallest such α is called the Lipschitz constant (of q) and is denoted by $L(q)$. If $L(q) < 1$ then q is called a *uniform contraction*.

Stable Manifold Theorem   Let $A : \mathfrak{R}^n \to \mathfrak{R}^n$ be a hyperbolic linear map with stable and unstable spaces E^+ and E^- respectively, and let $\| \cdot \|$ be a norm adapted to A such that $\lambda = \max\{\|A^+\|, \|(A^-)^{-1}\|\} < 1$. Let $q : \mathfrak{R}^n \to \mathfrak{R}^n$ be Lipschitz such that $\lambda + L(q) < 1$. Then the perturbation h of A defined by $h = A + q$ satisfies the following:

• h has a unique fixed point ω. Moreover, if $\ldots z_{-1}, z_0, z_1, \ldots$ is a bounded sequence for which $z_{i+1} = h(z_i)$, then $z_i = \omega$ for all i.

• There exists a Lipschitz function $w^+ : E^+ \to E^-$ whose graph W^+ (the *stable manifold*) is invariant under h (where E is identified with $E^+ \times E^-$), and the restriction of h to W^+ is a uniform contraction with fixed point ω.

• There exists a Lipschitz function $w^- : E^- \to E^+$ whose graph W^- (the *unstable manifold*) is invariant under h (where E is identified with $E^- \times E^+$), the restriction of h to W^- is invertible, and the inverse of the restriction is a uniform contraction with fixed point ω.

• The intersection of W^+ and W^- is ω. The sequence $z_0, z_1, \ldots$, where $z_{i+1} = h(z_i)$, is bounded if and only if $z_0 \in W^+$, and then the sequence converges to ω. The sequence $\ldots, z_{-1}, z_0$, where $z_{i+1} = h(z_i)$, is bounded if and only if $z_0 \in W^-$, and then the sequence (z_i) converges to ω (as $i \to -\infty$).

• *Shadowing Lemma*   For $\ldots z_{-1}, z_0, z_1, \ldots$ a bi-infinite ε-chain ($\|z_{n+1} - h(z_n)\| < \varepsilon$), there exists a bi-infinite 0-chain $\ldots w_{-1}, w_0, w_1, \ldots$ such that $\|w_n - z_n\|$ is uniformly bounded by $O(\ )$.

Frequently, one would like to apply the stable manifold theorem using a perturbation function q which has suitably small Lipschitz constant only near 0 (i.e., in the case where $\lambda + L(q) < 1$ does not hold on account of the necessity to define q away from the origin where it may not be as nicely behaved). In that case, it is customary to work with the perturbation $g \circ q$ where g is a *retraction*,

$$g(x) = \begin{cases} x & \text{if } \|x\| < \varepsilon \\ \varepsilon x/\|x\| & \text{otherwise} \end{cases}$$

The retraction g is Lipschitz and $L(g) \leq 2$.

Existence of Lyapunov Function   Suppose $\mathcal{G}$ is continuous and for every x the sequence $x, \mathcal{G}(x), \mathcal{G}^2(x), \ldots$ converges. Let $y = \mathcal{G}(x)$. If, for all $x \in \Lambda$, the existence of an ε-chain from y to x for every $\varepsilon > 0$ implies that y is a fixed point, then a Lyapunov function exists for $\mathcal{G}$.

Theorem Index

Symbol Index

$\vee$	disjunction	4
$\implies$	implication	4
$\iff$	logical equivalence	4
$\lceil \cdot \rceil$	ceiling	4
$\lfloor \cdot \rfloor$	floor	4, 162
$(\cdot)^-$	negative part	4
$(\cdot)^+$	positive part	4, 57
$[\cdots]$	indicator function	4, 53, 68, 70, 119
$[\cdot]$	induced function on representatives	188-191, 203, 206
$[\cdot]$	equivalence class	186, 188, 195, 200-201, 203, 206
$[\cdot, \cdot]$	closed real interval	4
$\equiv$	equivalence relation	4, 185-218
$\oplus$	integer "xor"	22-24, 28, 30, 33, 42, 49-50, 53, 55, 57, 62-63, 65-66, 71, 98, 111-112, 114, 119-120, 126, 195, 207-208, 212
$\otimes$	integer "and"	22-24, 30, 57-58, 114-115, 119, 196, 210-214
$\ominus$	subtraction modulo c	24, 53, 65, 72, 98, 117, 121
$\overline{(\cdot)}$	integer "not"	22-24, 30, 212
$(\cdot, \cdot)$	inner product	225
$\#$	number of nonzero components	30, 117
$\widehat{(\cdot)}$	transform	50-67, 70-72, 112, 213
$(\cdot)^*$	twist	50-53
$*$	convolution	52, 214
∇	gradient	74
$(\cdot)^{-1}$	vector with ith component $1/(\cdot)_i$	169-173
$\prec$	is dominated by	186, 197, 200-201
$\tilde{(\cdot)}$	quotient	190-191, 193, 199, 206-208, 215-216
$\alpha_{u,v}$	cost of a step in a path	151, 153-154

Index